52 WEEKE[ND]
DIGITAL PHOTO
PROJECTS

INSPIRATIONAL PROJECTS · CAMERA SKILLS · EQUIPMENT · IMAGING TECHNIQUES

THIS IS A SEVENOAKS BOOK

This edition published in 2015 by Sevenoaks
an imprint of the Carlton Publishing Group,
20 Mortimer Street, London W1T 3JW

First published by Carlton Books Ltd in 2013

Text © Carlton Books Limited and Bauer Media Limited 2013
Images © Bauer Consumer Media Limited 2013 (except page
134: Motodan/Getty Images)
Design © Carlton Books Limited 2013

A CIP catalogue record for this book is available
from the British Library.

ISBN 978 1 78177 331 4

Printed in China

52 WEEKEND
DIGITAL PHOTO
PROJECTS

INSPIRATIONAL PROJECTS • CAMERA SKILLS • EQUIPMENT • IMAGING TECHNIQUES

SEVENOAKS

SPRING

SUMMER

AUTUMN

WINTER

ESSENTIAL ACCESSORIES

CORE CAMERA SKILLS

Introduction

THERE HAS NEVER BEEN A BETTER TIME TO ENJOY PHOTOGRAPHY, whether it is snapping magical moments of your family's adventures through life or as a form of creative expression.

Taking, making and sharing pictures has never been easier, thanks to the huge strides made in digital imaging technology, explaining why photography's popularity has soared in recent years. Just take a look, for example, at the camera kit used for capturing pictures. A few years ago, taking high quality pictures meant that you needed a big, heavy single-lens reflex (SLR) camera. While that camera type remains massively popular there is a new breed of compact cameras with interchangeable lenses, called CSCs (compact system camera) that give almost identical picture-taking versatility but in a small body form. The decrease in body size is matched by their partner lenses, too, so a versatile outfit now is readily portable.

If you want to travel even lighter, the latest compact cameras have resolutions in excess of 10 megapixels, creating images that are easily high enough quality to produce poster-sized prints and, with their powerful zoom lenses, make photographing distant objects extremely simple.

Last, but by no means least, are camera phones and tablets with integral cameras. It is true that such devices do not have the versatility, quality or controllability of a true camera but this will inevitably change in time. Their benefit, however, is that you are likely have them with you when the camera has been left at home. Having something to take pictures with is better than nothing, regardless of their limitations.

To put all this technology into some sort of context, the truly remarkable fact is that digital imaging has been with us for less than 20 years and the very first consumer-level digital cameras had resolutions of 0.5 megapixels or fewer, and even a top-end model boasted a mere 1.5 megapixels.

Back then, digital could not compete with the image quality that was possible with film. Of course, this has completely changed, and today's digital cameras easily match or even surpass what was previously only possible with a fine quality film. The latest DSLR cameras have resolutions in excess of 20 megapixels with one particularly hi-tech model boasting a huge 36 megapixels.

The creative and convenience features of a typical digital camera open up many opportunities that were, until now, impossible – and make creating beautiful photographs easier than ever. When taking quick and simple snapshots, cameras can detect whether your subject blinked as a picture was taken and tell you to reshoot, or only let you take a shot when your subject is smiling. Most cameras also have art functions to simulate creative effects, can deal with capturing high contrast images, have GPS functionality so you know precisely where an image was taken, and are able to produce panoramic images without any special accessories. Models are becoming available that have Wi-Fi connectivity, meaning that sharing images to social networking sites can be done seconds after they were taken. Yes, the modern digital camera is an amazing technology-packed picture-taking machine, yet shooting the image is just the beginning.

The availability of image editing software that won't break the bank, such as Adobe Photoshop Elements, means that a picture can be enhanced on the computer to accurately reflect what the photographer envisaged at the time of taking the shot. Post-capture editing can comprise of one or two clicks of the mouse or several hours in front of the screen – it really depends on how you want to enjoy your pictures and what style you are going for in your work.

The pivotal word here is 'enjoy', and that is where the 52 projects in this book come in. With a mix of in-camera and post-capture software editing projects, they aim to help you get more from your photography, regardless of your level of expertise, and are achievable with a typical DSLR and lens together with bits and pieces you might have around the house. Techniques like using flash to stop the action, dealing with backlighting and shooting a panorama are among the in-camera techniques covered; while a little bit of Photoshop magic can help you defy gravity or make your own pop art Andy Warhol-style poster.

Our editing projects are based on using Adobe Photoshop or Photoshop Elements, softwares that are 'industry standard' in the world of imaging. Elements is the pared down version of Photoshop and therefore much more affordable. However, it is hugely capable and has more than enough useful and professional standard features for keen photographers.

There are a year's worth of weekly projects to try, experimenting with new skills and techniques. But if you'd like to brush up on your core camera know-how, or find the essential accessories to make even better pictures possible, then we've got that covered too. Modern cameras are packed with features and festooned with controls that can sometimes be daunting to even the keenest photographer. We'll help you to discover which features are right for you and how to get the best from them – whether it's using the mode dial, understanding exposure, or reading the histogram.

Whether you're just starting out or already an accomplished photographer, there will be many nuggets of information here to help you take your photography a little bit further, always presented in a clear, fun and accessible way.

With all this knowledge at your fingertips you probably can't wait to get started. We wish you a wonderful year of photographic adventures.

LYNNE MAXWELL

Simple indoor flower photos

Shoot stunning images from the simplest of set-ups

WHAT YOU NEED
DSLR WITH KIT LENS
FLOWER
TABLE
ANGLEPOISE LAMP
BLACK CARD
WHITE PAPER

DIFFICULTY LEVEL
EASY

FLOWERS ARE A GREAT PHOTOGRAPHIC SUBJECT because of their colour, shape and form. They can be shot outdoors in the garden or, for more controllable results, indoors. The great thing about shooting inside is that you don't have to worry about messy backgrounds or it being the right time of day. Shooting indoors gives you total control over the two things that can make outdoor flower photography difficult – light and background.

The next thing you need to consider is the overall treatment of the photo. Will you go for a moody low-key shot, like the rose, or would you prefer a high-key photo like the lily? Alternatively you could try both styles to see which one you prefer. Either way, here's everything you need to know to achieve both options.

CAPTURE A LOW-KEY BLOOM

Low-key photos are made up of a high proportion of shadow areas, with the midtones seemingly emerging from the shadows. It is possible to have highlights in a low-key shot but this is, by the very nature of the lighting style, quite rare. It's a common style for portrait photography but works just as well, if not better, for still life.

For this shot, the deep red petals and strong shape of the rose made it the perfect bloom for a moody lighting treatment. With no highlights in sight and dark midtones, this is a very subtle yet sophisticated photo that doesn't follow normal photographic conventions.

FINISH

USE CARD FOR A BACKGROUND Attach a black piece of paper or card to the wall behind the flower. You could use A3–size card but this would make things tight. Ideally use A2 card or larger for a bigger background and a larger workspace.

MAKE A LIGHT TUBE A light tube made out of white paper produces extremely soft light, albeit only a very small amount.

USE EXPOSURE COMPENSATION With black taking up most of the frame and shooting in aperture priority, you'll need to use exposure compensation. Depending on composition this could be 1 stop of underexposure, but is most likely to be 2.

ADD STABILITY Working in extreme low light means shutter speeds will be very slow, even with an aperture like f/5.6. Make sure you use a tripod and a cable release to keep the camera steady and avoid camera shake.

SET WHITE BALANCE

Getting white balance right in-camera is essential if you shoot JPEGs because you can't change it later. If white balance is set incorrectly your shots will suffer from a colour cast. If you shoot in RAW white balance can be changed later during image processing, but it's better to set it to match the light source before you shoot. This is because detail can appear to be lost, making it difficult to judge exposure on the LCD screen when there's a colour cast, as illustrated in the examples here.

Daylight balance Leaving white balance set to Daylight has produced a very strong orange cast, as the light source is actually tungsten. This has produced blocks of colour on the flower, making detail impossible to see.

Tungsten balance Setting white balance to Tungsten gives a much more neutral result with visible detail (left).

SHOOTING TECHNIQUE: LOW-KEY

1 SET UP THE WORKSPACE Setting up on a dining room table next to a wall provides a good working height and a place to attach the cardboard. Use A2 black card stuck to the wall using Blu-Tack. If your table can't be placed next to a wall, prop the card up at one end of the table and shoot from the other.

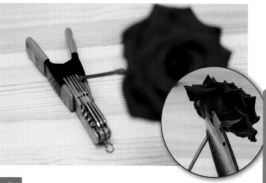

2 PREPARE THE FLOWER Even if you find the most perfect flower, be prepared to trim leaves and sometimes petals to make it look even better. The small leaves at the back of the rose stuck out and didn't look very good in the photo – the simple solution was to cut them off. Then make the flower stand up with a clamp or bulldog clip.

3 CAMERA SETTINGS Set up on a tripod and use a cable release if you have one. If you don't then the self-timer will help you avoid camera shake during long exposures. Set the ISO to 100 for best quality and the camera to aperture priority at f/5.6 for a shallow depth-of-field. Zoom the lens out to its longest focal length and recompose the shot.

4 CONTROL YOUR LIGHTING With a black background and when shooting in aperture priority you'll need to dial in 2 stops of underexposure to ensure it's exposed correctly. Once this has been done roll a white sheet of paper into a tube and hold it over the lamp to make a light tube. Draw the curtains and angle the tube to light the flower. To avoid the bulb overheating do not leave the paper over the lamp for too long. Shoot in bursts of 5–10 minutes with a break in-between.

TIP

CHOOSING THE MOST PHOTOGENIC FLOWERS

If you're not familiar with flowers choosing the right ones for a photo needs a bit of thought. Check your garden for something suitable, if the season is right, or buy from a florist or supermarket. The latter offers very good value for money, but flowers can be damaged and you may have to buy a whole bunch when you only want one stem. Buying from a florist allows you to pick flowers individually so you can be sure you have perfect specimens, but it will be more expensive.

THE ROSE is a classically beautiful flower, with the numerous folds of petals creating a great texture for the main image.

THE PASTEL colours of the lily made it ideal for the high-key photograph.

THE GERBERA is great for photos but didn't work for the low-key shot – the colour was too bright and the bloom too spread out.

IRIS   **ALLIUM**   **TULIP**   **ORCHID**

BEST FLOWERS When choosing flowers for photography, look for strong and bold shapes, and bright, eye-catching colours. Iris, orchid, allium and tulip are other good choices.

CAPTURE A HIGH-KEY BLOOM

FINISH

High-key photography refers to a lighting style where shadows are kept to a minimum, if not completely non-existent. This requires even lighting of the subject, typically, but not exclusively, against a white background. High-key photography is possible under natural light using reflectors or flash, or a mixture of the two. For the shot of the lily a mixture of window light and diffused flash bounced off the ceiling was used. For this technique a flashgun is the best option but you could use a pop-up flash with a piece of card positioned in front to make the flash bounce upwards. It's easiest to shoot in landscape format when doing this.

SHOOTING TECHNIQUE: HIGH-KEY

1 PREPARE THE FLOWER Attach a sheet of white card to the wall behind the table or prop it up in position if your table isn't next to a wall. With a flower like a lily, a drinking glass can be used to hold it in place. The weight of the flower head will help it to naturally sit in roughly the right position.

2 CAMERA SETTINGS Set your camera to ISO 100 for best image quality, in aperture priority at f/4 for a shallow depth-of-field. Use a tripod as the shutter speed (¼ sec in this case) will be too slow to handhold. Now dial in 2 stops of overexposure to make sure the white background exposes as white rather than grey.

3 SET UP FLASH Set the flashgun to TTL mode and aim it up at the ceiling. Since you're working in aperture priority with 2 stops of overexposure the camera will choose a suitable shutter speed. Now simply focus manually on the part of the flower you want to be sharp.

Get floral flashes of inspiration

Use fill-in flash to add drama to your outdoor shots

WHAT YOU NEED
DSLR, COMPACT
SYSTEM CAMERA OR
CREATIVE COMPACT
WITH BUILT-IN FLASH

DIFFICULTY LEVEL
EASY

WHEN YOU'RE SHOOTING FLOWERS with a bright background, such as a midday sky, you'll often find that your subject will come out dark and under-exposed. You can try to correct this by altering your exposure values for the subject, but this will mean your background becomes too light. It's a frustrating situation but one that's easy to fix once you know how. Pop a little bit of flash into the scene and you'll have the best of both worlds – a correctly exposed background and a bright, well-lit subject, too.

With your camera alone you can't set your exposure individually for different parts of the scene – for example, you can't choose a different exposure for your subject and background. However, activate your pop-up flash and this will no longer be a problem, as the light from the flash illuminates the subject and not the distant background. This evens out the brightness difference between the two for an even exposure across the image. All you need to do is switch over to aperture priority and pop up the flash on your camera, then dial in the correct exposure settings.

With your flash lighting the subject, you're free to play with the exposure of the background. If the camera's suggested exposure is leaving it looking a bit flat and underwhelming, you can try underexposing it to add punch and a more moody feel, because the flash will still light the subject correctly to give you great-looking results.

WITHOUT FILL-IN FLASH

These two pictures haven't quite worked. Why? Well, without flash to balance things out, the difference in brightness between the subject and background is too great. Exposing for the background makes the subject too dark and exposing for the subject makes the sky blow out, so it's something that needs to be tackled by exposing for the sky and using flash to fill in the shadow.

With the camera set to expose for the subject the background is too light...

... and when the background is correctly exposed the subject is too dark.

Right: A burst of flash balances the exposure of the flowers with the bright sky behind, giving punchy, attractive floral shots

HOW FILL-IN FLASH WORKS

Often overlooked and under-used, your pop-up flash is an incredibly useful tool – and not just when the lights go out. Follow this technique to control its power and use it in daylight to balance your exposures.

Using fill-in flash is all about creating a balance between the lighting in different parts of your picture. The natural light will take care of the background while your flash then adds light to your subject, balancing the two for an even exposure across the image. You can then use your shutter speed to change the exposure of the background without changing the flash power. Using fill-in flash in this way means you don't need to worry about your subject being in shadow, in fact, you can even shoot directly towards the light and still get a balanced exposure. This makes it a great technique, not only for florals but for shooting portraits as well.

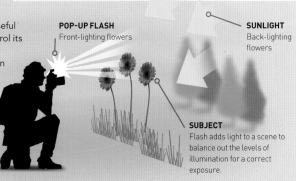

POP-UP FLASH
Front-lighting flowers

SUNLIGHT
Back-lighting flowers

SUBJECT
Flash adds light to a scene to balance out the levels of illumination for a correct exposure.

FINISH

Securing your subject will make it easier to shoot.

SHOOTING TECHNIQUE

1 SET UP THE FLOWERS Choose your floral subject wisely to get the best images – to get that contrast between the sky and subject you'll be shooting from slightly below the flower, so it helps to use one that doesn't point directly up, allowing you to see the petals.

Find a small wooden stick, shorter than the flower stem, to set in the ground and attach your flowers to – if they're secured in place they won't wobble around so much if there's a gust of wind. This also leaves you with both hands free to operate the camera.

Finally, the higher off the ground the flower head is positioned, the easier it will be to shoot from below, so either place it on something, or pick examples with a long stem – if they're very near the ground you'll have to practically lie on the ground to get the shot!

Ensure that your shutter speed remains below 1/200sec.

2 SET THE EXPOSURE Switch over to aperture priority (A or Av on your Mode dial) and dial in an aperture of f/11. In this mode, the shutter speed will take care of itself, but you want to make sure it's lower than 1/200sec for the fill-in flash to function. If it isn't, you'll need to decrease the aperture to f/16 or smaller, or lower your ISO setting. Next, make sure you are set to multi-zone metering mode and set the Exposure Compensation to -1.0 (this is denoted by a +/- symbol on most cameras or the scroll wheel on most Canon DLSRs). A value of -1EV will underexpose the image a little, causing the sky to darken and look more moody, while the flash will light the subject correctly.

3 ACTIVATE THE POP-UP FLASH Now you need to bring the camera's pop-up flash into play as, unlike in auto mode, it won't pop up automatically. This is done with a button located on the camera body and it will have the symbol of a lightning bolt. With the flash up, your shutter speed will automatically be limited to the camera's flash sync speed setting, usually a maximum of 1/200sec or 1/250sec. This shouldn't be a problem thanks to the way you set the exposure in Step 2, but if you see 'HI' or a flashing value where the shutter speed should be, you're beyond the sync speed and will need to use a higher f/number. Also, if you have a lens hood on your lens it's wise to remove it as it may cast a shadow, owing to it blocking some of the light from the flash.

Increase the aperture value if you get warning signs or symbols.

4 TAKE THE SHOT AND CHECK IT With your settings dialled in, frame up and take the shot, then check your picture on the camera's screen. Pay particular attention to the exposure on your subject and on the background. If the background is coming out too dark you can decrease the Exposure Compensation to -0.7EV or perhaps -0.3EV to brighten it up. If, on the other hand, your background is too light you may need to push it up to -1.3EV or -1.7EV, which will darken the image. With the background sorted, look to your subject and check for any over- or underexposure. The flash power can be controlled in a very similar way – see the box below to see how to do this.

Get low to shoot your subject against the sky.

TECH TALK

GETTING THE BEST FROM YOUR FLASH

If your background is spot on, but the subject is too light or dark, you'll need to control the power from your pop-up flash, or alter your distance from the subject. The first of these you can do with Flash Exposure Compensation, available either through your menu system or via a button with a flash symbol and a +/-next to it. So,if your subject is too dark you can increase the flash power, or if it is too bright, you can decrease the power.

Flash compensation works in 'stops' of light with one stop being twice the brightness of the previous stop. The scale moves up in increments of 1/3rd, usually up to +1 and down to -3.

Alternatively, in manual mode, you can alter the strength of the flash on your subject by changing the distance between them. If you move back the flash has to reach further and will appear less powerful, while getting closer will make the flash appear stronger. In the default TTL mode on your flash menu the camera will automatically factor this distance into its output, so moving back and forward won't change your exposure.

FLASH EXPOSURE COMPENSATION
The power of your pop-up flash can be controlled using Flash Exposure Compensation.

FLASHGUN
If you've enjoyed this technique and want to take your flash options further it's worth investing in an accessory flashgun. Flash power is described by the guide number (GN), and this denotes the distance from the flash to the subject, multiplied by the f/number required for a correct exposure. Accessory flashguns have much higher guide numbers than those of pop-up flashes, allowing you to throw the flash further. The majority will also feature swivel heads, allowing you to alter the direction of the flash.

Give freelensing a go

Shoot with your lens off-camera and achieve an ultra-low depth-of-field

WHAT YOU NEED
DSLR
FAIRLY 'FAST' LENS

DIFFICULTY LEVEL
ADVANCED

REMOVE THE LENS FROM YOUR DSLR MOUNT, hold it in front of the camera, and then start shooting. Seriously. This is, in fact, a technique known as freelensing. Taking the lens off and shooting like this allows you to capture an extremely shallow depth-of-field, resulting in images similar to that created by a tilt & shift lens. This technique is probably the most advanced in-camera technique to master and, therefore, one of the most rewarding when you get it right.

As you are separating the lens from the camera and increasing the distance between the optics and the sensor you can make your life easier by using certain equipment. A fast lens (wide aperture) is better for this technique, as the glass on the lens is bigger. You may think this means shelling out lots of

money on an expensive f/1.4 lens, but you can pick up 50mm f/1.8 lenses for less than £100 or you may be able to find an old but fast manual lens that would be perfect. The great thing about freelensing is that you don't even need to use the same make of lens as your camera. After all, they're not making contact with each other.

Other things to look out for are a focusing ring and an aperture ring. It is essential you are able to focus manually with your lens, and if your lens has an aperture ring it means you can simply open the aperture wide. A lot of modern lenses don't have an aperture ring, which means that you will have to hold back the pin/catch that opens and closes the aperture. This is found on the back of your lens.

FINISH

SHOOTING TECHNIQUE

You're shooting at the widest aperture so you'll need to set your ISO to the camera's lowest setting. Detaching the lens from the camera means you'll have to shoot in manual mode and adjust exposure by changing the shutter speed.

With your lens you need to open the aperture so as much light as possible can get through. To get an accurate exposure remember to keep viewing the LCD screen and altering the shutter speed. If you aren't getting a shutter speed faster than 1/60sec you'll probably need to place the camera body on a tripod or increase ISO. With your camera on a tripod you can then concentrate on where you place the lens and use one of your hands to focus it.

You may find that you get better results and focusing is easier when you keep the bottom of the lens close to the camera mount and tilt the top of the lens away from the body. It's also useful to use continuous shooting mode and shoot bursts of images to ensure one sharp frame. Try this technique and you'll be hooked!

START

HOW TO FOCUS Shooting with the lens detached from the body can conjure up quite a few obstacles, the first being major focusing issues. Stick with it, though, and try everything from moving closer to your subject, to making the most minimal of rotations on the focus ring.

CHOOSING YOUR EFFECT By tipping the lens up and down you create a horizontal focal plane, and moving the lens from side to side adjusts the vertical focal plane.

THE PROS AND CONS OF FREELENSING

➕ The effects created can be very dramatic and help transform an image into an extremely creative shot with lots of depth.

➕ Stunning results can be achieved by light leaking into the gap between the lens and the camera. Try shining a small torch covered with a coloured gel here to add a vibrant effect.

➕ Using a full-frame DsLR makes the technique slightly easier because there is a bigger area on the sensor for the light/image to be projected.

➕ Because the lens doesn't have to fit, this is a very versatile technique that allows you to use any make of lens 'on' any make of camera.

➖ Removing your lens and exposing the camera's sensor leaves it open for dust to get in, so you may need to clean it afterwards.

➖ Holding the lens and trying to rotate the focus ring with one hand is a tad tricky. Losing your grip and dropping a lens is a real possibility, so use a tripod whenever possible.

Create a small world with macro

Your macro lens is good for more than flowers –
try something a little more surreal

WHAT YOU NEED
DSLR
MACRO LENS
TRIPOD
FLASH
RAILWAY FIGURES

DIFFICULTY LEVEL
INTERMEDIATE

FINDING NEW WAYS OF APPROACHING POPULAR SUBJECTS is part of what photography is about, and inspiration can come from absolutely anywhere. If you're looking for a new direction for your macro photography, take a look into the world of the model railway enthusiast. You're probably familiar with photography where everyday objects are made to look like models, so how about the opposite: photographing tiny models and making them appear real.

Model railway figures come in a variety of sizes and scenarios, and with 00-gauge people being roughly 2cm tall they're perfect for macro photography. These detailed and hand-painted models are available in sets of construction workers, hunters, photographers, fashion models, sunbathers, emergency workers and many more. By carefully choosing locations and everyday objects to photograph them with you can achieve interesting results, and shooting them is a lot of fun.

HANDHELD OR TRIPOD? Shooting handheld gives you the freedom to move about and try different compositions, but using a tripod makes things easier once you've settled on a composition.

LIGHTING Natural light provides realistic results, but if you're looking for something more dramatic try using TTL flash with an off-camera cable or even wireless off-camera flash.

LOCATION You can find miniature locations in the most unlikely places. Remember to think about scale when you're looking for suitable locations.

Flash can be used on this shot to create dramatic lighting. Here a figure was placed in some moss and the result is a lumberjack chopping wood in a dark forest.

SHOOTING TECHNIQUE

1 FIND A MINIATURE SCENE The first and perhaps most difficult step is finding a suitable location for the tiny figures. Try to think differently, because you're working on a different scale. Conversely, use normal everyday objects in the scene to add a surreal element to the shot (left).

2 PLACE THE FIGURE Some settings make it easy to position your figures but, if you're shooting on concrete or another a smooth surface, making the figures stand by themselves requires more thought. Blu-Tack and Pritt Stick are two solutions, just make sure you only use a tiny amount so you can't see it under the model's feet (below).

3 SETTING YOUR LENS Most such lenses have a focus limit switch that limits focus between two distances. This makes focusing easier since the lens doesn't go through its entire range to lock onto subjects. Set your lens appropriately according to the distance you are away from the subject, or try focusing manually.

4 CHOOSE YOUR CAMERA SETTINGS If you're shooting with a flashgun on a cable, set the flash to TTL mode and the camera to Manual mode. This will produce dramatic side lighting. Depth of field is very shallow at such close focusing distances, so experiment with different apertures in order to get as much in focus as you want. Aperture priority mode is good for this.

PROPS Placing figures in miniature environments results in a more natural image, whereas using everyday-sized objects wreaks havoc with our expectations of size and scale. The idea of snails the size of a truck is humorous and terrifying at the same time.

DEPTH-OF-FIELD Allowing the background to go out of focus keeps attention on the main subjects and cuts out the background. It's important that the shot is taken outdoors to create a believable illusion.

VIEWPOINT When photographing model-rail figures, adopting the right viewpoint couldn't be more important. Shooting from too high up makes the scene look less believable; get down low and it'll look more authentic.

TIP

HOW TO BUY THE FIGURES

Model-railway suppliers are the best place to find tiny figures like this. There are hundreds of different model people available, including ones you just wouldn't expect, so there's no reason to compromise on creativity. Have a look at figures from a German company called Noch, which sells sets at about £6–10. Figures can be purchased from modelling shops and online. check out www.ontracks.co.uk for a huge selection.

This pack of six Bachmann 00 gauge figures provides a wealth of creative macro options.

ACCESSORIES

If this type of close-up photography floats your creative boat, try using accessories to add to your compositions. You can buy all sorts of scale objects, such as cars and workmen's tools. The idea is to add more realism to model-railway scenes, but they'll work equally well for your surreal macro photos.

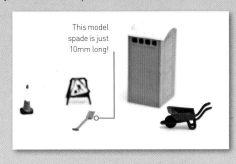

This model spade is just 10mm long!

Creating the impossible

Use Photoshop to create amazing composite special effects

WHAT YOU NEED
PHOTOSHOP
DSLR
FLASH
TRIPOD
REMOTE RELEASE

DIFFICULTY LEVEL
INTERMEDIATE

SELF-IRONING CLOTHES WOULD SURELY BE one of the greatest inventions ever made. Sadly, it's probably never going to happen, but you can at least dream of the possibilities with a little help from Photoshop. While this technique won't actually get you out of doing the chores, creating a surreal photo based on the idea is very achievable and enjoyable to complete. You can even use your own arm to hold the iron if you have a wireless remote, but asking a friend to lend a helping hand will make life a lot easier. Plus being able to check shots on the camera's LCD screen as you shoot means you can get the shots you'll need for the composite in as little as 10 minutes.

As with any composite, the key to success is minimising movement between shots. This is the most difficult aspect of the self-ironing shirt image, but get this part right and you'll save yourself a lot of trouble in Photoshop later when masking the component images. Shooting against a plain, painted wall will help if there is a slight shift of the ironing board or shirt. The Photoshop element of the project requires only two images and one Layer Mask for the blend, making this is a more simple technique than you might think.

START IMAGES

FINISH

SHOOTING TECHNIQUE

Composition and viewpoint are just as important for composite photographs as they are for more conventional pictures. Remember aids like the rule of thirds, and experiment with different viewpoints: here the photographer has looked down at the ironing board to add depth. Being such a simple composition, this depth is essential to show more of what's happening on the ironing board. The best way to do this is to set up using a tripod at full height and stand on a chair to compose and focus.

PLAN AHEAD

A tripod is absolutely essential for this type of shot, and with the camera positioned above head height a cable release is a great help too. Don't forget, with the tripod set so high you'll need a chair or stepladder to focus and compose. The order in which you take the two shots is also very important.

1 CHOOSE YOUR CAMERA SETTINGS Set your camera to Manual mode, choose a mid-range ISO setting like ISO 400 and an aperture of about f/11. This will give you the depth-of-field you need in the shot. A shutter speed of 1/80sec is a good start too. Under natural light these settings would produce an underexposed shot, but you're going to use a flashgun, so exposure will be fine. Attach the camera to a tall tripod, compose and manually focus.

2 SETTING UP YOUR FLASH Attach the flashgun and set it to TTL mode so that the camera and flashgun will work together to determine flash power output automatically. Now swivel and tilt the flash head so that it's facing backwards and at a 45° angle and bouncing off a wall behind you. This will provide even lighting with soft shadows.

3 FLASH EXPOSURE COMPENSATION Everything is nearly ready for the shot but with the flash set as it is you're likely to experience underexposure. To combat this, dial in some flash exposure compensation (FEC). Check your user manual for exactly how to do this as all DSLRs differ slightly in how FEC is applied.

4 SHOOTING THE IMAGES Using a cable release when shooting will prevent the camera moving between frames. Take a with-arm photo first, then help your model remove their arm from the shirt without moving the fabric too much. Now take the second shirt-only shot. Check that movement between images is minimal using the camera's LCD screen.

LIGHTING Fire the flash backwards so light bounces off the wall behind you creating a soft and even lighting. Flash exposure compensation can help achieve a correct exposure.

COMPOSITION Stand on a chair to focus and compose. It's a good idea to switch the camera and/or lens to manual focus mode so focus doesn't change from shot to shot.

ORDER Take the shot with the arm first, then carefully remove the model's arm from the sleeve making sure the shirt doesn't move. Lay the sleeve out pointing away from the shirt.

CONTROL Using a cable release means you can shoot without looking through the camera's viewfinder and the camera won't move between shots.

PROCESSING TECHNIQUE

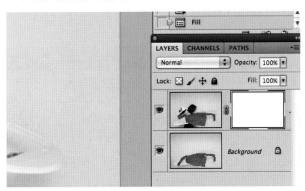

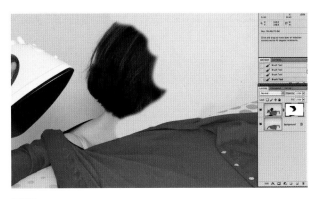

1 CREATE A LAYER MASK Open the two images in Photoshop and drag the 'with-arm' background layer onto the 'shirt-only' photo. This will ensure the with-arm shot is at the top of the Layer stack. The top Layer will be active, so click on the Layer Mask icon at the bottom of the Layers Palette – the rectangle with a circle in the middle.

2 BLEND THE LAYERS Press D to make sure black and white are set respectively as foreground and background colours. Choose a soft-edge brush and begin painting out the head of the person holding the iron. If you make a mistake, hit X to switch the foreground colour to white and paint over the mistake. Press X again to reset black as the foreground colour and continue masking.

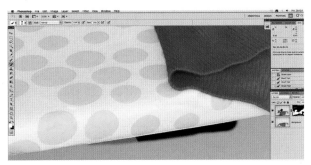

3 REMOVE THE SHADOWS The shot with the model in will have a light shadow on the wall behind the ironing board, and this will have to be carefully masked out. Choose a hard-edged brush, then hold down Shift and press the left square bracket key two or three times to soften slightly. Now carefully paint out the darker areas on the wall.

4 CORRECTING FOR SHIFTS If there has been any movement between shots, more precise blending is required. Continue to blend the Layers using the Layer Mask, but use a brush with a slightly soft edge to paint right up to the edges. To do this, again choose a hard brush, then hold down Shift and press the left square bracket key two or three times.

5 DESATURATE THE IMAGE Click on the Adjustment Layer icon at the bottom of the Layers Palette – the small half-black/half-white circle. Choose Black & White, close the window and change Blending mode to Screen. Copy the layer (Ctrl+J), change Blending mode to Multiply, hold down Ctrl and left-click on the lower B&W layer so both are active. Group them (Ctrl+g) and lower opacity until you're happy.

6 FLATTEN AND SAVE With editing completed it's time to save the image as a JPEG. Click on the small black arrow with lines to the right of it at the top right of the layers palette. Choose Flatten Image to merge all layers into one. Press Ctrl+Shift+S to Save As and choose the JPEG file format. If you want to keep all your layers intact, don't flatten the image and save it as a TIFF or PSD file.

Use shallow focus on landscapes

Concentrate attention to your scenics with some selective blur

WHAT YOU NEED
PHOTOSHOP
OR ELEMENTS
DSLR AND STANDARD
ZOOM LENS
OPTIONAL:
WIDE-APERTURE
50MM LENS, TRIPOD

DIFFICULTY LEVEL
EASY

TREES OFTEN DESCRIBE NICE SHAPES but, ordinarily, don't work as a landscape photograph by themselves because there's no foreground to balance the composition, and no lead-in lines drawing the eye to the subject. So, you need to think a bit more creatively.

By defocusing the grass that leads up to the tree, the bland foreground is lost and your eye immediately falls on the sharpest part of the picture – the tree itself. With a sufficiently strong subject, this is a technique you can try out almost anywhere and, ultimately, creates more of a 'tree portrait' than a traditional landscape – something that'll really help it stand out from other shots.

SHOOTING TECHNIQUE

This technique is all about positioning and setting up the camera to create as shallow a depth-of-field as possible, leaving only the subject sharp. Shooting from a very low position will also thrust the subject up into the sky, so there's less chance of it getting lost in its surroundings, making it even more striking.

CHOOSE THE RIGHT SHOOTING MODE
Because you want to control depth-of-field, shooting in Aperture priority mode is the sensible choice here. Set your Mode dial to A or Av and you'll have full control of the aperture, so you can set it as wide as possible.

SHOOT LOW TO THE GROUND
The closer the grass is to the lens the easier it is to blur, so spread the tripod's legs as wide as possible and tilt or reverse its centre column if you can.

CAMERA SETTINGS
Set the lowest f/number that your lens allows to blur the foreground (f/5.6 will do the job fine, so long as you're close enough to the ground). And zoom in as far as you can to exaggerate the defocusing effect.

START

FINISH

PROCESSING TECHNIQUE
ADD MORE BLUR USING PHOTOSHOP

If you weren't able to shoot from a low enough position, or if your lens doesn't have a wide enough aperture to get the shallow depth-of-field you wanted, it's easy to replicate the effect in Photoshop using Selections and the Gaussian Blur filter. Or you might just want to try this look out on an already existing shot.

It's quick and easy to do, but it's important to do things the right way so the effect looks realistic. For example, don't try to add the blur all in one go; it's better to add it slowly, increasing the strength towards the bottom of the frame.

1 MAKE A SELECTION Open your tree picture in Photoshop and pick the Rectangular Marquee tool from the Toolbox. Drag it out over the picture starting just below the base of the tree and then click on Refine Edge. In the box that appears use about 75px of Feather and click OK. Press Ctrl+J to copy this Selection to a new Layer.

2 GAUSSIAN BLUR With the new Layer active in the Layers Palette, choose Filter>Blur>Gaussian Blur. In the palette that appears set the Amount slider to 1.5px and click OK. You won't see much difference in the image yet but the point is to add the effect gradually. Press the Ctrl key and click on the Layer 1 thumbnail to load it as a Selection.

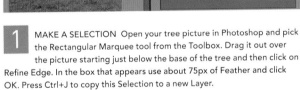

3 DRAG SELECTION With the Selection back on screen, click within it and drag it down slightly towards the bottom of the picture. As you do this hold down Shift so it doesn't move out of alignment. Now go Filter>Blur>Gaussian Blur once more, this time doubling the Amount to 3px. Click OK to apply the effect.

4 FINISH MORE BLUR Drag the Selection down again and use the shortcut Ctrl+Alt+F to re-enter Gaussian Blur, this time using 6px. Click OK, drag the Selection again, but this time click Refine Edge and use 100px of Feather. Now blur (12px), and keep dragging and blurring until you reach the bottom. Finally go to Layer>Flatten Image.

Have fun with unique abstracts

Bubble with enthusiasm for these weird and wonderful colour abstracts

WHAT YOU NEED
ELEMENTS
DSLR WITH MACRO LENS
TRIPOD
WIRE COAT HANGER
DESK LAMP
WASHING-UP LIQUID

DIFFICULTY LEVEL
INTERMEDIATE

FINISH

PHOTOGRAPHING BUBBLES IS A POPULAR TECHNIQUE that's most commonly geared towards bubbles being blown against a dark background to make them show up. But get in close with a macro lens to focus and you'll find incredibly colourful swirls on the surface of soap film when it's suspended in a wire frame. You get only about 30 seconds to shoot each soap film, but that's more than enough time to shoot some amazing abstracts. Even adults can have fun with a little washing-up liquid and water!

This is a technique that takes a lot of trial and error because focusing and catching the light can be tricky. You'll need a macro lens set to manual focus at the full 1:1 ratio, then you simply move the wire and soap film backwards and forwards to focus. You also need to tilt and change the angle of the wire frame to catch light from a desk lamp and show the swirling colours. The camera should be locked onto a tripod because you'll need both hands free to hold the wire and depress the shutter button.

For the best results hold the soap film at the same angle as the light source. The light source should shine straight through the film, both of which should be at an angle to the lens.

SHOOTING TECHNIQUE

1 CAMERA SETTING Set your macro lens to manual focus at full 1:1 ratio and your camera to manual mode at ISO 400 to keep the shutter speed to about 1/30sec. You'll need a fairly narrow aperture to help increase depth-of-field, so dial in f/11. The shutter speed will need to be set according to the power of your light source, but expect to use something between 1/30sec and 1/125sec.

2 POSITION YOUR SOLUTION It's best to use a tripod, so attach your camera just above where your solution will be. Place the solution bowl in front of the camera, close enough to catch any drips, and position a sheet of black card behind the solution. This should be at an angle so it isn't lit by the light source – at roughly the same angle as the light should be about right.

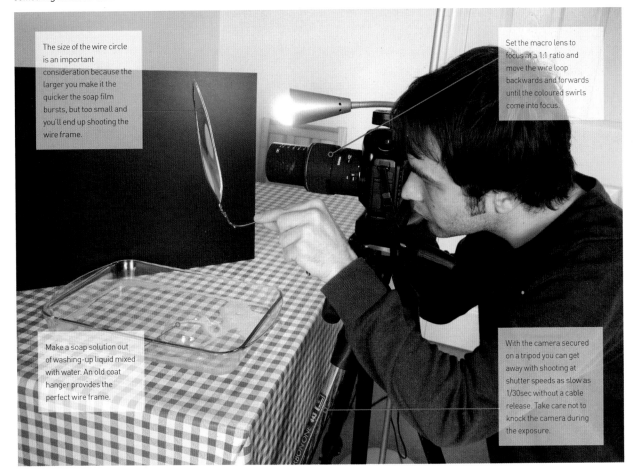

The size of the wire circle is an important consideration because the larger you make it the quicker the soap film bursts, but too small and you'll end up shooting the wire frame.

Set the macro lens to focus at a 1:1 ratio and move the wire loop backwards and forwards until the coloured swirls come into focus.

Make a soap solution out of washing-up liquid mixed with water. An old coat hanger provides the perfect wire frame.

With the camera secured on a tripod you can get away with shooting at shutter speeds as slow as 1/30sec without a cable release. Take care not to knock the camera during the exposure.

No two shots are ever the same, because the exact angle of the light in relation to the soap film constantly changes, as does the film itself once it begins its short life. Shoot the swirling patterns next to the edge of the wire and then concentrate on the centre of the soap film for very different results.

HOW TO INCREASE YOUR SUCCESS RATE

The difficulty in this technique comes from having to move the wire and soap solution backwards and forwards to focus, not to mention finding the best angle for it to catch the light correctly. Until you hone your technique it's not uncommon to shoot out-of-focus shots and photos with black bands across the frame, although this can, occasionally, add to the composition. The key to success is to shoot a large number of frames to increase your hit rate.

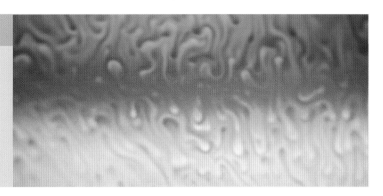

PROCESSING TECHNIQUE
ELEMENTS

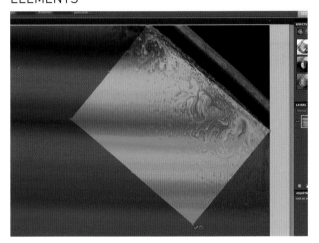

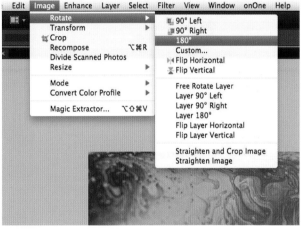

1 CROP THE IMAGE The best parts of the frame will be tiny, so some cropping is absolutely necessary. Activate the Crop tool by pressing C on your keyboard, and then left-click and drag to define the crop area. To rotate the crop area, move the pointer to one of the corners of the crop until the rotate arrow appears, then simply left-click and drag to rotate it.

2 ROTATE THE IMAGE Rotating the crop area is one thing but there's a reasonable chance you may need to rotate the cropped image for the best result. To do this, go to Image>Rotate and then enter the most appropriate amount for your image. This crop required the final image to be rotated by 180°. If the result isn't right, press Ctrl+Z and try again.

3 INTERPOLATE THE IMAGE Hold down Ctrl+Alt+I to open the Image Size dialogue box. Make sure the Constrain Proportions and Resample Image check boxes are ticked and increase either the Width or Height to the desired length. With proportions constrained the other edge will increase automatically. Try to limit size increase to about a third for the best interpolation results.

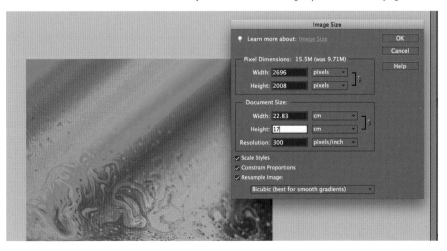

Freeze motion with off-camera flash

Stop moving objects in their tracks and get pin-sharp images with your flash

CAPTURING A CRITICALLY SHARP IMAGE of a moving subject isn't the easiest of tasks. Without enough available light to allow for faster shutter speeds, speedy movement can create an unwanted blur (see example), but flash can help. By filling the scene with a super-fast burst of bright light it's possible to capture pin-sharp shots of even the fastest subjects and freeze them dead in their tracks, making for fantastic images that would otherwise have been missed with the naked eye.

Splashing liquid is an ideal candidate for freezing in this way as its fast movements and unpredictable shapes make for brilliant pictures. Some ordinary household items – a glass tumbler, a lime and some soda water – are good subjects for some simple but effective splash photos.

WHY USE FLASH?

A burst of light emitted from a flashgun set to manual can last 1/1000sec or less, and by removing all other lighting and making the flash the only light source in your scene, the flash burst effectively becomes the length of the exposure. So, when the camera's shutter is opened and the flash is fired, the burst of light illuminates the subject, imprinting that moment onto the camera's sensor and nothing else before or after. It's so fast that it freezes the subject in place.

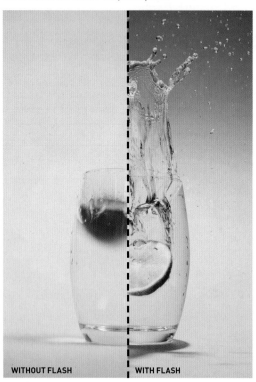

WITHOUT FLASH   WITH FLASH

FINISH

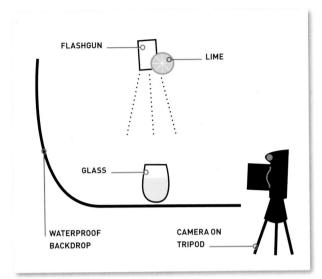

A flashgun and touch of careful timing is all you'll need to capture some fascinating splash photography.

SHOOTING TECHNIQUE

Shooting against a waterproof backdrop is always a good idea when dealing with liquids. A 1x2m piece of vinyl flooring can be picked up for about £15 from a local DIY store. Then use gaffer tape to secure it to the wall and table, creating a smooth curve behind the subject. Alternatively, you can shoot on a tiled or vinyl floor at home and place a white piece of paper behind it to create a background.

1 SET UP YOUR FLASHGUN Once your flashgun has powered up, start by switching it over to full manual mode, giving you complete control over its settings. Dial down the power to 1/16 and if your flashgun has a zoom function, adjust it to the widest setting available so that the burst of light will cover the broadest possible area.

2 CAMERA SET UP Grab your DSLR and set it to full manual mode (M on the mode dial) so that you can control the exposure settings yourself. Now set the shutter speed to 1/160sec and the aperture to f/8. Make sure that the ISO is set to its lowest setting for best picture quality (ISO 100 or 200), and then finally switch the white balance over to flash.

3 SELF-TIMER. Use self-timer mode to help carefully time the drop of the lime into the soda water. In your camera's Drive Mode settings, select 10sec timer, giving you enough time to fire the shutter and ready yourself for the drop. Alternatively, if you have someone to help, get them to drop the lime while you fire the shutter manually.

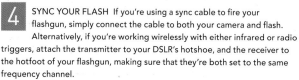

4 SYNC YOUR FLASH If you're using a sync cable to fire your flashgun, simply connect the cable to both your camera and flash. Alternatively, if you're working wirelessly with either infrared or radio triggers, attach the transmitter to your DSLR's hotshoe, and the receiver to the hotfoot of your flashgun, making sure that they're both set to the same frequency channel.

5 FOCUSING Attach your camera to a tripod and compose, zooming in to about 50mm so you're not too close to the water, and framing the glass in the lower part so there's room for the splash. Press the shutter halfway to lock the focus on the glass (focusing on the base will make this easier) then switch over to manual focus to stop your camera 'hunting' when you press the shutter button later.

6 TAKE THE SHOT Turn off any room lights and fully depress the shutter to activate the self-timer. Hold the flashgun in one hand and the lime in the other, and position them about 60cm above the glass of soda water. When the camera is just about to fire, drop the lime into the water, being careful not to get any of the splashing liquid onto your flashgun. Check the results on your camera screen and if the image is too bright, try holding your flashgun further away from the subject on the next go. Alternatively, if it's too dark, increase the flash power to 1/8.

7 CLEAN UP AND REPEAT It may take you a few attempts to get it just right, but you'll soon master the correct timing. Before reshooting though, and especially with electric gadgets nearby, it's important to keep things dry. Make a note of where the 'splash zone' is and keep all equipment out of that area. Clean up any spillages with a cloth or kitchen roll and without moving the glass, or you'll need to refocus.

PROCESSING TECHNIQUE

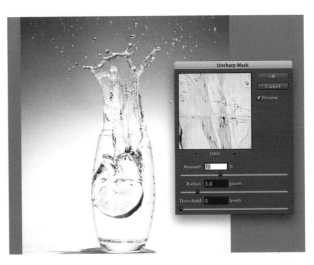

1 CORRECTING EXPOSURE It can be hard to get the exposure exactly right when working with flash, especially if you have a white background. Open up your image in Photoshop or Elements and correct any exposure problems with a Levels Adjustment Layer (Layer>New Adjustment Layer>Levels). Move the White Point Slider to the left slightly to brighten up a dark background.

2 LOOKING SHARP Highlight the Background Layer in the Layers palette by clicking on it, before choosing Enhance>Unsharp Mask (or Filter>Sharpen>Unsharp Mask for Photoshop users). In the window that appears, set the Amount to 70%, the Radius to 3 pixels and the Threshold to 0 levels, and then click OK to confirm the settings.

3 BURN IN THE DETAIL Choose the Burn tool from the Toolbox, or press O on the keyboard a few times until it appears (Shift+O for Photoshop). Move up to the Brush preset window in the Options Bar, choose a nice soft brush of about 65 pixels and make sure that the Range is set to Midtones, and that the Exposure is at 5%. Now run it over the centre of the lime to bring back some of the midtone detail.

4 TIDY THE FOREGROUND Hit Ctrl+Shift+N to create a new Layer, then choose the Brush Tool from the Toolbox with a soft Brush of about 200px in size. Hold down Alt and you'll see the Eyedropper icon appear. Left-click on a clean white area around the base of the glass to select that colour and proceed to paint over the bottom of the image to remove any offending shadows.

Power up to defy gravity

Be a superhero for the day, and capture your super powers on camera

WHAT YOU NEED
PHOTOSHOP
DSLR AND STANDARD
ZOOM
TRIPOD
WIRELESS REMOTE
CONTROL

DIFFICULTY LEVEL
ADVANCED

FINISH

BE HONEST – HAVING SUPER POWERS is something we've probably all dreamed of at one stage or another, and makes a great basis for a quirky, enjoyable self portrait. Picking the right superhero to hoax requires some thought: flying through the air like Superman is possible, but a lot of hard work, while the Invisible Man is not a particularly visual concept. How about the wall-crawling abilities of Spider Man for a great image that will surely have your friends thinking you lead a secret double life.

To make the shot believable, try to come up with a rough story for the character you are about to become – having this makes it easier to think about how the end result will look. From this you can choose costume, location and props to ensure your photo idea is complete.

If you're stuck for an idea, how about the moment when, walking to work one morning, you suddenly realize you have a superpower. Unable to control the power, the person is surprised and slightly scared by what is happening as they stick to the wall as if it's a giant magnet. Sounds adventurous, but attention to detail is the key to a good result here – dressing in a suit and using props like a laptop bag, which you can tape to the wall to make it stick.

SHOOTING TECHNIQUE

This technique is a more advanced version of making someone appear to levitate (see Floating Portraits Project 35 on page 136). The principles behind the two techniques are very similar, but attaching someone to a wall some way off the ground requires more subtlety. As always, the key to success is consistency between shots, so a tripod is absolutely essential. Off-camera flash can be used to add a 'caught in the headlights' effect, but this is optional and the technique works perfectly well under normal daylight conditions.

When it comes to self portraits there are a few ways of being both photographer and subject. For this type of shot, where you won't have much time to scurry between the camera and your pose, a remote control combined with the camera's self timer is a good bet: the 2sec or 10sec delay will give you enough time to stash the remote out of sight in your pocket.

Alternatively, ask a friend to play assistant and fire the camera Or shoot the picture with a model and stay behind the camera.

1 SET UP THE SCENE Find a location with a wall to pose against, and position a ladder or footstool to stand on. Set up your DSLR on a tripod and find a good composition for the scene. Make sure the tripod is locked securely in position because even a small amount of movement between shots can create hours of extra editing time.

2 CHOOSE YOUR FOCUS POINT Manually focus on the model's face, or if you're the model then focus on the wall behind where your head will be – depth-of-field will ensure your face is sharp. Engaging manual focus mode will ensures the focus point in every shot is the same.

3 SET UP THE CAMERA Shoot in manual exposure mode so the camera settings are identical in every shot. Set the ISO to between ISO 100 and ISO 400, depending on conditions and set the aperture to a medium setting. With a wide-angle lens depth-of-field will be pretty good at f/5. If you're shooting at more telephoto settings, use an aperture of at least f/8.

4 USE PROPS TO ADD NARRATIVE Props can really add life to photos like this. They must be relevant, otherwise they'll stick out like a sore thumb. This laptop bag was stuck to the wall using tape; it didn't keep it up there for long, but it was enough to get one shot of it. The end of the red tie was also stuck to the wall with tape.

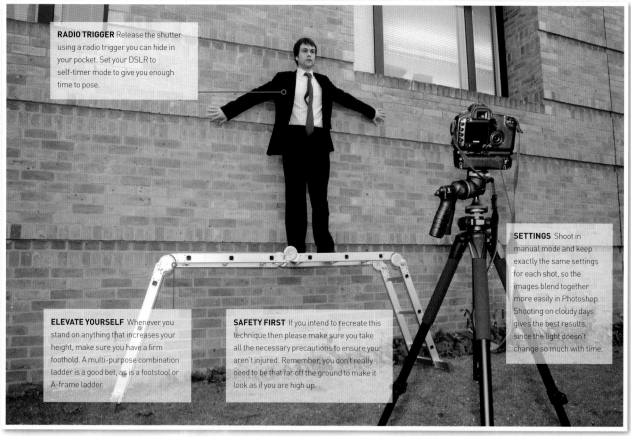

RADIO TRIGGER Release the shutter using a radio trigger you can hide in your pocket. Set your DSLR to self-timer mode to give you enough time to pose.

SETTINGS Shoot in manual mode and keep exactly the same settings for each shot, so the images blend together more easily in Photoshop. Shooting on cloudy days gives the best results, since the light doesn't change so much with time.

ELEVATE YOURSELF Whenever you stand on anything that increases your height, make sure you have a firm foothold. A multi-purpose combination ladder is a good bet, as is a footstool or A-frame ladder.

SAFETY FIRST If you intend to recreate this technique then please make sure you take all the necessary precautions to ensure you aren't injured. Remember, you don't really need to be that far off the ground to make it look as if you are high up.

TIP

HOW TO GET THE BEST RESULT

For the individual photos, attach your camera to a tripod to prevent variation between frames. Camera settings and flash power (if you are using flash) should be kept constant too by using manual modes where possible. This will ensure a successful blend in Photoshop later.

The end result is made up of five separate photos: one for the laptop bag, one for the empty scene, one for each leg and one for the face.

PROCESSING TECHNIQUE

1 STACK THE IMAGES Open your shots in Photoshop using the empty scene photo as the base image. Drag the other four shots onto it in this order – right leg, left leg, bag and then face. Add a Layer Mask to the top layer by clicking on the Layer Mask icon at the bottom of the layers palette and paint black with the Brush Tool to blend the shots of the model's legs.

2 REVEAL PROPS Type Ctrl+E to merge the top layer with the second layer. Add a Layer Mask to the new top layer and paint with a black brush where the bag should be. The bag will appear, but if at any point during the masking process you make a mistake, switch the Foreground colour from black to white and erase the mistake.

3 CHANGE FACIAL EXPRESSION Hold down Ctrl+E to merge the top layer with the second layer and add a Layer Mask to the new top layer. Again, paint with the Brush Tool set to black and reveal the shot of the face with the best expression. If one of your leg or bag shots has a good expression you can use this but you must reveal it using masking when that layer is being edited.

4 REMOVE THE LADDER Hold down Ctrl+E to merge the top layer with the second layer and add a Layer Mask to the new top layer. Again, paint with the Brush Tool set to black and this time remove the ladder from the shot along with any stray pieces of leg that may not have been cleaned up in previous layers.

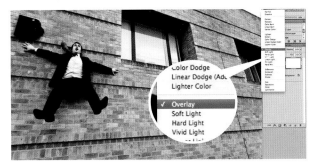

5 ADD SPECIAL EFFECTS Hold down Ctrl+E to merge the top layer with the background layer, so now there will be just one layer. To add a graphic look to the shot, go to the Adjustment Layers icon in the Layers palette (the half-black/half-white circle icon) and choose Black & White. Set the layer blending Mode to overlay and reduce the opacity to 50%.

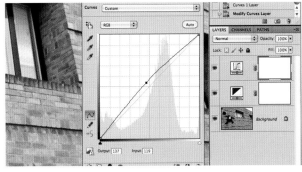

6 FINAL TWEAKS Every shot is slightly different, so final tweaks can vary. If your image looks a little too dark or light, add a Curves adjustment layer by clicking adding another Adjustment Layer – this time a Curves one. Push up the middle of the Curve to brighten the picture; pull it down to darken the scene.

Create a water droplet effect

Add virtual water drops without getting your camera wet

USUALLY, RAIN AND PHOTOGRAPHY DON'T MIX so here's a great alternative to running the risk of getting your delicate camera gear wet. This project helps you create realistic water drops on any surface. No special filters or images are required – everything you need is already built into Photoshop.

Adding water drops to a subject can really make an impact but it's important to choose the right start image.

Obvious subjects are flowers and plants, and a close-up of a leaf is exactly the kind of thing that would collect water drops. Of course, you can apply the same technique to any photo and some will work better than others, but it's great fun to experiment!

And once you've mastered the technique, you'll be adding water drops to everything!

CHOOSING A START IMAGE

This is a nice, clean close-up of a leaf and ideal for adding water drops to. The uniform surface allows you to experiment with different-sized droplets for a more realistic-looking final effect. The leaf fills the frame and so makes a striking subject, and the subtle colours make it easy to add in water droplets which reveal the surface below.

START IMAGE

FINISH

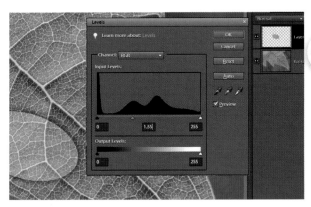

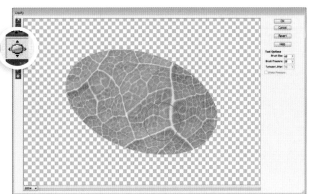

1 ADD A DROP Pick the right kind of image from your files, then start by using the Elliptical Marquee tool to make a Selection where you want your first water drop. If you go to Select>Transform Selection you can reshape or rotate it. Copy the selected area by pressing Ctrl+C and then hit Ctrl+V to paste it as a new Layer. Now go to Layer>Layer Style and, in Elements only, click Style Settings. Choose the Drop Shadow effect and change Size to 75 and Distance to 0. A real water drop acts like a mini lens, magnifying and brightening whatever's below, so to lighten it hit Ctrl+L to open Levels and move the mid point slider to about 1.55.

2 LIQUIFY THE LEAF Next, you need to open Liquify, which is usually found under Filter or sometimes Filter>Distort. Once inside Liquify, select the Bloat tool and carefully paint on the leaf with a small brush, using a brush pressure of about 25. Try not to move the edges if possible so you keep the water drop as a perfect oval and therefore make it look more realistic. If you do go over the edge and spoil the shape, press Ctrl+Z to undo the last step then continue painting.

TIP

HOW TO MAKE IT REALISTIC

The key to keeping it real is to ensure that the direction of light remains constant. This means when adding the gradient or the white reflection, make sure they're always on the same side of every drop. A great tip is to make all your drops different sizes and it doesn't matter if you're making big ones or small ones – the technique is exactly the same. In fact, once you've learnt how to make one drop, adding more becomes much quicker and easier.

LIGHT

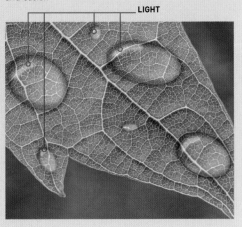

3 ADD SOME LIGHT Now add some lighting effects for a more 3D feel to the drip. Press Ctrl+Shift+N to make a new Layer, click Select>Reselect and then press D to reset the colour swatches to black and white. Start with the Gradient tool; check in the Options bar at the top that it's a Linear Gradient and the Foreground/Background gradient is selected. Drag a diagonal gradient across the Selection and change the Blending Mode to Soft Light.

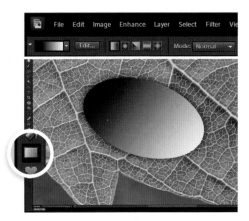

4 ADD SPARKLE All that needs doing now is a bit of painting. Press Ctrl+Shift+N to make a new Layer and go to Select>Reselect. Use a soft-edged paintbrush about 200px in size and paint around, but just outside, the Selection. Change the Layer Opacity to about 30%. Now make another new Layer and press X. This time reduce the paint brush size to about 80px and paint a white arc well inside the Selection. Lower the Opacity to about 50% and you're all done!

Add extras to architecture

Three great ideas to add a new dimension to your architectural images

WHAT YOU NEED
ELEMENTS
PHOTOSHOP

DIFFICULTY LEVEL
INTERMEDIATE

FROM CASTLES TO COTTAGES, and superstructures to street scenes here are some simple ways to add wow factor to your pictures.

FROM PICTURE TO PAINTING

Street scenes can be bustling with life or be more subtle still lifes – as here – gentle shots that are simply about shapes working together. As photos, these can work nicely as a set to reveal the nature of a place, but viewed in isolation they can look a bit, well, underwhelming – especially when the backdrop is cluttered and busy.

But what they can do is make an excellent starting point for a painterly masterpiece. They're
exactly the kind of scene that a painter would look for – packed with detail, colour and texture – so, provided you have a reasonable composition and a little bit of light, you've got everything you need.

Although pen & wash style paint effects can be generated just by using filters, this technique puts the art back into the process, as it involves you making real brushstrokes and painting directly on the pic. It's great fun, thoroughly addictive, and produces fab results.

FINISH

EDITED SHOT (Left)
A great effect is easy to achieve, and you really get to paint, too!Modes.

THE IMAGE (Below)
Taken in a side street in Istanbul, Turkey, the original pic is pleasant enough, but it doesn't really hold enough interest to work as a photo in its own right. It does, however, offer lots of detail and colour, and is nicely composed with the scooter on the lower-left third and the pharmacy 'E' sign balancing it on the top-right.

DETAIL AND TEXTURE
To make a painterly effect work, you need to start with a picture with lots of intricate detail. You have it in abundance here, with the shapes and lines of the scooter and street signs dominating the frame. On the less detailed areas, you still have some texture, and that will come in handy to create an authentic look with your brushstroke effects.

VIBRANT COLOUR
Vivid, highly saturated areas give a sense of depth to the scene, and the main components are again the bright red of the pharmacy signs and the punchy blue of the scooter. You can accentuate these colours to give your painterly effect more warmth.

PROCESSING TECHNIQUE

1 COPY THE PICTURE Pick a colourful, detailed photo from your collection, then the first job is to get your Layers palette on screen. If yours isn't already there, go to Window>Layers and it'll appear. You need to make two copies of the Background Layer, so hit Ctrl+J twice on the keyboard and you'll see them stack up in the palette. You need to create a simplified, sketched version of the pic, and you're going to use the charcoal filter. It's worth noting that this filter takes its information from Photoshop's foreground and background colours, so you need to set them to Black and White before opening it. The fastest way to do this is to hit D on the keyboard. With the colours set, make sure the top Layer is highlighted, and go to Filter>Sketch>Charcoal. In the dialogue box, for this image, charcoal was set to a thickness to 2, detail to 5 and light/dark Balance to 50, but with your own images have a quick play with the settings to get the best effect. You want an unfussy sketch that has a reasonable level of detail but doesn't look too dark. When you're happy, click OK to run the filter.

CHARCOAL FILTER
The charcoal filter works well with settings of 2, 5 and 50 on this example, but experiment with the sliders to get the best results on your own pics. colours to give your painterly effect more warmth.

2 DEGRADE COLOUR LAYER Now you have a good-looking sketch, click where it says normal in the Layers palette and change the Blending Mode to Soft Light – this will allow the Charcoal Layer to be overlaid on the Layer beneath. You need to do some work on this middle Layer, so click on it to make it active. You're going to apply a paint filter to deconstruct it, so go to Filter>Brush Strokes>Spatter and try setting Spray Radius to 22 and Smoothness to 9. You might want to tweak these settings on your own pics, but they work pretty well on this example, and are a good starting point. Click OK to run the filter, and then to further degrade the image, select the Eraser tool. Switch off the Background layer at the bottom of the stack by clicking the 'eye' icon alongside it, and then, up in the Options bar at the top of the screen, click on the downward-facing arrow next to the Brush size and pick the Dry Brush (39) option from the list. If you can't see it, pick the Large List view option from the Brush Preset Picker (see Tech Talk).

Now set Opacity to 35, and Flow to 100, and then increase brush size to about 500px – you can do this by hitting the right square brackets key. Paint quickly over the entire image to make it more mottled and less distinct. You now need to boost the colours to inject a bit more vibrance into the scene, so when you're done with the mottled Eraser, hit Ctrl+U to open the Hue/Saturation palette, and crank up the Saturation slider to about +50. Click OK and your image should be taking shape.

3 GRAB A BRUSH It's time for the fun to begin! You're going to start painting to add a real human feel. In the Layers palette, click on the top Layer, and then click the Create a New Layer icon at the bottom of the palette. Set the Blending mode to multiply, click on the Brush tool, and from the list, select the Watercolor Loaded Wet Flat Tip (WlWFT) brush. In the options bar, set Opacity to 35 and Flow to 100.

Now open the Swatches palette (Window>Swatches) and pick a colour. Paint directly onto the image, using repeated strokes to build up the colour depth, or single strokes to give a subtle colour wash. Change brush size with the square brackets keys, and change colours using the Swatches palette. You don't have to cover the entire image – that's why you've got your degraded layer in place – or to be too neat, either – the effect will be all the better with a few rough edges. The WlWFT brush was used throughout, but there are dozens to choose from if you want to try some different brush textures and flow rates.

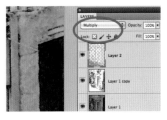

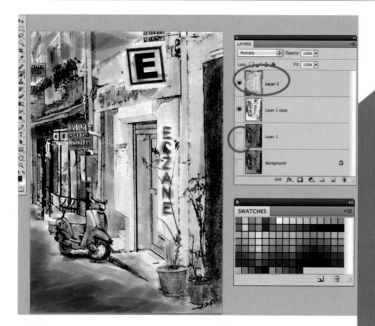

BRUSH PRESETS

Click on the Brush tool and then pop up to the Options bar at the top of the screen. Click the downward-facing arrow next to the Brush size box and you'll bring up the Brush Preset Picker. This can be displayed in various ways, but one of the most convenient is the Large List option, which gives you a small image of the brush head and a description alongside. To set this, click on the fly-out arrow at the top-right of the Brush Preset Picker and select Large List.

4 IMPROVE YOUR BRUSHWORK Once your hand-painting is underway, switch off your degraded colour Layer by clicking on the 'eye' icon alongside Layer 1, and you'll be able to see your brushwork over the charcoal. If you like the look of this then continue painting in this mode to get a really loose, watercolour feel to the picture. It's a good idea to switch on the colour Layer from time to time to use as a reference. If you do this, you can see which colours and tones are in the original, and that'll guide your choices when you're selecting colours from the Swatches palette.

Vary your brush size as you go, and before long, you'll have built up a great-looking effect, all of which you'll have painted yourself. Once you're happy, switch Layer 1 back on again, and see whether you prefer the richer look with it in place, or the looser look with it switched off.

5 CREATE AN ARTISTIC EFFECT You're getting there, but you need to sort out the edges of your piece of art. Very few watercolours would have a squared-off edge, so you need to introduce a more ragged effect to give a painterly feel. You're going to do this by covering the pic with a white 'page' and painting a hole in the middle of it. This will give a ragged surround, but it'll also give you white at the very edges – just what you need for when you make a print. Your paper will be white, so you want the painting to 'bleed' out of it, giving an ultra-realistic look and feel.

To do all this, click on the top Layer, and then click the Create a New Layer icon to make a blank Layer at the top of the Layers stack. Hit D to ensure you've got black and white as the foreground and background colours, and then hit Alt+Backspace to fill with the background colour. This will flood your top Layer with white, and the white layer will cover the whole image. To make a hole that reveals the picture beneath, select the Eraser, and pick the same WIWFT brush you used before.

Set your Opacity to 35 and your Flow to 100 in the Options bar, and paint inside the edge of the frame in short strokes to reveal a strip of the picture. It'll take a few minutes, but paint all the way around, and once you have a ragged-edged strip you can increase brush size and paint out the middle. With an opacity of 35, you'll need to use repeated strokes to bring the painting through, but this will add a bit of texture. Once you've completed painting the hole in the white Layer, you'll have a painting! The human feel is there in the brushstrokes and the ragged edge effect, and all that remains is to add some extra texture to it.

6 APPLY A TEXTURE LAYER You'll have built up a good number of Layers so far in creating the image, but there's always room for one more. You can stop here but if you have a suitable texture image then open it up and then hit Ctrl+A to select it all. You'll see the 'marching ants' surround the image and, when you do, hit Ctrl+C to copy the texture into system memory. You can now close it down with the shortcut Ctrl+W and, once it's off the screen, you'll go back to your main image. Hit Ctrl+V to paste the texture in place, and then, in the Layers palette, drag the new texture Layer so it sits below the top Layer with the ragged edge.

Now click where it says Normal, and change the Blending Mode to Soft Light (for a bolder texture, try using Overlay instead of Soft Light). This will allow the texture to show through the image and give some extra depth. Once you're happy, go to File>Save As and save your work in the Photoshop format. this will retain all the Layers so if you want to jump back in at a later date and do a bit more brushwork, you can.

TIP

USING SPECIAL BRUSHES

When you're using special brushes, like the Watercolor Loaded Wet Flat Tip in this project, you may find that the angle of the brush tip isn't what you want. The good news is that it's easy to change – just open the Brush panel(Window>Brush in Photoshop or click on the Brush icon on the right of the Options bar in Elements). Once the panel is on screen, you'll see an 'angle' icon (a circle with crosshairs and an arrow). Click and drag the arrow and you'll change the angle of the brush tip, so if you want it to be vertical instead of horizontal, just drag it to 90 degrees.

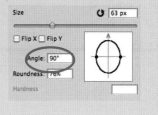

EXPERT ADVICE

GET FAMILIAR WITH FILTERS

There are so many filters in Photoshop and Elements that it can be hard to know where to start. Because of this, it's a really good idea to spend some time trying out each filter on an image, just so you can familiarise yourself with the sort of effect that's produced. While you're looking at the effects generated by the filters, have a play with the settings and sliders, as this will give you a rough feel for how they change the results on the pic. Keep a pad by your PC and, as you go through each filter, make a quick note of any you particularly like the look of. This is really important as there's nothing worse than knowing the effect you want to create but not knowing how to get there! It's normally a combination of filters that produces the best results but an hour of experimenting/ note-taking will prove invaluable as your experience grows.

PROCESSING TECHNIQUE
BLURRED VIGNETTE

Using a shot of Groombridge Park in Kent – with its nicely balanced lighting, great sky and plenty of depth-of-field – as a start image here are a couple of other ideas to add an extra dimension to your architectural images.

The first is vignetting. Cool, slick and arty, this effect focuses attention on the centre of your shot by darkening and blurring the edges. It's handy one for symmetrical scenes, or ones with a nice lead-in line, like the path in this example.

ORIGINAL IMAGE

ORIGINAL SHOT
Both techniques work on images with finely detailed subjects, and here you have that from the lead-in line of the path, through to the brickwork and windows of the house.

FINISH

A Open the pic into Photoshop or Elements and then in the Toolbox, click and hold on the Rectangular Marquee so you can select the Elliptical Marquee tool.

B Click in the top-left corner of the image and drag down to the bottom-right to make an elliptical Selection, then click the Refine Edge button in the Options bar and move the Feather slider to an amount of about 150px. This will soften the edge of the selection you've made. When you've done this, click OK.

C Hit Ctrl+Shift+I to get the inverse of the Selection and then go to Filter>Blur> Gaussian Blur, using a Radius setting of 25. Click OK to confirm this.

D Hit Ctrl+U to open Hue/Saturation and move the Lightness slider to the left to about -40. Click OK, then get rid of the 'marching ants' by hitting Ctrl+D.

E Finally, to boost the colours, hit Ctrl+U again and move the Saturation slider to the right to about +30. Click OK.

PROCESSING TECHNIQUE
ANTIQUE TONING

This technique combines two different toning effects to give a really rich, sumptuous finish. It produces a rich sepia-style result, but if you look closely, you'll see that all the highlights have a subtle glow to them, which really adds a touch of class. Try this one on older buildings and barns, as it'll be a bit over-the-top for a modern semi on a housing estate!

A With the pic open in Photoshop or Elements, hit Ctrl+J to make a copy of the Layer, then hit Ctrl+U. In the Hue/Saturation palette, tick the Colorize box and set both the Hue and Saturation sliders to about 30 for a sepia toning effect. Click OK.

B Go to Filter>Blur> Gaussian Blur and use a Radius of about 15px to really blur out the sepia-toned Layer. Now in the Layers palette (Window>Layers), click where it says Normal and from the options provided change the Blending Mode to Overlay.

C In the Layers palette, click on the Background Layer to make it active, then hit Ctrl+U. Tick the Colorize box and use settings of 0 in Hue and 15 in Saturation to give a gentle red toning. Click OK to this and you'll see a wonderful blend of colour and contrast.

D To strengthen the effect, click on the top Layer and hit Ctrl+J again to copy it. This will reproduce the blurred sepia Layer and apply the overlay Blending Mode in one fell swoop, producing very warm, rich tones. If this finish is looking too strong for your image, click on Opacity in the Layers palette and reduce the strength of the effect by moving the slider to the left a little.

FINISH

Shoot X-ray effects

Create amazing X-ray pictures of everyday objects

WHAT YOU NEED
PHOTOSHOP OR
ELEMENTS

DIFFICULTY LEVEL
INTERMEDIATE

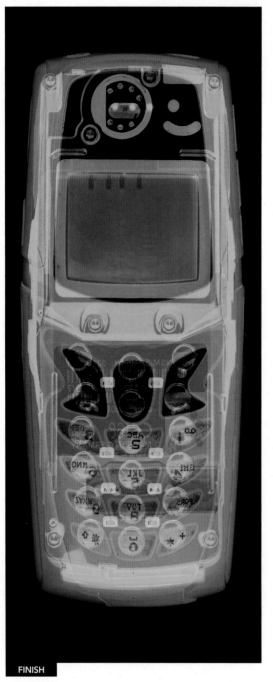

FINISH

EVER WISH YOUR CAMERA HAD AN X-RAY FUNCTION, so you could reveal the complex inner layers of everyday objects? Well, sadly technology hasn't progressed that far yet, but what if there was a way to create realistic X-ray-style images using nothing more than a bit of Photoshop trickery? The beauty of this technique is that it's very simple but the result speaks for itself, leaving you with an image that's bound to impress. The whole thing works by carefully dismantling your chosen subject and taking a snap of each of its layers. These photos are then blended together in Photoshop to create the illusion of an X-ray picture. Choose your subject wisely, though: you'll need to make sure that whatever you choose to take apart is also easy to put back together again if you still need to use it. An old mobile phone with an interchangeable case is a good example since it offers easy access to its inner workings without causing any unnecessary damage.

SHOOTING TECHNIQUE

A total of four shots are blended together to make the final X-ray-style image, each taken in a well-lit area to avoid harsh shadows. To keep background clutter to a minimum place your subject on an A4 sheet of white printer paper. Use Aperture priority, setting a small aperture of about f/11 to ensure that each shot is sharp from front to back and shows maximum detail – as indeed a real X-ray image does.

START IMAGES

PROCESSING TECHNIQUE

1 STARTING OUT With either Photoshop or Elements opened up, make a new document by hitting Ctrl+N. In the New Document dialogue set the Preset to International Paper, the size to A4, the Color mode to grayscale and make sure Background Contents option is set to White. Click OK. The next step is to import your images into the new document: go to File>Open and locate your photos and open each one. For each image hit Ctrl+A followed by Ctrl+C to copy it to the clipboard. Go back to the blank document (Window>Untitled-1) and press Ctrl+V to paste the image as a new layer within the Layers palette (Window>layers). Repeat this process for your remaining images until they're all on their own layers within the document. You can close the component pictures when you've combined them all.

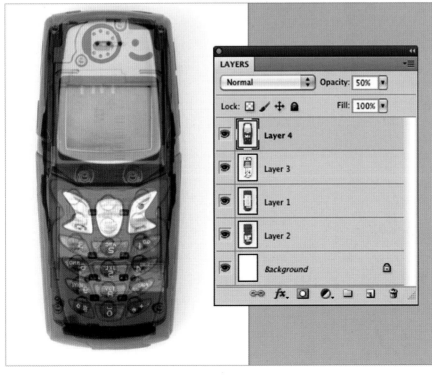

2 GETTING ALIGNED With all of your images open and combined in the new blank document, the next step is to make sure that all of these image Layers line up correctly and the easiest way to do this is to simply click the top layer within the Layers palette – Layer 4 – to make it active, then reduce its opacity to 50% to expose some of Layer 3 beneath it. Now click Layer 3 in the Layers palette to make it active and, using the Move tool, carefully reposition it so that it lines up with Layer 4. Once you've done this, click the eye icon next to Layer 4 to turn it off and reduce the opacity of Layer 3 to 50%. Repeat the process, lining up Layer 2 with Layer 3 and Layer 1 with Layer 2 until all of the Layers match up. If one of your shots isn't quite the same size, hit Ctrl+T to enter Free Transform mode and pull on one of the corner handles to resize it. Hit enter to confirm. Once finished, make sure that the layers are visible again by clicking where their eye icons should be.

3 INVERTING THE IMAGE Now that all of the layers are lined up correctly, start by reducing the opacity of each (except the Background layer) to 50%. Doing this will allow you to see through each layer, which is the start of the X-ray treatment. The real secret to this effect, however, is inverting the colours of each phone layer so that they're turned into a negative. Do this by clicking on the top Layer in the Layers palette and hitting Ctrl+I to invert it. Repeat this process for all the other phone Layers, working your way down the list until you get to the Background Layer at the very bottom. This layer will also need to be inverted to change it from its current White state to pure Black – click it to make it active then simply press Ctrl+I to turn it Black in an instant. Your image will now look much closer to the finished product, though there are a few finishing touches you can apply to really add impact.

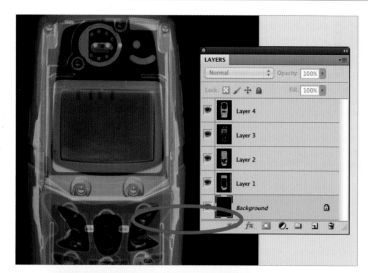

4 ADD GLOW AND TONING Now it's time to add a blue glow effect, just like the effect seen on many types of X-rays. To do this, first make a duplicate of the top Layer by clicking it in the Layers palette to highlight it, then hit Ctrl+J on the keyboard. Click where it says normal in the Layers palette, choose the Lighten Blending mode and increase the opacity to 100%. Drag the Layer down the list so that it's positioned above the Background layer. Next, go to Filter>Blur>Gaussian Blur and set the radius to 250px before clicking OK. Finally, hit Ctrl+L to bring up a Levels adjustment and move the white-point slider to brighten the effect and give the image a boost.

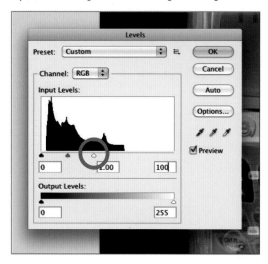

Now change the Color mode for the whole document from Grayscale to RGB by selecting Image>Mode>RGB Color. Next, make the top layer active by clicking it in the Layers palette and click the Adjustment Layer icon. From the list choose Photo Filter and, in the window, set the Filter to Cyan to create a cold blue tone. Next, boost the strength of the effect by increasing the density to 80%, and make sure that the Preserve Luminosity option is ticked at the bottom of the window.

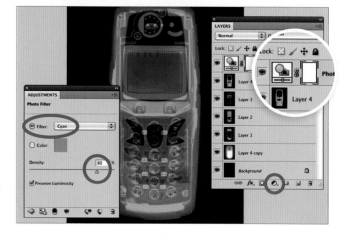

5 BOOSTING CONTRAST Most of the construction work is now complete but there's still one last trick you can do to improve the results, and that's to increase the contrast and make the whole thing pop. In the Layers palette, make sure that the top layer (the Photo Filter Adjustment Layer you created in the previous step) is highlighted. Click the adjustment layer icon at the bottom of the palette and select Levels.

In the Levels dialogue, all you need to do is move the White-Point slider below the histogram to the left to brighten up the highlights. Once you're happy with the results, finish things off by flattening the Layer using Ctrl+E on the keyboard. Then save the image as a JPEG by going to File>Save as.

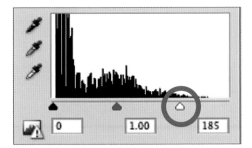

LINE UP LAYERS

Making sure that all of your layers are aligned correctly will give you the best results for this technique. If you're finding it difficult to line up your layers using your computer mouse, try using the directional arrow keys on your keyboard to gently nudge the layers in the right direction. It's a really useful feature that's ideal for making small, precise adjustments.

After choosing the Move tool from the toolbox, position the Layer you want to align as close as possible to its correct location. Now simply tap the directional keys in the direction you want the layer to move. Each press moves it one pixel; holding down Shift while you nudge will move it 10 pixels.

ALIGN LAYERS

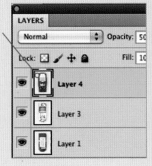

HOW TO GIVE OTHER SUBJECTS THE X-RAY TREATMENT

Once you've practised the technique you can apply it to all manner of subjects. The only limit is your imagination. Here are some tips for shooting your pseudo X-ray photos.

• Choose a subject that's easy to dismantle – and to put back together again if you are going to need it in the future. Small electrical items, like an old computer mouse or remote control, are a good place to start as their inner circuit boards provide plenty of interesting details. Fruit, vegetables and flowers are also a good choice of subject.

• With a subject decided on, you'll now need to take snaps of its individual layers. Shooting in an evenly-lit area is a must, as any harsh light will cast shadows that will look unnatural when the colours are inverted.

• Shooting outdoors on a cloudy day gives a pleasant diffused lighting, and a sheet of white paper provides a nice, clean background.

• Switch your camera over to Aperture priority mode (A or Av on the mode dial), setting an aperture of f/8 to ensure front-to-back sharpness. To make aligning your images as easy as possible, lock off your camera on a tripod to prevent the shooting angle altering as you photograph the subject's layers.

• If your shots are too light or dark, dial in some exposure compensation, starting with ±1 stop and moving to 2 stops if necessary.

Retouch to make the most of your models

Improve your portraits in just a few minutes in Photoshop

WHAT YOU NEED
PHOTOSHOP OR
ELEMENTS

DIFFICULTY LEVEL
EASY

PORTRAIT RETOUCHING IS OFTEN painted as a contentious subject because parts of the fashion and advertising industry have taken its application to the extreme. But retouching doesn't have to be a dirty word – when used in moderation it's an extremely useful tool. Everyone has woken up to find a huge spot where just the day before there was a perfectly clear patch of skin. It's not the way you normally look, so removing such blemishes with Photoshop or Elements means the image is actually more in keeping with reality.

The Healing Brush is a highly effective tool for skin retouching and can be used for everything from basic spotting to non-destructive editing and more. It can really help you to get the best from your portraits.

START

WHY USE THE HEALING BRUSH TOOL

The Healing Brush Tool allows you to cover up imperfections by blending in pixels from elsewhere in the image. A sample is taken from an area close to the problem, and used to paint over the imperfection. The sample area is cloned and blended with the problem area, giving a result that is often seamless, a perfect match in tone, texture and lighting. This makes the Healing Brush perfect for detailed areas, like skin, where a perfect blend is essential.

PROBLEM AREAS
This model only has a few blemishes to remove, so we're not going to change his appearance too much. The Healing Brush Tool is perfect for the job.

FINISH

SHOOTING TECHNIQUE:
BLEMISHES

1 SET UP FOR HEALING Zoom in to about 100% so you can get a good view of the face. To do this, click on the Zoom tool in the Tools palette and left-mouse click on the face. To zoom out, hold down the Alt key when clicking. You may need to zoom in more or less, depending on how large the subject is in the photo. If you need to move the photo hold down the spacebar, left-click and drag.

2 REFINE THE HEALING BRUSH Press J to activate the Healing Brush tool or choose it from the Toolbox – look for the plaster icon (a plaster with a circle off to the side is the Spot Healing Tool). If the Spot Healing tool is selected when you press J, hold down shift and press J again. Click on the brush icon at the top-left of the Elements interface and drag the Hardness slider to 0% and set a small diameter.

3 HEAL THE BLEMISHES Make sure the Caps Lock is off so you have a visible brush cursor. The Aligned option should be checked to keep the sample area in line with the healing point as you paint. Now hold down the Alt key and left-click to sample close to the area you want to heal. Release the Alt key, hover the brush over the blemish and left-click with your mouse to heal the imperfection. Use short clicks rather than dragging.

WORKING NON-DESTRUCTIVELY

Using the Healing Brush in the way described means the image's pixels are physically changed. Once these changes have been made they are permanent; to reverse the change you'll have to step back using Undo, which undoes everything else you've done since, or edit the picture again. Alternatively, you can start to work non-destructively by making the Healing edits on an empty Layer.

The advantage of this approach is that, once you've edited a photo, you can easily remove or change those edits by deleting or altering their Layer, without having to go all the way back to the beginning and starting again. To give this method a try perform the following steps before you embark on the main Healing process described above.

A CREATE EMPTY LAYER To clone non-destructively create an empty Layer to work on. To do this either press Ctrl+shift+N, or click the 'Create a new Layer' icon at the bottom of the Layers palette – the square with an upturned corner.

B SAMPLE THE RIGHT LAYER Make sure the Healing Brush Tool is active, and the Sample All Layers box is checked. This means the sample point is taken from both the empty Layer and the Background Layer. If this is set to Current Layer nothing will be sampled.

4 CORRECT MISTAKES Don't work too quickly until you're confident with your skills. If you do make a mistake press Ctrl+Z to go back to a previous image state. Every time you press Ctrl+Z you go back one step. To go forward through the steps press Ctrl+Y. (In Photoshop press Alt-Ctrl-Z/Shift-Ctrl-Z to step back/forward, or use the History palette.)

5 LOOK FOR FINE DETAILS If you notice smaller imperfections surrounded by detail, like facial hair, zoom in even further and use a smaller brush to avoid mistakes. If you remain at 100% you could set a poor sample point so the healed area doesn't blend successfully with the surroundings. Once the finer imperfections have been fixed, zoom back out to about 100% to make sure the blend has been seamless.

6 CHECKING THE RESULT Once you've completed your retouching it's best to zoom back out to make sure all healing blends are unnoticeable. To do this, press Z to activate the Zoom Tool and click on the Print Size button. If you're happy you can save your work, but if there are areas you're unhappy with simply use Ctrl+Z (as in step 4) to go back to a previous image state and try again with the Healing Brush.

TECH TALK

HEALING DIFFICULT AREAS ADVANCED LEVEL

When shooting portraits outdoors you're at the mercy of the elements: a common problem is the wind blowing hair around. This can sometimes produce dramatic results, but most of the time it just blows stray hairs over difficult-to-clone areas like the eyes. These are often individual stray hairs that are still noticeable, but removing them with the Healing Brush (or Clone Stamp tool) will improve things. The main issues here will be sampling from the wrong area, not sampling often enough and using the wrong brush size.

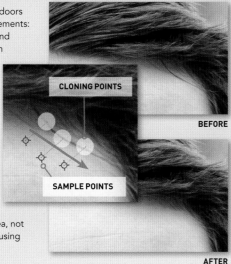

CLONING POINTS

SAMPLE POINTS

BEFORE

AFTER

A SAMPLE THE FRINGE Choose the Clone Stamp tool and tick the Aligned box in the Options bar to keep the sample point in line with the brush as it moves. Start sampling from points along the main line of the fringe, slightly above the stray hair. This will make the healing blend more seamless. Left-click to paint from the sampled point, and resample every few clicks to avoid a repeating pattern.

B CLICK, DON'T DRAG Setting the sample point so it's aligned with the brush usually works well and individual clicks along the length of the stray hair often work more effectively than clicking and dragging. Dragging the pointer when healing or cloning can create blurry areas with mismatched colours. Healing fine details can be fiddly and isn't always necessary, so don't create work for yourself unless the shot really needs it.

THE EYES HAVE IT

START

ORIGINAL IMAGE

FINISH

EYE LIGHTENED

PROCESSING TECHNIQUE: EYES

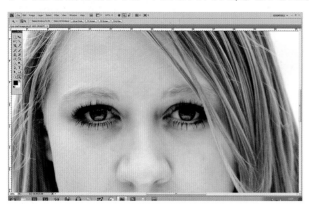

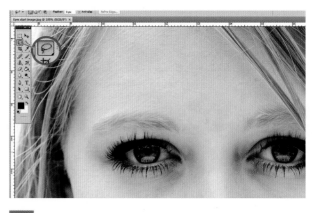

1 OPEN THE IMAGE Open your image and zoom in using the Zoom Tool to a comfortable working distance – 100 % is about right but it really depends on how big in the frame the eyes are, so choose a working distance that is right for you. Remember, with the Zoom Tool selected you can click the mouse to zoom in further or hold down the Alt key and click the mouse to zoom out.

2 FREEHAND LASSO TOOL Press L to get the freehand Lasso Tool and hit the Caps Lock to give you a more precise cross-hair cursor to draw with. This is important as you have to go around both eyes and you'll want to be as careful as you can be. This is the hardest bit of this technique and you'll need a steady hand, but keep trying until you can do it smoothly. A graphics tablet might help if you don't get on with a mouse.

3 DRAW AROUND THE INNER EYE Using the mouse, move the cross hair around the inner contour of the eye, keeping it fractionally within the natural frame of the eye. If you go wrong don't worry, just hold the Shift key down and redraw the bit you messed up and it'll sort itself out. Or hit Ctrl+Z to start the whole process again. But it really won't take you long to get the hang of it.

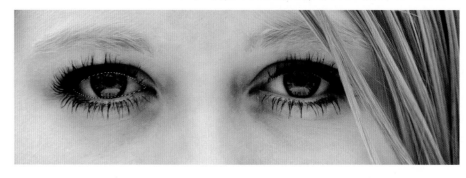

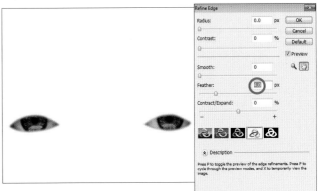

4 SELECT SECOND EYE You're now well practised, so repeating the process with the second eye will be easier. Hold the Shift key down so you don't lose the first selection and click in the corner of the eye with the cross hair and start the process over again. Go smoothly and steadily. When you are done, both eyes will have a selector line around them.

5 REFINE THE EDGES Now click on Refine Edge in the top bar. Go to the square icons with the symbols inside that you can see at the bottom and change the view to On White to make it easier to see how the edge softens. Move the feather slider to 3 or 4 for a subtle feathering that will just take the edge off the changes you are going to make so they appear natural. Click OK.

6 USE ADJUSTMENT LAYERS Now you are going to work in a separate Layer. If you've not done this before it's very straightforward. If the Layers palette isn't already open, hit F7 on your keyboard to open it. Click on the little symbol at the bottom of the palette that looks like a half-black/half-white circle; this is the Adjustment Layers icon. Click on the icon and select Levels from the options that are revealed.

7 LIGHTEN EYES USING LEVELS
In the Levels box that opens, pull in the white-point slider on the right hand side of the histogram to lighten the whites. You may want to tweak the middle slider (midtones) to lighten things even more, but take care not to overdo it or the eyes will be too white and will look unnatural.

8 REDUCE THE RED IN THE EYES Hold down Ctrl and click on the Layer Mask in the Layers palette so the eye selections reload. Go back to the Adjustment Layers and choose Hue/Saturation. Go to the drop-down menu, set to Master and choose Reds. Take Saturation to -50 and Lightness to +20. You can repeat this with Yellows but it may alter the iris colour. Go to Layers>Flatten Image and save as a JPEG or TIFF file.

Too much

Make a splash without flash

Freeze the movement of water with the simplest of camera equipment

WHAT YOU NEED
DSLR
TRIPOD
GLASS OF WATER
STRAWBERRY OR SIMILAR

DIFFICULTY LEVEL
EASY

GIVE THIS WATER SPLASH PROJECT a try and you'll find it's a hugely rewarding technique, capturing some amazing results that are sure to impress all who see them. It couldn't be easier to tackle, either and, best of all, you don't need any fancy studio gear or special flash set-ups.

The trick to freezing the action and getting the shot is actually quite simple. The secret lies in only exposing your camera's sensor for a very short amount of time; the less time the sensor has to record the splash, the less movement will show up in the image, leading to that wonderful 'frozen in time' look.

More often than not shots like these are taken in a studio using a super-fast burst of light from a flashgun, but move outside and suddenly you don't need any of that pro set-up and the whole process becomes much, much simpler. Shooting outside in bright sunlight should give you more than enough illumination to push your shutter speed up to 1/1000sec or faster, and that's quick enough to freeze the motion of water drops in mid air and give you strikingly clean and crisp-looking images without the need for flash.

FINISH

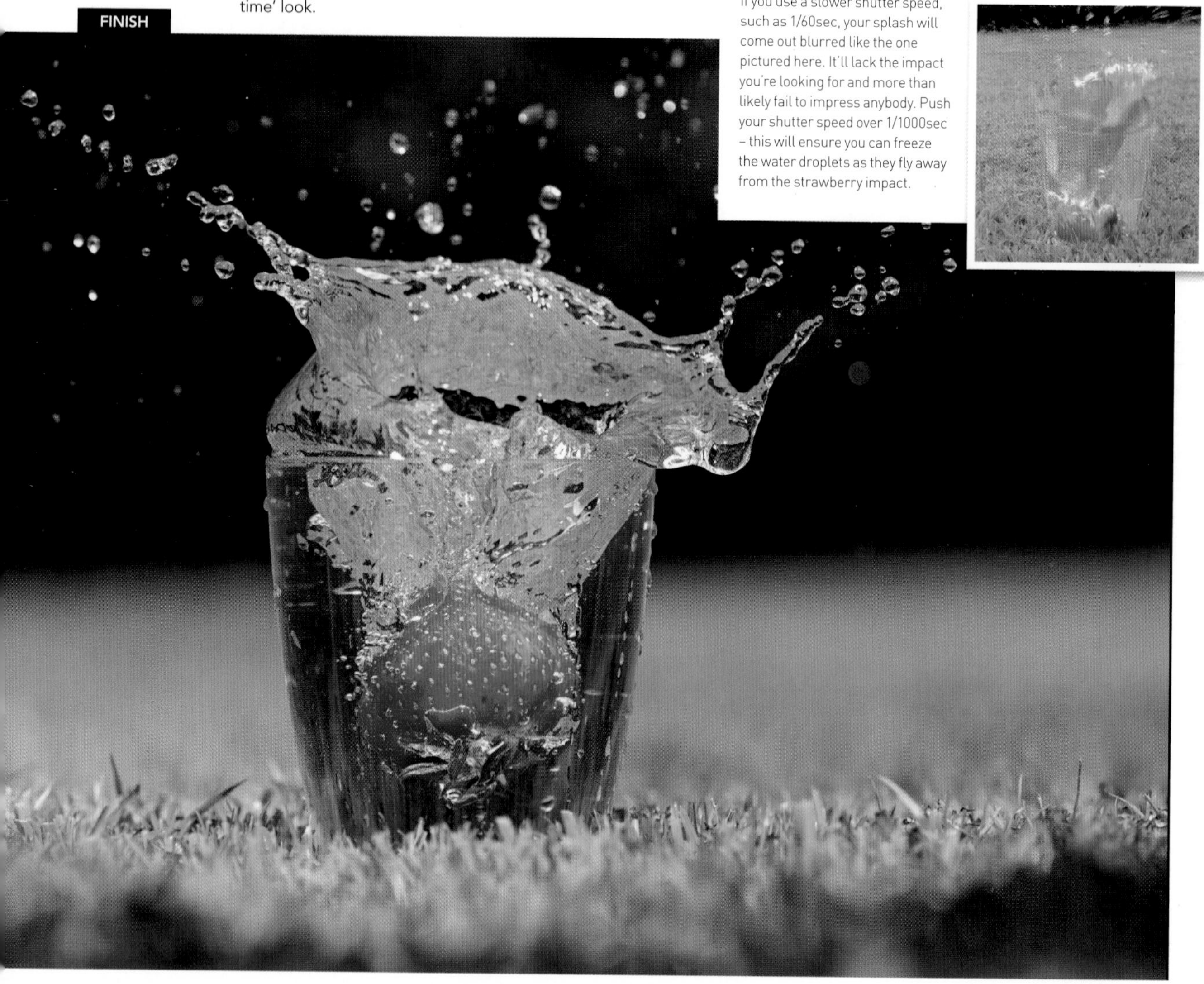

If you use a slower shutter speed, such as 1/60sec, your splash will come out blurred like the one pictured here. It'll lack the impact you're looking for and more than likely fail to impress anybody. Push your shutter speed over 1/1000sec – this will ensure you can freeze the water droplets as they fly away from the strawberry impact.

SHOOTING TECHNIQUE

Head outside and set up in an area where there's plenty of light, then position yourself with the sun behind you. You'll need a nice clear area of ground with a simple backdrop – a hedge or fence is perfect as it won't interfere with the subject – while using grass as a backdrop looks great as the green makes the red of the strawberry stand out. Finally, take plenty of water to avoid having to run back to the tap every few minutes.

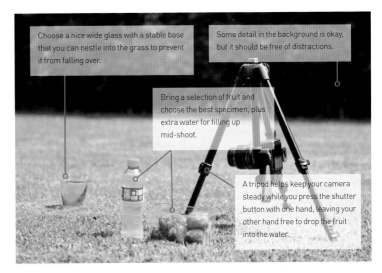

Choose a nice wide glass with a stable base that you can nestle into the grass to prevent it from falling over.

Some detail in the background is okay, but it should be free of distractions.

Bring a selection of fruit and choose the best specimen, plus extra water for filling up mid-shoot.

A tripod helps keep your camera steady while you press the shutter button with one hand, leaving your other hand free to drop the fruit into the water.

1 SET UP THE GLASS Position your glass on an even area of ground and nestle it into the grass, making sure the top is level – if it's at an angle it could fall over when the strawberry hits the water. Next, fill up the glass to the top as filling it right to the brim will create a bigger splash and give you that lovely crown-like shape (a half-filled glass won't look as good).

2 SET SHUTTER SPEED AND ISO With the shot roughly composed and the camera's position locked off, switch over to Shutter priority mode (Tv or S on your mode dial). Now set the shutter speed to 1/1000sec and, to start with, set your ISO to its lowest value, usually 100 or 200. If you notice your aperture value blinking or the letters LO where the f/number should be, then your aperture can't open wide enough to balance the shutter speed, so raise the ISO until the blinking stops.

3 CHOOSE YOUR SUBJECT Choosing a good subject is vital, so dive into your box of fruit and look for one with a nice bright colour and an archetypal shape. Make sure it's free from blemishes and bruising as the better the condition of your subject, the better your final images will look. It helps to pick a few examples and keep them to one side as replacements – repeated dropping is likely to bruise the fruit and after a few attempts it can begin to look battered.

4 SET FOCUS Once you've chosen the subject you need to use it to set your focus. Hold the strawberry by the stalk and dip it into the centre of the glass of water with one hand while framing up with the other; be sure to remember to leave enough room to allow for the splash coming out of the top of the glass. Now move your autofocus point so it sits on your strawberry. Half depress the shutter button to focus and, once locked on, switch over to manual focus to prevent your camera from re-focusing on the wrong part of the image when it comes to shooting.

5 SHOOT THE SPLASH With everything set up and your strawberry at the ready, keep your index finger poised on the shutter button. Drop the strawberry into the glass and try to fire the shot a fraction after the moment of impact for best results. Keep refilling the glass, dropping the fruit and shooting until you've got a few examples to assess. Dropping from a greater height is easier to time and gives a bigger splash, but it does make it harder to aim!

6 CHECK ON SCREEN Because this technique is so wonderfully unpredictable, you'll be itching to check the results. If your splash is coming out blurred then your shutter speed isn't fast enough, so raise it to 1/2000sec, or faster. Remember, higher shutter speeds mean less light so if your aperture value flashes or reads LO, you'll have to boost your ISO to compensate. If in doubt, wait for sunnier conditions as pushing up the ISO will inevitably degrade image quality.

TECH TALK

KEEP AN EYE ON YOUR ISO!

The easiest way to get the fast shutter speed you want is to crank up your ISO sensitivity to its highest setting. However, the higher you go, the more noise (digital interference) will be visible in your pictures, and this could ruin a good shot. While you'll often need to raise the ISO a certain amount, it's best to keep it below the ISO 1600 mark, to avoid heavy noise. That could even mean waiting for a brighter day, but a little patience means you'll be rewarded with better shots.

Going from ISO 400 to ISO 25,600 results in unsightly Noise.

This shot (right) was taken on ISO 25,600 giving a really fast shutter speed, but also leading to an image that was full of Noise, spoiling the shot.

OTHER IDEAS TO TRY

The great thing about this technique is its versatility, so don't feel limited to shots of simple splashes with your garden as the backdrop. There are all kinds of stunning images you can create using the same fast shutter speed set-up, from trying different fruits to bursting water-filled balloons and even introducing coloured backgrounds. Just think of something that involves a bit of a splash and let your imagination run wild.

If you'd like to try freezing action with flash turn to Project 8 on page 32.

BURST A WATER BALLOON

Set up a tripod and extend it to its full height, then from the centre column tie some string and hang a balloon filled with water. Next, follow the rest of the steps in this technique in just the same way as before, except instead of dropping a strawberry into a glass of water you need to burst the balloon using a pin. Pressing the shutter to take the photo as the pin hits and the balloon bursts should result in an impressive spray of water going in all directions – and a brilliant shot!

GET THE STUDIO LOOK

Try placing some white card behind a glass to create a superb white background to shoot against. It will give your splash pictures a classy, high-key, studio look.

Capture animal antics at the zoo

Create wonderful wildlife shots from a trip to the zoo

WHAT YOU NEED
DSLR WITH ZOOM
TELEPHOTO LENS
(LENS USED HERE WAS
A 120–300MM ZOOM)

DIFFICULTY LEVEL
EASY

A DAY AT THE ZOO sounds like fun and the perfect opportunity to grab some wildlife shots. But the emphasis here is on 'wild' – you have no control over the animals' behaviour. They may snooze through your photography or be in a location at the furthest point away from your lens or under a tree. And even if they are close-up, chances are there will be a high fence or glass between you and them.

But follow these shooting tips and you'll walk away with some animal antics' pictures to be proud of.

SHOOTING TECHNIQUE

Eager as you are to take a walk on the wild side, be patient. The animals aren't going anywhere and a few minutes perusing the zoo map will pay dividends, both in planning the best route and making sure you get to shoot the animals you particularly want as there will almost certainly not be enough time to see and shoot everything.

Patience really is the key to unlocking the best images. Be prepared to spend time at each enclosure simply watching the animals and studying their behaviour, without even looking through your screen. By staying still and not messing around with your kit you'll give the animals time to get used to you and eventually forget you're there. They'll act more naturally and you'll get the chance to get some images you're really happy with. All that's left for you to do is concentrate on exposure, composition and focusing on their eyes.

If you shoot on Aperture priority it allows you to dial in the aperture you want to use and leave the camera to set the shutter speed. This allows you to open the aperture to its widest, perhaps f/2.8, and ensure that the background, or foreground, is out of focus. This is perfect for not only isolating the animal in the shot, but it also throws obvious distractions such as posts and fences out of focus, too, making the shots look more as if they were taken in the wild and less like a zoo, which is always what you'll be aiming for. Of course, there are always going to be occasions where you can't avoid the image looking like a zoo portrait, but the more the viewer concentrates on the animal, and the less on the surroundings, the better!

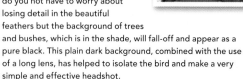

SPOT-ON EXPOSURES This bird is standing right in the harsh light. Not an ideal situation, especially as it is pure white. But by using spot-metering you can ensure that the bird is exposed perfectly. Not only do you not have to worry about losing detail in the beautiful feathers but the background of trees and bushes, which is in the shade, will fall-off and appear as a pure black. This plain dark background, combined with the use of a long lens, has helped to isolate the bird and make a very simple and effective headshot.

GET A GREAT GROUP SHOT Find a high vantage point or location that allows you to eliminate the fencing if possible, for any shot. A zoom lens allows you to get in close and large mammals like these elephants will fill the frame better than, say, a bunch of meerkats! Images of them on their own, from a distance, may lack punch. Wait for them to group together and interact.

HOW TO SHOOT THROUGH GLASS

This is the main problem people encounter when they take photos at zoos but, even if you can't get rid of it completely, you may be able to alter your position so that the glare is in a less important part of the picture. With this monkey cheekily posing on his back the photographer quickly re-positioned a few feet to the right so that the glare covered the animal's body and not its face.

Avoid glare by holding your lens close to the glass and put a dark coat or jumper over your camera to block out any light coming in between the lens and the glass. Overcast days will produce fewer unwanted reflections than bright sunny ones. Take a non-scratch cloth with you to rub away grubby fingerprints.

ABSTRACTS With enclosures for large herbivores, such as giraffes, there may be plenty of space between the fence wires to shoot without including them. However, getting the whole animal in shot without a distracting background might be trickier. If that's the case, opt for an abstract. This simple headshot was framed by aiming high through the fence as the giraffe grazed on a branch and using spot-metering to get an accurate exposure for the giraffe against a bright sky. Or go even more abstract and focus on the patterns of the giraffe's coat without including any identifying features.

COMPOSE FOR A NATURAL LOOK This image of a bird really could've been taken in the wild. It has this appeal because of the way it was composed. By positioning the bird over to one side of the frame and using the leaves in the foreground to fill the left side of the scene, it has created plenty of depth and has no distracting features such as wires anywhere on show.

SHOOTING THROUGH WIRE FENCES

Wire fences are sometimes more of a challenge for photographers than shooting through glass. You're on one side and (thankfully) on the other is a potentially sharp-toothed, beautiful animal that you'd like to capture looking as if it's in more natural surroundings.

With a medium to long telephoto lens you can make the fence 'disappear'. If it's a zoom, take it to its longest setting and then have the end of the lens as close to the fence as possible without risk of damaging the front element. Position the lens so any gap in the wire mesh is as close to the centre of the lens as possible, then focus on your subject. The wire mesh of the fence will pretty much disappear, although some of it may show on your image if you use an aperture that gives a lot of depth-of-field. Take a look at our three example shots below and left.

Above: A 200mm lens focused on the fence so the cheetah can be seen out of focus in the background. Not the shot you want.

Above: Focusing on the cheetah with an aperture of f/8 you can get a much better image of the animal but there's still enough detail to make the out-of-focus wire rather intrusive.

Left: Changing the aperture to f/4 means that the combination of focal length, focal point and aperture finally renders the fence almost invisible.

Take your time with long exposure scenics

Be a smooth operator with ND filters and even calm choppy water

WHAT YOU NEED
DSLR WITH KIT LENS
TRIPOD
ND FILTER

DIFFICULTY LEVEL
INTERMEDIATE

USUALLY, BLURRED PHOTOS are something that we all try to avoid, but sometimes a bit of softness can be used creatively to change the way you portray a subject or scene. There are some brilliant examples of this, such as blurring the motion of people to give busy urban scenes a sense of movement, and one of the most successful and rewarding applications is when you're shooting water.

To record moving water as a blur you need a slow shutter speed – usually 1sec or longer – and the first thing to do to achieve this is to minimize the amount of light entering the camera. You can do this by setting a low ISO and dialling in a small aperture (f/16 or f/22), but if there's still too much light to get a slow enough shutter speed, especially in daylight conditions, that's where a Neutral Density (ND) filter comes in handy. Once screwed onto your lens or slotted neatly into a filter holder, you'll be able to use much slower shutter speeds, blurring anything that moves, while fixed objects in your shot will appear perfectly pin-sharp in focus.

A stark contrast between moving and stationary subjects in landscape images can turn mediocre scenes into spectacular shots, so if you enjoy getting outdoors with your camera and experimenting with new techniques you'll definitely want to try this one out.

SHOOTING TECHNIQUE

There's a lot more to shooting with an ND filter than simply attaching it to your lens and firing off a few shots Before rushing outdoors and giving long exposures a try read this step-by-step guide.

1 LOCATION To get a great long-exposure landscape shot you'll first need to find the right location. Look for a scene that has either flowing water, such as a waterfall, or an expansive area of water like a lake or reservoir (a windy day is better for the latter). Whichever you choose, find some foreground interest, like this jetty, that'll remain sharp and contrast nicely with the water.

2 SET UP YOUR TRIPOD When you're happy with your location, set up your tripod in a spot where it won't move or sink (avoid shifting sand and mud), then mount your DSLR on top. It's vital you use a tripod for this technique as without one it'll be impossible to keep the camera still throughout the exposure. Any movement and you'll get a completely blurred shot and not just blurred water!

By attaching a strong 10-stop ND filter to your lens you can cut out a lot of light and will be able to use a slow 6sec shutter speed, making the water blur into a smooth surface.

3 COMPOSE AND FOCUS Next, carefully compose your shot. For the image featured here the jetty was composed in the centre of the frame to keep it symmetrical and the railings used as lead-in lines. Set your DSLR to autofocus (AF) and decide on a point of focus in the image (this shot was focused halfway down the jetty). Once focused, set your DSLR to Manual focus (MF) to prevent the lens hunting later on.

4 ATTACH THE FILTER Finally, it's time to attach your ND filter to the front of your lens. If you have a screw-in type make sure you place one hand under the lens to catch it should it fall. For this technique the filter used was a square-shaped 10-stop ND filter that cuts out 10 stops of light passing through the lens to the sensor. It was slotted in front of the lens using a filter holder.

Reviewing images as you shoot will give you a better idea of whether the exposure is long enough to blur the water.

5 CAMERA SETTINGS Set your DSLR to self-timer mode to prevent you from knocking it and introducing shake when it's time to fire the shutter. Now switch to Aperture priority mode (A or Av on most DSLRs). Dial in a high f/number, like f/16, before checking the ISO is set to its lowest value; in this case ISO 100. Now check the shutter speed – if it's 1sec or longer you're good to go.

6 TAKE AND REVIEW IMAGES Fire off a shot, wait for the self-timer to count down and review the image on screen, zooming in to check the smoothness of the moving parts. If you'd like to accentuate the blur, use a longer exposure by dialling in an aperture of f/22 and try again. If the shutter speed still isn't long enough, you'll need to use a stronger ND filter or wait for dimmer conditions.

UNDERSTANDING ND FILTERS

Neutral Density filters come in many different strengths and sizes to fit any lens, and they can be screwed into your lens's filter thread (check you've got the right size for your lens when buying) or placed in front using a filter holder. When picking one, you'll first need to decide on the strength you want (how dark it is) and this is measured in 'stops'. For every stop of strength you'll cut out enough light to double the length of the unfiltered shutter speed, so for example a 1-stop ND will change a 1/60sec shutter speed into 1/30sec, whereas a 3-stop ND will change a 1/60sec shutter speed to 1/8sec.

ND filters that cut out 1, 2 or 3 stops of light are useful, but mainly when light is already weak, so if you want to get long exposure effects in daylight you'll need something stronger.

In this technique an extreme 10-stop ND filter was used. This type of ND is so dark that you'll barely be able to see anything through it when you hold it up to your eye. Although they don't come cheap (expect to pay about £70–£100 for a high-quality 77mm 10-stop filter) they are an essential accessory for landscape photographers or anyone who likes to get creative with blurring moving subjects in daylight, making it a great addition to your kit bag.

Extreme 10-stop ND filters are well suited to landscapes and can turn waterfalls and fast flowing water silky smooth.

Make the perfect panorama

Shoot panorama frames correctly to make stitching easier

WHAT YOU NEED
DSLR OR COMPACT CAMERA

DIFFICULTY LEVEL
EASY

THERE'S A SPECIAL QUALITY ABOUT PANORAMIC IMAGES, something that really captures the imagination. Maybe it's the vast scenes they're able to convey, usually showing more width than the eye can see, and certainly more than a conventional camera. Or maybe it's just that their instantly recognizable wide format is so much rarer than the standard 3:2 or 4:3 photo formats.

Either way, panoramas are great fun to shoot and very satisfying to look at. Done in the right way, they'll fill you with a sense of pride and accomplishment that you just don't get from a standard, one-shot snap.

There are two ways to make a panoramic image. First, you can shoot a scene with a wide-angle lens and crop the resulting image into a panoramic format. This is the easiest route, but does mean throwing away many of the pixels you captured and achieving no wider angle of view than normal. In contrast, the second method involves taking a sequence of pictures from the same location and merging them using software like Photoshop or Elements. This route gives greater image quality and allows you to capture scenes that are too big for even the widest of lenses.

Although panoramas are fundamentally about recording very wide views, it's important to remain selective in what you shoot, just as you would with a regular landscape. This means the first step is always to find a great subject – after all, a wide view of nothing isn't going to impress anyone.

START IMAGES

 +  +  +  +

These five pictures were shot in Manual mode to ensure the exposure was the same in each. This helps frames match up later when stitching.

SHOOTING TECHNIQUE

Once you've found yourself an exciting subject, it's time to start shooting. You'll need to take several shots in sequence which can then be merged in Photoshop, but doing this in the right way guarantees the best results.

FINISH

PORTRAIT
Keeping your camera in portrait orientation will give you a higher quality final image – you'll need to shoot more frames this way, but this means you'll also have more pixels to play with in the final image.

ELBOWS
Keep elbows in to create a stable platform to shoot from.

STRAIGHT
Keep your body straight, you don't want to be moving up and down between the individual shots.

STANCE
Stand with your feet shoulder-width apart to keep your balance as you turn through the sequence.

1 VISUALISE AND PLAN Panoramic images may be a lot wider than regular pictures, but they still work on the same principles of composition. You'll be shooting numerous photos to join later, so composition can be quite tricky. To get this right, first scan the scene and visualize your framing within it. Where are you going to start shooting, where are you going to stop? Keep in mind the same things that work in regular photos: is it a strong subject? And could you include foreground interest or lead-in lines to draw in the viewer's attention? Shoot with some excess space around the subject area, as the final panorama stitch will always need some cropping after it has been put together.

HOW TO SHOOT SUCCESSFUL PANORAMAS

Alignment is important to the software doing the stitching, so misalignment and overlap are two things to look for when shooting the frames of your panoramic photograph.

To fight the effects of perspective and avoid the background and foreground becoming misaligned between shots you'll need to rotate around your lens's nodal point, rather than twisting from your waist. The nodal point is usually close to the front of the lens so the best bet is to rotate around this point.

For the best results you need to overlap each shot you take by about 40% so the software can work out how to stitch them.

2 SET SHUTTER SPEED AND APERTURE Since you'll be shooting multiple photos to stitch into the panorama you need to ensure that exposure stays constant in each, otherwise the lighting won't be consistent. That means using Manual exposure mode. To get your exposure settings switch to Aperture priority (A or Av on the mode dial) and dial in the f/number you want to use (f/11 in this case). Next, set your ISO to its lowest value and point your camera at the brightest part of the scene (not the sun). Take a look at the settings, then switch over to Manual mode (M) and dial in the same aperture, shutter speed and ISO. It's also well worth switching your image quality to RAW as you'll have extra control over the exposure later in editing.

USING A PANORAMIC TRIPOD HEAD

Panoramic tripod heads attach to your tripod and allow more precise rotation of your camera around its nodal point.

Once you've had a go at this technique, you'll notice that rotating around the front of your lens takes some practice, although it's vital to shoot in this way for the best quality. But it can feel very unnatural.

A panoramic tripod head can save you this effort and ensure top quality results. Simply set up your tripod so it's level and use the adjustable sliders to position your lens's nodal point over the point of rotation. This sounds a bit complicated but it's actually relatively easy, and most heads come with easy-to-follow instructions.

With this extra precision you'll get the best-quality results and guard against any distortion in your stitched pictures. Heads can be a bit pricey, but if you're serious about shooting panoramas and want to work on more complex subjects like architecture, the investment will pay off.

TRY THIS!

What if you have a really tall subject? Well, this technique will work vertically too. Just change the camera from a portrait orientation to landscape and follow the steps, rotating upwards rather than side-to-side for some stunning vertical panoramic images.

3 SET AND LOCK FOCUS It's important to ensure the focus doesn't change between photos; the best way to do this is to use Manual focus mode. First, while still in autofocus place your AF point on the focal point of your scene. Half press the shutter to set the focus there and switch the camera over to Manual to lock it in place. Once you've done this be sure not to move back or forwards and don't knock or change the focus ring on your lens, or you'll have to start again.

4 START SHOOTING Frame up on the far left of your composition, remembering to leave a little extra room for cropping later. Take the first shot, but before you move, check where the frame ends and pick a marker in the scene that you can use to line up the next shot. Now step to your left, rotating around the front of your lens, rather than twisting from your waist, and frame up on the next section. You need to leave an overlap between the frames (about 40%) so include the spot you remembered from the previous shot and place that about a third of the way in from the left.

5 CHECK YOUR PICTURE SEQUENCE Review your images on screen. Rotating your view around the front of the lens, rather than the usual method of twisting from the waist can be tricky so check each frame is level and includes sufficient overlap between each. Assess the exposure – if there was a change in light during shooting (perhaps the sun went behind a cloud), you'll need to shoot again. Keep at it until you've got plenty of material to stitch later on.

PROCESSING

With the pictures captured all that's left is to stitch them together using Photoshop or Elements. Turn to Project 25 on page 102 to see how this is done. You'll soon be creating impressive ultra wide-angle panoramas at huge sizes that make great fine-art prints.

Be subtle and surreal

How to create a surreal image that's good enough to eat

WHAT YOU NEED
PHOTOSHOP
DSLR
105MM MACRO LENS
OR SIMILAR FOCAL
LENGTH
STUDIO LIGHTS
IDEALLY

DIFFICULTY LEVEL
INTERMEDIATE

SUBTLETY IS A POWERFUL TOOL when it comes to the world of surreal photography and this image demonstrates that. Although it would be possible to recreate it in-camera with the right props, professional make-up and appropriate lighting, it would be a laborious process. But, with careful planning and a little help from Photoshop absolutely anything is possible. In the time it would take a make-up artist to carefully apply strawberry seeds to bright red lips, you can shoot lips and strawberry shots, and then edit them in Photoshop, with delicious results.

In theory you could blend any fruit or vegetables with someone's lips, but you have to make sure there is at least some curvature to the food. If you're prepared to experiment and put in the hard graft you could try a pineapple or an orange. The key to blending is matching the lipstick to the fruit, although it doesn't have to be an exact match. The thing is, in reality it's much easier to blend a fruit like a strawberry because colour and shape are fairly similar to a pair of lips. But be prepared for this technique to take a few hours at the editing stage because precision is required alongside a little trial and error.

SHOOTING TECHNIQUE

This technique borrows much from high-end beauty photography because the focus is on the lips. For this shot it's important your model wears high-gloss red lipstick to make the blend between lips and strawberry more believable. Asking her to wear a light foundation is helpful because it will decrease the amount of skin retouching required at the editing stage. With these considerations taken care of, it's time to think about how to light the model. It's essential to shoot the model's lips and the strawberry under identical lighting. This shot was lit by two small softboxes to create a high-key/shadowless lighting effect. This helps mimic beauty photography, but if you don't have studio lights you could shoot outdoors in the shade with white paper attached to a wall. If you decide to take this option, shoot in Aperture priority, set metering to spot and add 1-stop of overexposure.

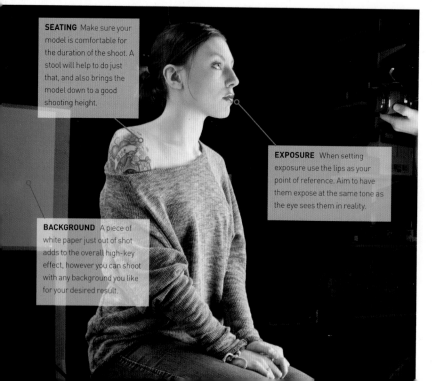

SEATING Make sure your model is comfortable for the duration of the shoot. A stool will help to do just that, and also brings the model down to a good shooting height.

EXPOSURE When setting exposure use the lips as your point of reference. Aim to have them expose at the same tone as the eye sees them in reality.

BACKGROUND A piece of white paper just out of shot adds to the overall high-key effect, however you can shoot with any background you like for your desired result.

1 CAMERA SETTINGS If you shoot in the studio, set the camera to manual mode at ISO 100, with shutter speed set to 1/200sec and aperture at f/11. Use a macro lens if you have one, preferably 105mm, otherwise use a telephoto lens at this focal length or longer if necessary to achieve a tight crop on the image.

3 SHOOTING THE LIPS Once you're happy with exposure and lighting it's time to photograph the lips. You can either manually focus or autofocus, but manual tends to be more reliable when working close to the model. Shooting the lips straight on is easier to blend with the strawberry at the editing stage, but photographing the face at an angle looks better.

4 SHOOTING THE STRAWBERRY With the lips shot it's time to move onto the strawberry. For this, simply shoot the strawberry straight on because this will allow a small amount of depth-of-field fall off at the edges that will work with the lips. If you shot the lips straight on you'll need a large depth-of-field for the strawberry, so stop down to f/22 and increase the power of the lights.

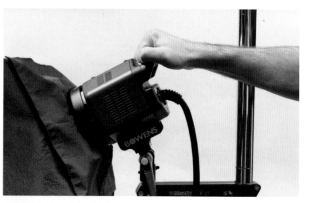

2 POSITION LIGHTS Set up your lights so that shadows are kept to a minimum – either one to each side of the model or one just above head height and one just below will do the trick. Set their power output and keep adjusting it until you get a correct exposure with the camera settings dialled in, as per the previous step.

MACRO LENS A 105mm macro lens is ideal for this technique, but if you don't have one then use a lens with a focal length as close to this as possible.

LIGHTING Whether you shoot in the studio or under natural light, always ensure you photograph the model and the strawberry under the same lighting conditions for consistency.

PROCESSING TECHNIQUE

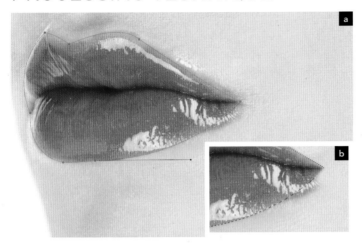

1 RESHAPE THE LIPS Open your lip photo then press P to activate the Pen Tool. Click on the small black arrow along the Application Bar – next to the grey blob – and make sure Rubber Band is ticked. Now make sure the Auto Add/ Delete box next to the shape is not ticked. Place an anchor point just inside the edge of the bottom lip (so the messy edges are cloned out later) by left-clicking. Click on the point again and drag a control arm in the direction of where the pen path will go. (a) Click the mouse again to place the next point, but don't put it too far away from the last point. Then hold down Ctrl and left-click on the control arm to adjust the shape. Repeat until the path has been closed/completed. If at any point you make a mistake press the backspace key to delete the last point made. Press Ctrl+Enter to convert the path to a selection and go to Select>Modify> Feather and set radius to 5. (b) Press Ctrl+Shift+I to invert the selection. Hold down Ctrl+Shift+N to create a new empty layer. Press S to activate the Clone Stamp Tool, press Alt to sample skin near to the lips, then left-click over the rough parts of the lips to reshape them.

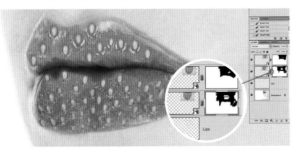

2 COPY THE STRAWBERRY Open the strawberry photo and press Ctrl+A to select the entire image. Go back to the lips photo and press Ctrl+V to paste the strawberry shot over it. On a PC right-click, on a Mac Ctrl-click on the strawberry layer and convert it to a smart object. By doing this you'll be able to resize the strawberry shot any number of times without pixelating the image.

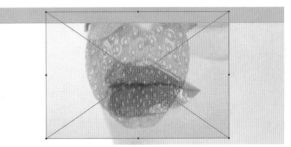

3 RESIZE THE LAYER Reduce the opacity of the strawberry layer to 50% so you can see the lips. Press Ctrl+T to add Transform controls to the strawberry Layer. Hold down Shift to Constrain Proportions and resize the strawberry to cover half the top and bottom lips, drag the Layer (left-click and drag) within the main image box. Press enter when size and position are right.

4 BLEND THE IMAGES Copy the strawberry image (Ctrl+J), resize and reposition to cover the lips. Click on the eye to turn off visibility. Click on the rectangle with a white circle in it (bottom of Layers palette) to Add a Layer Mask to the first strawberry Layer. Use a black brush to remove parts of the picture, and a white one to bring them back. Repeat blending on other strawberry Layer.

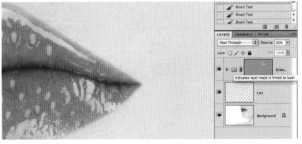

5 IMPROVE THE SEEDS Hold down Shift and left-click on both strawberry Layers to select them. Press Ctrl+G to group them and then add a Layer Mask. Press Shift+F5 to open Fill dialogue box and choose 50% Gray. Press B to activate the Brush Tool and set foreground colour to white. Paint over just the seeds on the lips to increase their visibility. Done!

Enjoy fast-action flower portraits

Think about movement and motion in still-life pictures with a twist

WHAT YOU NEED
DSLR WITH KIT
ZOOM LENS
TRIPOD
ADOBE PHOTOSHOP

DIFFICULTY LEVEL
INTERMEDIATE

THINK OF STILL LIFE PHOTOGRAPHY and you'll instantly think of subjects that are… well, still. Static objects like fruit, books, antiques and, of course, flowers are usually what photographers spend their time looking at, but it doesn't have to be this way. Many such objects can also be made to move about and catching them in motion is a great alternative to the usual static approach to still-life.

Flowers are easy to find and make colourful subjects. Look in your local florist or supermarket and, of course, your garden where you can shoot them 'on location' without cutting a single stem. A dandelion clock makes a great subject for a moving still-life picture; gently blowing on it from the side will scatter its seeds in the wind, which we can capture fleetingly on camera.

To make your subject stand out a simple background is a must. Plain mounting board from your local art shop is good, or why not create something graduated in Photoshop or Elements and print it on your photo printer to make a bespoke background?

SHOOTING TECHNIQUE

To freeze movement you'll need to set a fast shutter speed using either Shutter priority (S), Manual (M) or Aperture priority (A) exposure mode. Plenty of light is required for this approach–another reason for taking the shoot outside into the daylight. Putting your DSLR on a tripod will let you fine-tune the composition during the shoot and allow you to move freely around the set-up.

One of the greatest skills any still-life photographer can have, though, is patience. Be methodical about setting up your shot. Make small changes and look at the effect each one has.

1 SETTING UP Arrange your backdrop behind the subject, making sure there is plenty of distance between the two. This will help keep the background out of focus, so it doesn't distract from the main subject. Compose the shot so that the background completely fills the frame. If you find working at low angles difficult and your DSLR has a flip-out Live View screen, try composing this way instead.

2 SUPPORT THE FLOWER Support the dandelion about 20cm in front of the background and check you're happy with the composition. There are many accessories to help hold things in position for shots like this, but the Plamp by Wimberley (about £30) is absolutely ideal for the job.

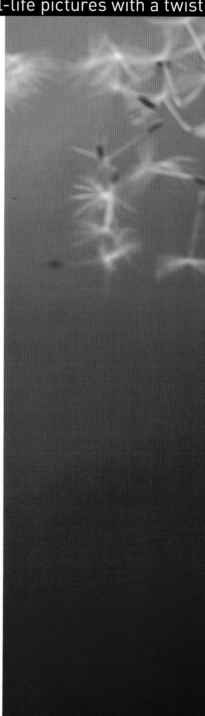

FINISH

3 LOCK THE FOCUS With one of your camera's AF points covering the head of the dandelion half-press the shutter to focus there, then switch over to Manual focus to prevent your lens hunting for focus if the dandelion moves sideways when blown. Set your ISO to 400 and check your DSLR is set to its Continuous shooting mode, ready to record a fast burst of images.

4 DIAL IN THE CORRECT APERTURE Set your DSLR's shooting mode to A or Av for Aperture priority then dial in an Aperture of f/8 which should keep the head and seeds in focus and give a shutter speed of about 1/2000sec in good daylight–fast enough to freeze the seeds in flight. If you're getting a speed much lower than that, increase your ISO by a stop to 800.

5 BLOW & REVIEW Hit the shutter and at the same time gently blow through a straw to release some of the seeds. After a few frames, take a look at your shots on screen. If you're not happy with the results go back and try again with another dandelion. Remember, patience and persistence are the keys to success here.

PROCESSING TECHNIQUE

After the shoot you may well have hundreds of images to trawl through on your PC. Load them into your file browser and work out which are best, ranking your favourite with your software's star-rating system, if it has this feature. If you use Adobe Bridge or Lightroom, the shortcut Ctrl+5 will assign five stars to an image or group of images. Once this has been done you can use the shortcut Ctrl+Alt+Shift+5 to reveal all your shots with a selected five-star rating alongside each other. These can then be saved to your computer. This housekeeping process will save you clogging up your hard drive with images that are no good.

1 ENHANCE EXPOSURE Open the files you wish to use for the final image into Elements or Photoshop. If you are shooting in Raw the Camera Raw interface will load. Hit Ctrl+A to highlight both files before increasing the Exposure by dragging the slider right somewhat. Click Open Images to load the files into the full editing area of Elements or Photoshop. (If you are shooting JPEG and you need to tweak exposure, do this with a Levels adjustment by choosing Image> Adjustments> Levels.)

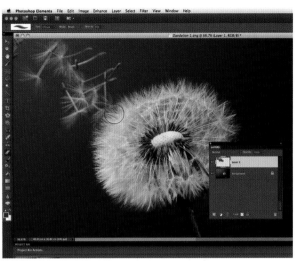

2 COPY THE SEEDS Select the Lasso tool and make a selection around the moving seeds in one of the images. Go to Select>Feather, set a Radius of 50px and hit OK. Press Ctrl+C to copy the seeds and go to the second image window before hitting Ctrl+V to paste and combine to the two elements. Use the Move tool to drag the seeds into the best position.

3 CLEAN UP THE BLEND Zoom into the dandelion (Ctrl+) and pick the Eraser tool (E). Use a soft 150px brush with the Opacity set to 75% and run this between the dandelion and the extra flying seeds to create a seamless blend between the two. Now pick the Crop tool (C) and drag a crop box over the image to tidy up the composition a little if this is needed.

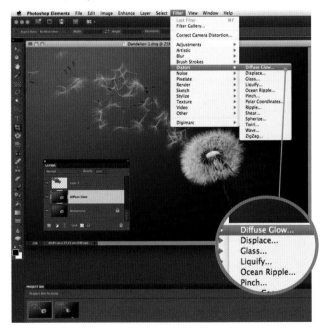

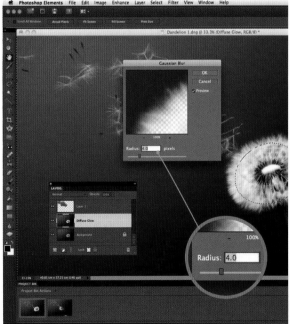

4 ADD THE GLOW In the Layers palette (Choose Window>Layers to display this if it's not already showing) click the Background Layer and go to Layer>Duplicate Layer. Rename it 'Diffuse Glow' and go to Filter>Distort> Diffuse Glow. Set Graininess to 0, Glow Amount to 7 and Clear Amount to 16. Hit OK then, using the Eraser again, (Opacity 30%) run it around the dandelion's fringe to bring back edge detail.

5 CREATE A SHALLOW DEPTH-OF-FIELD. Using the Lasso tool, make a Selection of the dandelion's head, then Feather it by 50px. Hit Ctrl+Shift+I to invert the Selection and go to Filter> Blur>Gaussian Blur. Set the Radius to 4px and hit OK. Now press Ctrl+D before going to File>Save As... to save the results of your still-life picture.

Create a colour infrared picture

Give a landscape image an other-worldly feel

WHAT YOU NEED
PHOTOSHOP OR
ELEMENTS
DSLR WITH LENS
TRIPOD

DIFFICULTY LEVEL
EASY

CAPTURING A GOOD TRUE INFRARED IMAGE with your camera can be tricky. You have to think differently and visualize how the scene before you will look; those green leaves, for example, will appear magenta. You'll need a special infrared filter which blocks out all visible light from the colour spectrum, leaving just the infrared light which passes through onto the camera's sensor.

The resulting images can then be opened in Photoshop and converted to colour for some spectacular results, just as

you see here, where the sky turns a deep cyan/blue and foliage and green vegetation, which reflects infrared strongly, adopts a distinctive pinkish hue. But there are pitfalls for those without the right equipment and knowledge.

However, with Photoshop or Elements, it's possible to mimic the infrared effect and convert an existing colour landscape into a colourful infrared scene. So, seize your camera and take the opportunity to create some other-worldy scenes.

START IMAGE

SHOOTING TECHNIQUE

You're looking for a landscape with a nice blue sky and some brightly lit foliage. If you don't already have something that fits the bill on your hard drive here's how to shoot the pictures you will need.

CAMERA SETTINGS Although the Photoshop aspect is the major part of creating this effect, a crisp landscape shot is the foundation. Use a tripod and shoot in Aperture priority mode and use a mid-to-high f/number to keep all the details sharp.

LUSH GREENERY As the foliage is going to be the main focal point of the shot once it's been processed in Photoshop, make sure it's brightly lit and there's plenty of it in your scene.

FINISH

EXPANSE OF SKY
The infrared effect also has a big impact on the blues in your shot, and you'll need these to balance the red of the foliage, so pick a day with broken cloud and lots of blue sky on show.

PROCESSING TECHNIQUE

Once you've decided on a suitable landscape image, it's time to take the shot into Photoshop and get to work with processing it. The way in which you apply the infrared effect will vary depending on whether you own a copy of Photoshop or Elements. Follow the relevant step-by-step for which version of the software you use.

PHOTOSHOP

1 CONVERT TO INFRARED Open your image into Photoshop and start by left-clicking on the Create New Fill or Adjustment Layer icon at the bottom of the Layers palette (Window>Layers), choosing Channel Mixer from the list. In the window, make sure that Monochrome is ticked, then take Red to +100%, Green to +175% and Blue to -175% (you may want to vary these depending on your image).

2 SAVE AS A JPEG Save this image as a JPEG by going to File>Save As... and in the window that appears, change the Format to JPEG, renaming the file as, say, Infrared.JPG. Make sure that you save the file in an easily accessible location – your Desktop is fine – then click Save. In the next window, increase the Quality to 12 to retain maximum quality, and then click OK.

3 SWITCHING COLOUR CHANNELS Re-open your start image into Photoshop again and go over to the Channels palette (Window>Channels). Left-click on the Green Channel to highlight it, then press Ctrl+A to select the entire image, followed by Ctrl+C to copy it. Next, left-click on the Blue Channel and press Ctrl+V to paste the Green Channel into the Blue Channel.

4 MORE CHANNEL SWAPPING Now perform a similar process on the Red and Green Channels; the Selection should still be active, so left-click on the Red Channel and press Ctrl+C to copy it, then left-click on the Green Channel and press Ctrl+V to paste the Red Channel into the Green Channel. Now, go to File>Open, locate the Infrared.JPG image, and open it up into Photoshop.

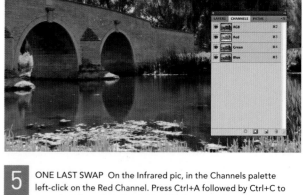

5 ONE LAST SWAP On the Infrared pic, in the Channels palette left-click on the Red Channel. Press Ctrl+A followed by Ctrl+C to copy the information. Head up to Window>your Start image.JPG to bring the main landscape image back in front of you once again, then left-click on the Red Channel and press Ctrl+V. Finally, left-click on the RGB Channel at the top of the Channels palette to see the results.

6 ADD SOME CONTRAST Press Ctrl+D to deselect, then left-click on the Create New Fill or Adjustment Layer icon at the bottom of the Layers palette again, and choose Brightness/Contrast from the drop-down menu. In the window that appears, increase the Contrast to 45 and the Brightness to 10, then close the window.

7 DIFFUSE GLOW AND SAVE Press the D key to ensure that your Background colour is set to pure White, then click the Background Layer in the Layers palette to highlight it. Next, go to Filter>Distort>Diffuse Glow and, in the window that appears, set the Graininess to 0, the Glow Amount to 2 and the Clear Amount to 20, then click OK. Save your work as a JPEG by going to File>Save As.

ELEMENTS

For Elements users, giving your landscape image a colourized infrared effect is a slightly different process, as there are a few options in Photoshop that aren't available in the stripped-down Elements package. However, all is not lost and, like a lot of other creative techniques in Photoshop, there's a workaround which will help you achieve similar results. Simply follow these four easy steps and you'll soon be giving your landscapes a new lease of life with this fantastic effect!

1 ADJUST HUE/SATURATION Begin by opening your start image, probably a JPEG. With the image open, go to Enhance>Adjust Color>Adjust Hue/Saturation and in the window that appears, push the Hue slider to -85 and hit OK to confirm the changes. This will add the desired pinkish hue in the greenery, but the other colours, like the green sky, need sorting out.

2 ENHANCE THE SKY Now go back to Enhance>Adjust Color>Adjust Hue/Saturation, this time left-clicking on the Colour Edit Menu (where it says Master) and selecting Greens from the list. Change the Hue to +65 and the Saturation to +50. Grab the Add To Sample eyedropper from the bottom of the window and left-click on any parts of the sky that are still green to turn them blue. Hit OK.

3 CORRECT BRIDGE COLOUR Go to Enhance>Adjust Color>Adjust Hue/Saturation for a final time, selecting Magentas from the Colour Edit Menu and setting the Hue to +55 to correct the colour, in this example, of the bridge and water. Finally, choose Reds from the Colour Edit Menu and reduce the Saturation to -50 to reduce the intensity of the pink foliage. Click OK to confirm.

4 FINAL TOUCHES Go to Filter> Distort> Diffuse Glow and set Graininess to 0, Glow Amount to 2, Clear Amount to 20, and click OK. Click Create Adjustment Layer at the bottom of the Layers palette (Windows>Layers) and select Brightness/Contrast, increasing the Contrast to 40. Finally, click Create New Fill or Adjustment Layer again, picking Levels and moving the Midtones to 1.20. That's it!

Surrealist still life

Turn reality on its head with a quirky composite

WHAT YOU NEED
DSLR, CSC OR
COMPACT CAMERA
TRIPOD, WINDOW LIGHT
SOURCE, BACKGROUND
PAPER, PHOTOSHOP
OR ELEMENTS

DIFFICULTY LEVEL
ADVANCED

START IMAGE 1

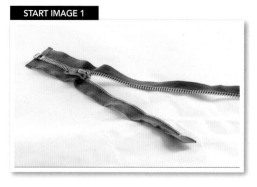

START IMAGE 2

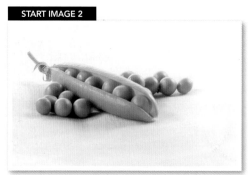

ONE OF THE BEST WAYS TO MAKE AN IMAGE that gets people thinking is to juxtapose regular everyday objects in a unique or uncommon way. The familiar in an unfamiliar fashion – for example, combining a peapod and a zip. The result is an eye-catching surreal still life that is sure to make people smile.

The trick is to make your finished pictures as believable as possible. The more realistic they look, the more at odds they are with our in-built perception of reality and the harder they are to dismiss as fantasy.

This peapod photo was shot using nothing more than a tripod, window lighting and some white paper used as a background. The zip was shot using exactly the same settings, lighting and perspective to ensure the two components could be combined in a completely seamless way.

The compositing is achieved in Photoshop by cutting out the zip from its own photo and placing it onto the peapod using the Layers and Selections tools. A shadow added as a final touch helps tie everything together.

Combining nature's peapod with a man-made
zip results in a quirky and surreal image.

FINISH

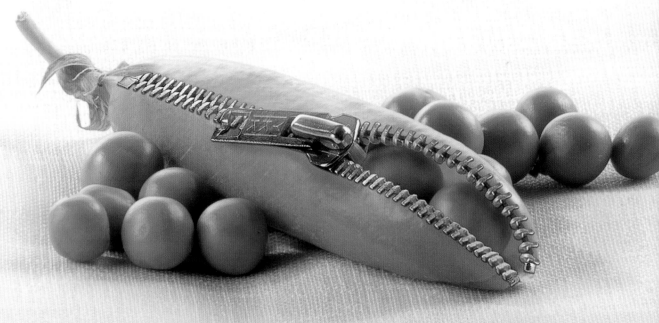

SHOOTING TECHNIQUE

You'll need to create a homemade still-life studio. First place some white textured fabric on a sunny windowsill. The window is going to be the main light source but taping a piece of white A3 paper over the window will soften the light slightly as it shines through. Make sure the paper isn't too thick – copy paper should be fine. Next, lean another piece of white paper against a sturdy object in front and slightly to the side of the textured fabric to act as a reflector. Finally, place the peapod in position.

Set up your camera on a tripod to keep it in one place. Shooting in Aperture priority mode (A or Av), set an aperture of f/8 or f/11, engage Manual focus mode and focus about one third of the way along the peapod. Changing the focus to Manual will ensure focus distance remains consistent when you come to photograph the zip, preventing a mismatch in sharpness between images.

With everything ready to go, and the peapod in position, take the first photo. Next, open the zip until the space between the pull and the stopper is roughly equal to the length of the peapod. Once done, carefully remove the peapod and place the zip in exactly the same location and at the same angle, then take the second photo.

PROCESSING TECHNIQUE

The two photos you've just taken form the building blocks of your final image. Combining them in Photoshop is where the fun really begins so it's time to open them up and get stuck in. You'll be using the Pen tool to cut out the zip, then using Layers to add it onto the peapod. Don't feel intimidated by the Pen tool; it's easier to use than you think. In Elements there's no Pen tool, so just use the Polygonal Lasso instead.

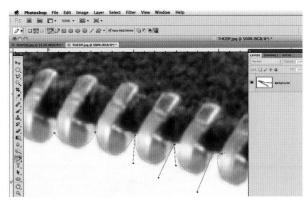

1 MAKE A PATH Open your zip image and select the Pen tool (P). Now click around the edge of the zip, creating a Path. Each click lays an Anchor Point and you can pull on the Control points that surround them to make curves around each tooth. Work around until you are back at the start and click on it to join up the ends and complete the path. In the Options bar, click on Exclude and make another Path around the gap, subtracting it from the first Path.

2 CONVERT PATH TO SELECTION   Once you've gone around your zip and removed the area of fabric visible through the pull tab you'll have your completed Path. With that done you need to bring up the Paths palette by choosing Window>Paths. Right click the Work Path that's visible and choose Make Selection. A dialog box will appear; type 0.5px into the Feather Radius option and click OK.

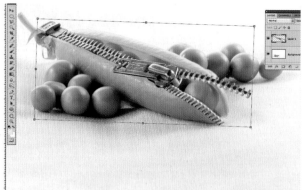

3 COPY TO THE POD Now you need to copy this Selection across to the peapod image. On the zip image head up to Edit>Copy. Bring up your photo of the peapod and choose Edit>Paste. You'll see a new layer appear in your Layers palette (Window>Layers). Now go to Edit>Free Transform. Drag the corners of the box to match the size of the zip to the pod and then drag it into position.

4 CLONE OUT THE GAPS With your zip in position on the pod you need to clone out the gaps between its edge and the pod. Pick the Clone Stamp tool and click on the Background layer in the Layers palette. Hold Alt and click on the near side of the pod to sample an area then paint over on the nearside of the zip to fill in the gap with the sample. Repeat on the far side edge.

5 MATCH THE ZIP TO THE CONTOURS Click on the zip layer (Layer 1) and choose the Polygonal Lasso tool. Make a rough selection around the far zip teeth starting at the point they seems to leave the peapod edge. Next, go to Layer>New >Layer Via Cut then Edit>Free Transform and rotate the strand into place. Repeat this process 2 or 3 more times until the whole strand lines up.

6 ADD SHADOW Click the Eye icon next to the Background Layer, then head to Layer>Merge Visible, to merge all of the zip layers into one. Click the Eye icon again. Go to Layer>Layer Styles>Blending Options (>Style Settings in Elements). Click Drop Shadow and set the angle to 45° and Opacity to 60%. Set the Distance to 1, Spread to 0 and Size to 2. Hit OK and this will add a shadow around the zip edges.

7 FINISHING TOUCHES Click on the Background Layer again and choose the Burn tool. In the Options bar, set Exposure to 5% and Range to Midtones, then paint in some shadow under the zip pull tab. Next click on your zip layer, choose the Dodge tool (5%, Highlights) and brush across the far side of the zip a couple of times to brighten it and create a highlight effect.

PEN TOOL

With so many Selection tools on offer in Photoshop, the Pen tool often gets ignored in favour of options like the Polygonal Lasso tool. But the Pen tool is actually one of Photoshop's most accurate and precise tools, and is especially good at creating Selections.

It works differently to other Selection tools because, rather than creating a Selection straight off, it first makes a Path. This Path can be bent and curved to follow the contours of even the most organic shapes.

To lay a Path you start by clicking Anchor points along the edge you want to follow, then drag the Tangent lines that appear to create curves. For a sharp edge hold the Alt key to break the Tangent line.

Continue laying points until you have reached the first point and the Path is complete, and can be made into a Selection.

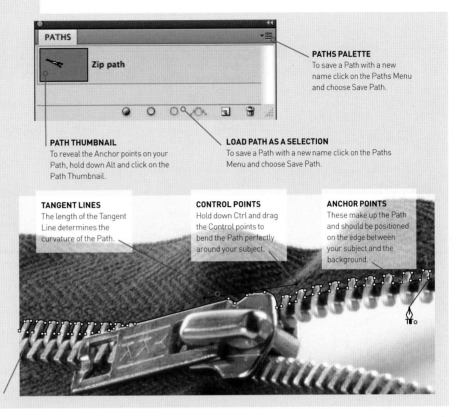

PATHS PALETTE
To save a Path with a new name click on the Paths Menu and choose Save Path.

PATH THUMBNAIL
To reveal the Anchor points on your Path, hold down Alt and click on the Path Thumbnail.

LOAD PATH AS A SELECTION
To save a Path with a new name click on the Paths Menu and choose Save Path.

TANGENT LINES
The length of the Tangent Line determines the curvature of the Path.

CONTROL POINTS
Hold down Ctrl and drag the Control points to bend the Path perfectly around your subject.

ANCHOR POINTS
These make up the Path and should be positioned on the edge between your subject and the background.

THE PATH
Your Path will appear as a thin grey line around your subject.

HOW TO KEEP YOUR IMAGES CONSISTENT

1 FOCUS To combine one picture with another in a realistic way, depth-of-field and focus are really important. For this reason it's helpful to shoot the pictures you're using at high f/numbers which will give the greatest front-to-back sharpness, therefore avoiding conflicts. Use a shallow depth-of-field and get the focus in the wrong place (see image) and the elements will look mismatched.

2 LIGHTING A big part of making a composite image look realistic is to do with keeping the lighting consistent because if it varies between the different elements your efforts will definitely look fake.

Shooting with your light source at the same angle in each picture is a good start, but adding shadows in the right places is important, too. In the image to illustrate this you'll see that the shadow on the zip and the peapod are at different angles, so they don't match, but get them the right way round and you're onto a winner.

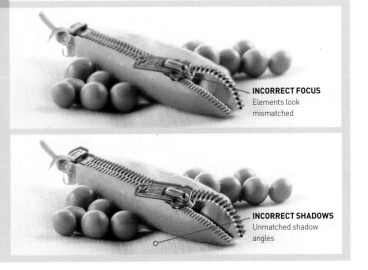

INCORRECT FOCUS
Elements look mismatched

INCORRECT SHADOWS
Unmatched shadow angles

Turn your friends and family into giants

They may only be small to you, but putting your children in a scene where scale plays tricks in the mind will make them look like giants

This trick was created in Photoshop to make it look as if a giant child is pushing a toy train across a viaduct

EVERYONE HAS A FAVOURITE SUBJECT they enjoy photographing, whether it's portraits, landscapes, wildlife or sport. Every now and then, though, it's a good idea to break out of the comfort zone and try a fresh, exciting new challenge. Which is exactly what this technique is all about.

You don't have to be a highly qualified photoshop whizz-kid to produce amazing digital images. The only things you really need are a bit of imagination, a novel idea and some Photoshop know-how to turn the idea into reality.

FINISH

SHOOTING TECHNIQUE

When combining subjects of different scales, it's vital they are shot correctly. Failure to match the perspective and lighting of your subjects to the background image will result in a poor composite and errors will stick out like a sore thumb, leaving you the painstaking job of having to reshoot the whole thing.

1 SHOOT BACKGROUND IMAGE This viaduct makes a great background. By shooting it from a low-angle you're able to make the child and train appear as giants in the final image. To ensure the background image is sharp throughout set an aperture of f/16 (as here) or even f/22 and inspect the results on your camera's rear view screen.

2 POSITION PROPS & SUBJECT To get the best shots for your final image, shoot the subject and props at the same location, the same angle and the same time of day as the background. This will allow the light to fall on every element of the image in exactly the same way and make it blend together perfectly.

3 SHOOT FROM THE RIGHT ANGLE Framing up from a low angle makes it look as though the train is running along the top of the viaduct. Keeping the camera in the same position, shoot a few shots of the child in the field pretending to hold the train.

GET THE LIGHT RIGHT

If you can't photograph all of your props at the same location and at the same time as your main background image, it's best to draw out a rough sketch of your set-up, taking note of where the light falls on your subject in relation to the position of your camera. Doing this will give you something to refer to when you return home and it'll allow you to try to match the same composition and lighting, saving hours of wasted time.

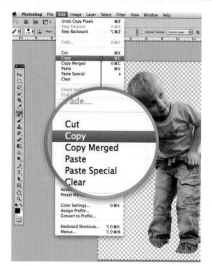

PROCESSING TECHNIQUE

When you've got your selection of shots in the can, it's time to start thinking about how these elements are going to be assembled in your software. As long as you've taken care of the perspective and lighting at the point of shooting, the job of bringing them together as one image is relatively hassle-free, creating a multi-layered composite image.

In this composite three images have been used – viaduct, boy and train – and it's important to load them into Photoshop in this order.

1 OPEN THE IMAGES Open up the images into Photoshop or Elements. You'll need to cut out the picture of the person in the shot, leaving them against a transparent background. Do this with the technique outlined in project 21 on page 86, using the Pen tool. Combine the person with the background by selecting the whole canvas with Select>All (or Ctrl-A) and choosing Edit>Copy. Go to the background window and paste the image as a new Layer (Edit>Paste, or Ctrl-V).

2 RESIZE ELEMENTS Using a Free Transform command (Ctrl-T) resize and reposition your subject matter so he or she looks natural in the background. Hold Shift while doing this to retain the right proportions. Hit Enter to apply the transformation. Hide this Layer (by clicking its eye icon) and pick the Polygonal Lasso Tool. Zoom in and click along the top of the viaduct (in this case) then everything beneath. You'll need to hide parts of the subject's legs to make it look as if he's standing behind the viaduct.

3 SET FOREGROUND COLOUR Go to Edit>Copy Merged and hit Ctrl+v. Layer 2 will now sit above Layer 1. Move down to Layer 1 and turn it back on. Make sure Layer 2 is highlighted and click on the Add Layer Mask icon at the bottom of the Layers palette before setting your foreground colour to Black. Select the Brush tool (B) and set up a 15px brush.

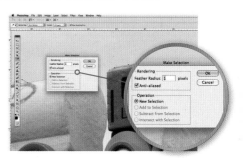

4 BRUSH INTO MASK Brush very carefully between the arch to reveal the child's jeans, giving the impression he's standing behind the viaduct. If you make a mistake, hit X to switch the foreground colour to white. Brush over the area to return the original detail before returning to a black brush (X). If you're using Elements, use the Eraser tool on Layer 2 for the same effect.

5 SELECT WITH PEN TOOL Open your foreground props (train here) in Photoshop (or Elements) and zoom in to about 200%. Pick the Pen tool (P) and click on the image to place an Anchor point between the edge of the blue train and the background. Click again to make Another anchor point further down, but hold down the mouse button and drag to bend the Path matching the edge. Work around the train, back to the first point and click it.

6 CUT AND PASTE Right-click inside the path and choose Make Selection, setting the Feather Radius to 1px before hitting OK. If you're using Elements, pick the Polygonal Lasso tool and click slowly around the train, then go to Select>Feather>1px. Now go to Edit>Copy and return to your equivalent of the viaduct JPEG. Check you're on Layer 1 in the Layers palette and hit Ctrl+V to paste in the train, dropping it behind the viaduct.

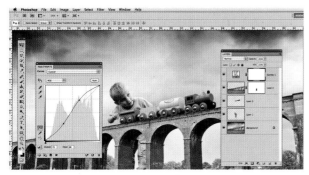

7 ROTATE THE TRAIN Press Ctrl+T and rotate the train anti-clockwise so it matches the angle of the viaduct. Drag it so the green carriage is in front of the child's arm and hit Enter. Click on Layer 2 before going to Layer>New Adjustment Layer>Curves. To improve contrast, click on the diagonal line and drag out a subtle S-curve. Now hit OK or exit the palette.

8 LOWER THE SKY Select the Lasso tool and make a Selection through the top half of the sky, selecting the clouds. Go to Select>Refine Edge and increase the Feather to 150px. Hit OK. Go to Edit>Copy Merged then Edit>Paste, select the Move tool and pull the sky down so it appears lower. Click the Add Layer Mask icon. Use a soft black brush to return detail to the child's hair and the train.

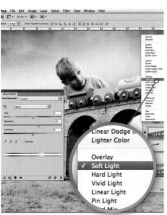

9 CROP THE IMAGE Select the Crop tool. Draw out a tighter crop box around the main subject and the viaduct. When you're happy with the new crop, hit Enter then go to Layer>New Adjustment Layer>Hue/Saturation. Boost the Saturation to about +20, hit OK and change the Blending Mode of the Hue/Saturation Layer to Soft Light. Reduce the Layer's Opacity to 70%.

10 RETURN SHADOW DETAIL Pick up the Brush tool and set up a soft brush with the foreground colour set to Black and the Opacity set to 75%. Click on the Layer mask next to the Hue/Saturation Layer and then brush over the child to reveal some detail in the shadows and any other areas where the shadows are too dark. Save your creation as a Photoshop (.psd) file to preserve Layers.

Create an abstract photo joiner

Make a picture that looks as if it's made of smaller prints – no glue required

WHAT YOU NEED
PHOTOSHOP
DSLR PLUS KIT LENS
TRIPOD

DIFFICULTY LEVEL
INTERMEDIATE

WHEN IT WAS FIRST CONCEIVED, the concept of joining photographs together to make a larger image was more rough and ready than the finely polished, seamless panoramas we can now produce in Photoshop and on our smartphones. Pioneering artists like David Hockney would shoot hundreds of pictures on colour print film, then arrange the 6x4in machine prints to form an abstract impression of the scene. If lines didn't quite match, or subjects got repeated then it didn't matter – this was all part of the desired effect. Today, with Photoshop and digital imaging, we can do this more easily than Hockney and his contemporaries could. We can shoot just one image, not hundreds, and apply the 'joiner' effect afterwards in Photoshop.

SHOOTING TECHNIQUE

To create a multi-shot joiner from a single image, compose with plenty of space around the subject using the wide-angle end of your lens. You'll need lots of space to play with once the image is in Photoshop.

1 CAMERA SETTINGS
Because the lion's share of work here is done in Photoshop, the camera settings are pretty straightforward. It is important to keep most of the subject in focus, though, so shoot in Aperture priority mode (A or Av), and pick an aperture of about f/8 or f/11 to ensure a decent depth-of-field. Shoot using a tripod for the sharpest possible results.

Any subject will do – from people to landscapes to buildings. The strong lines of this ice-cream hut respond well to the fractured look of a joiner.

PROCESSING TECHNIQUE

With the picture sorted it's time to apply the Joiner technique. A traditional joiner is one large picture made up of lots of smaller ones, but here you're going to replicate the effect by cutting up a single image in Photoshop.

Using the Layers palette will let you cut and paste parts of the picture onto new Layers and also move them around, ensuring that all the sections of the picture end up slightly out of line. You can also add a drop shadow to each Layer giving the impression that they're separate, and vary the lighting, which really add to the charm of the joiner effect.

1 PREPARE TO COPY First you need to break up the image into 20 smaller overlapping sections and for this you'll use one of Photoshop's Selection tools: the Marquee tool. In the Options bar, change the style from Normal to Fixed Size and enter 33% in both the Width and Height boxes.

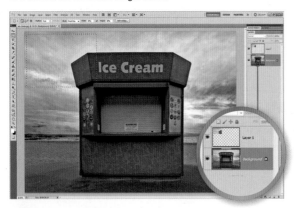

2 CUT OUT THE FIRST PIECE Click in the top-left corner of the image and, as if by magic, a rectangular Selection will appear. Next, click Edit>Copy followed by Edit>Paste. You've now made the first piece of the joiner – take a look in the Layers palette (Window>Layers) and you'll see it as Layer 1. Click the Background Layer again to prepare for the next step.

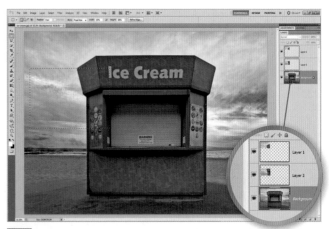

3 REPEAT THE PROCESS Click on the image again and the rectangular Selection will reappear. Drag it to a new position that's different, but slightly overlapping the previous one, then go to Edit>Copy followed by Edit>Paste to copy the new piece onto a new Layer. This time you'll see the chosen section appear as Layer 2 in the palette. Click the Background Layer and begin the process again.

4 MAKE MORE PIECES Now just keep repeating the cut and paste process, moving around the image until you've covered the whole area, or at least the areas that cover the main elements of the photo. Remember to keep selecting the Background Layer after you've pasted or you'll get a message saying you can't copy because 'the selected area is empty'.

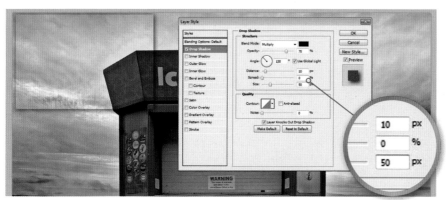

5 DROP SHADOW Once you've finished cutting and pasting the different parts of the picture, click on the top Layer in the Layers palette to make it active. It will probably be called Layer 1 and will turn blue or a darker grey to show it's active. Now go to Layer>Layer Style>Drop Shadow, set the Angle to 135°, the Distance to 10 pixels and the Size to 50 pixels, and press OK.

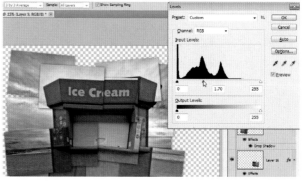

6 COPY THE STYLE Within the Layers palette you'll notice the word Effects just below Layer 1. Right-click the word Effects and from the drop-down list that appears, click on Copy Layer Style. Scroll down the Layers, find the Background Layer and click on the 'eye' icon to switch off its visibility. Hold Shift and click on the Layer immediately above the Background to select all the Layers.

7 PASTE THE SHADOW Right-click on any of the Layers (click the Layer name, not the thumbnail) and then choose Paste Layer Style. The drop shadow will appear on all the Layers. Click on any one of the Layers in the Layer palette (except the Background Layer) and drag it into a different position in the Layers stack. Repeat with other Layers to give the joiner a more random appearance.

8 ROTATE THE LAYERS Click Image>Canvas Size, change the units to Percent and enter 125 for both the Width and Height. To add further to the random look, click on the top Layer to make it active then press Ctrl+T (Free Transform) and move the cursor just outside the bounding box. Drag to rotate the image slightly. Repositioning the image a little also works well. Repeat this on the other Layers.

9 ALTER THE EXPOSURE Choose a Layer at random and press Ctrl+L to apply a Levels adjustment. Move the middle slider to either lighten or darken the image and click OK. Repeat this, lightening some Layers and darkening others. Finally click on the Background Layer, hit the 'eye' icon to toggle the visibility back on and go to Edit>Fill, choosing White as a colour and hitting OK.

Cross-processing effects

Create retro-looking photographs in Photoshop or Elements

WHAT YOU NEED
PHOTOSHOP OR
ELEMENTS

DIFFICULTY LEVEL
EASY

IF YOU'VE EVER DABBLED IN FILM PHOTOGRAPHY then you may well have experimented with cross-processing: asking your processing lab to develop E-6 slide film in C-41 print film chemistry, or vice versa. Typically this puts colours out of whack, adds contrast and often a bit of extra grain too. In a sense it's film abuse, but it's fun and unpredictable too.

In the digital era we can create the same effects more predictably using image-editing software like Photoshop or Elements and the results are much more predictable. The cross-processed look is a popular technique to try, especially with the rise of smartphone apps like Instagram and Hipstamatic offering cool-looking retro-effect filters. Cross processing is not restricted to people pictures, but it is is very popular with portrait photographers who add colour casts and shift hues within the colour palette of the picture.

The type and amount of cross processing you'll need for your own pictures may well differ from that shown here. When you follow the technique don't be afraid to use different values and experiment with shifting different colours, picking what works best for your particular image and tastes.

PROCESSING TECHNIQUE
CROSS PROCESSING
WITH CURVES IN PHOTOSHOP

If you are used to adjusting Curves for exposure compensation in Photoshop then applying cross-processing colour shifts is only a few steps away. Applying Curves adjustments to individual colour channels, instead of the component RBG colour channel creates strong colour casts.

FINISH

STAR IMAGE

1 OPEN THE IMAGE Open your image and go to Window>Layers to open the Layers palette.
Click on the half-black/half-white circle icon (Create new Fill or Adjustment Layer) and scroll along the drop-down menu to Curves. Select it to open the dialogue box. This box has a diagonal line running from the bottom left-hand corner to the top right-hand corner and it's this line you're going to use to manipulate each of the colour channels.

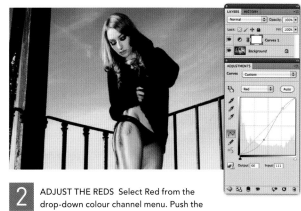

2 ADJUST THE REDS Select Red from the drop-down colour channel menu. Push the
diagonal line up at the top slightly and down much more dramatically at the bottom. Generally this will increase the blue tones within the image and make it look a lot cooler than the original. It's impossible to say exactly how much you should push it but an S-shaped curve is a good starting point.

3 ADJUST THE BLUES Now select Blue from the drop-down menu. Take the very top of the
Curves line down slightly and the bottom up. The change on the image will be very subtle at this stage, but the colours should go a little creamier. How much they change at this point will depend on the specific tones within your image and how much you've pushed the Curves line.

4 ADJUST THE GREENS Select Green from the drop-down menu and create another subtle
S-curve. Again, the exact nature of the Curve you create will depend on the tones in your image and what differences shifting the Blue and Red has already made, so experiment to see what you like. Playing with the Green channel often accentuates the turquoise blue of the sky beautifully.

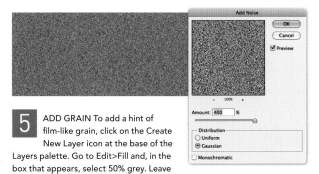

5 ADD GRAIN To add a hint of film-like grain, click on the Create
New Layer icon at the base of the Layers palette. Go to Edit>Fill and, in the box that appears, select 50% grey. Leave Blending Mode set to Normal and Opacity at 100%. Hit OK. Your Layer will now be grey; go to Filter>Noise>Add Noise and tick the Gaussian option. Go to the Amount slider and push it right up until you're happy with the effect – click OK.

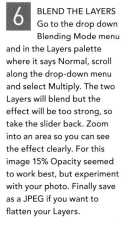

6 BLEND THE LAYERS Go to the drop down
Blending Mode menu and in the Layers palette where it says Normal, scroll along the drop-down menu and select Multiply. The two Layers will blend but the effect will be too strong, so take the slider back. Zoom into an area so you can see the effect clearly. For this image 15% Opacity seemed to work best, but experiment with your photo. Finally save as a JPEG if you want to flatten your Layers.

PROCESSING TECHNIQUE
CROSS PROCESSING WITH VARIATIONS IN ELEMENTS

Adobe hasn't blessed its Elements software with Curves adjustments, but there are other ways of creating colour shifts and casts. The Variations tool is a good choice since you can see the effect of each adjustment before you commit to it, and there is plenty of flexibility to restrict changes to shadows, midtones or highlights. This brilliantly simple effect basically has two phases: first change the colours for the retro look; secondly add more contrast to give your image some extra punch.

FIND BRIGHT AND BOLD COLOURS

Bright colours or subjects are the name of the game when it comes to eye-catching cross-processed images because the more varied the colours in your shot, the more striking the effect will be.

USE PICTURES WITH LOTS OF CONTRAST

The cross-process effect often pushes the contrast range through the roof but don't let that fool you into starting with a photo where the lighting is totally flat with no real shadows or highlights. Remember that this effect turns highlights one colour and shadows another, so if the picture is full of midtones, you won't see much happening.

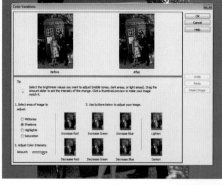

1 OPEN COLOUR VARIATIONS PALETTE Begin by opening the image you want to use then choose Enhance>Adjust Color>Color Variations to open the palette you need. If you're using this method in Photoshop then you'll need to access the Variations palette via Image> Adjustment> Variations.

The Variations palette is a large one and can look a little daunting at first, but in reality it's fairly easy to master. First, pick the Shadow tone option then move the slider to control the intensity of the change; it moves in jumps and to make the effect controllable make sure the slider is a couple of jumps back from the right edge, which is the maximum.

2 ALTER HIGHLIGHT AND SHADOW COLOUR Now, in the palette, locate the thumbnail image with Increase Blue underneath it and click it a number of times. With each click, the colour effect will become more intense and after about six clicks you'll add a very strong blue cast to the shadows, which is perfect for the cross-processed look. However, if you want to stop short of this, or apply more colour, the choice is yours. Now change from Shadows to Highlights, and apply a different colour effect to the brighter parts of the image. Here, Elements users should try six clicks on the Decrease Blue thumbnail. Photoshop users will do their six clicks on the More Yellow thumbnail before clicking OK. The wording in Elements may be a little unhelpful, but the effect is the same as in Photoshop – decreasing blue increases yellow.

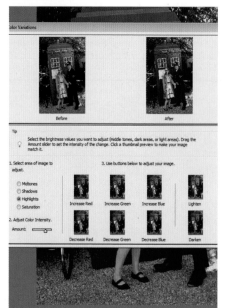

3 INCREASE BRIGHTNESS AND CONTRAST The only thing left to do now is to increase the contrast in the photo, giving it a more punchy look. In Elements this is done by clicking Enhance>Adjust Lighting>Brightness/Contrast; Photoshop users will need to click Image>Adjustments>Brightness/Contrast. Move the Contrast slider all the way to the right so it reads +100, then, as an optional step, you can also add a bit of brightness to even-up the tones in the image. In this case adding +10 to the Brightness is perfect.

Capture scenic panoramas

Create ultra-wide angle views by stitching images together

WHAT YOU NEED
DSLR OR COMPACT
CAMERA
PHOTOSHOP ELEMENTS
OR PHOTOSHOP

DIFFICULTY LEVEL
EASY

STITCHING TOGETHER INDIVIDUALLY SHOT IMAGES to form a long, thin panoramic photograph is easy to do and the results are seriously impressive. Such pictures cover very wide angles and the large file sizes produced means they can be printed big, too.

The Photomerge command in Adobe Photoshop or Elements pulls together individual frames into the same Layers palette, analyses and overlaps them and warps and stretches them so they line up perfectly. Layers masks are then used to create a seamless join between frames. Complicated though this sounds, there is only a little work required from you, the photographer. Just some extra cropping and general tidying up with the Clone Stamp tool at the end.

Photomerge is a really powerful tool and, in its most current version, it will cope admirably with even the most difficult of images. So, dig out some pics and have a go at creating your own panorama.

FINISH

SHOOTING THE START IMAGES

It's best to create the component images for your panorama by using your camera in the upright (portrait) position. This makes the most of the longest edge of the frame and increases the number of pixels in the final stitched image. Keep the same settings for each shot and allow a slight overlap of what's included in each frame. Also, try to shoot in Manual exposure mode and with a manual white balance setting. This will reduce the changes in colour temperature and brightness between frames, which results in abrupt changes in the final panorama. Project 17 on page 70 will help you shoot your panorama.

START IMAGES

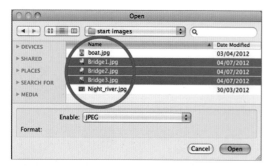

1 OPEN THE COMPONENT IMAGES

Once you've shot a panoramic sequence open the image files into Photoshop or Elements. It's best not to make any changes to them until after you have made the stitched panorama. The software works by matching up similarities between images, so editing the files beforehand can make things difficult for Photomerge to get it right. Additionally, if you leave editing until the end, you will only have one image to make changes to rather than three or more.

TECH TALK

VISUALISE YOUR CROP

Go to File>Preferences, choose the Display and Cursors option and you'll find a heading entitled Crop tool. This allows you to change what's known as the Shield and it's this that helps you visualize how your crop will look. You can turn it on or off altogether, or choose which colour to use, or even how opaque the Shield is. To see exactly how your image will look use 100% Opacity, but sometimes it's more helpful than it sounds to see what you are cropping out – somewhere between 75% and 90% works well.

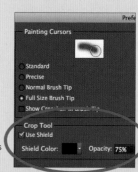

2 USING PHOTOMERGE

In Elements choose File>New> Photomerge>Panorama or, if you're using Photoshop, go to File>Automate>Photomerge. Click the Add Open Files button and choose the Auto Layout option (see Other Layout Options in box below). Click OK and the software will begin the merging process. This may take a while, so be patient. Once done, your finished panorama will appear; if you're using Elements you'll be asked if you want to fill in the edges of the panorama automatically. Click No, as clicking Yes can result in strange effects. Your panorama should now exist in three separate Layers in the Layers palette, with Masks being used to blend them together.

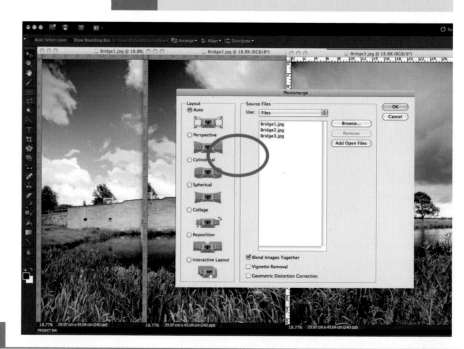

OTHER LAYOUT OPTIONS

Auto	Perspective	Cylindrical	Spherical	Collage	Reposition	Interactive Layout
Chooses to apply either a Perspective or Cylindrical layout, depending on your images.	Images are mapped out on a flat plane and then stretched and skewed to line up together.	Mapped out as if on an unfolded cylinder to reduce 'bow tie' distortions from using a wide lens.	The images are mapped out as if inside a sphere. Best used for 360 degree panoramas.	Overlapping content is aligned using only scaling and rotation to match it up.	Aligns the Layers to match overlapping content without transforming the image at all.	A manual option that allows you to align Layers yourself in a separate dialog box.

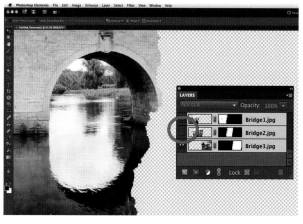

3 CROP INTO PANORAMIC FORMAT The odd shape of the resulting image is due to the transformations employed by the Photomerge command. You need to crop your image into a more pleasing form. To do this select the Crop tool from the Toolbox and in the drop-down menu at the top in the Options bar choose No Restriction or, if you're using Photoshop, click Clear to get rid of any pre-set sizes. Now, drag a long rectangular box around the image – don't worry too much about the corners, you can fill them in later, just concentrate on making a nice composition. Hit Enter on your keyboard to commit to the crop.

4 FILL AND REPAIR WITH CLONING Now clean up the panorama and fill in any gaps left with the Clone Stamp tool. The image is still in three separate Layers so you'll need to flatten to do this, but first check for any problems at 100% magnification. Zoom in on a seam between two layers and navigate along it checking for problems. Turning Layers on and off using the 'eye' icon in the Layers palette may help with this. Once you've identified any errors, go to Image>Flatten Image (Layer>Flatten image in Photoshop). Now choose the Clone Stamp tool, set to a soft brush of 100px diameter and Opacity of 100%. Alt-click to pick an appropriate sample point, and then release Alt and paint over any gaps.

5 FIXING DISTORTION To finish off, tweak the perspective using the Transform command. Right-click on your image in the Layers palette and choose Duplicate Layer. With this new Layer selected in your Layers palette hit Ctrl+T on your keyboard to bring up the Free Transform command. Right-click within the bounding box that will now be surrounding your image and choose Perspective. By left-clicking, drag the top right-hand box upwards to make the right-hand side of your image larger, which in turn makes it appear closer. Stop when the horizon is straight. Hit Enter on your keyboard to commit to the change.

TIP

HOW TO MOUNT YOUR PANORAMA

Panoramic images make great wall art and will look superb when framed and set above the mantelpiece. It's much more affordable than you'd think, too. There are plenty of options for getting your images framed. The most cost-effective is to buy a pre-made frame, and crop your pic to suit. The other option, to really make the most of your image, is to have it custom-framed by a professional company. It will fit a frame to the proportions of your image ensuring an exact fit. Prices vary with frame size.

Think about which frames will best suit your image. The simple black frame here had a neat white border and together they worked well with this mono panorama.

Turn a scene into a photo planet

Give your landscapes the 360° look

TURN YOUR HOME TOWN OR FAVOURITE LANDSCAPE into an amazing photo planet. It only takes a few minutes and the results can look intriguing. Look for, or take specially, pictures that have a clear area of sky right across the whole image and an uncluttered foreground. If your image also has things like trees or buildings breaking up the skyline, then that's even better as they'll give your planet a more defined, interesting edge.

FINISH

The end result has an almost imperceptible join making a perfect photo planet!

START IMAGE

PROCESSING TECHNIQUE

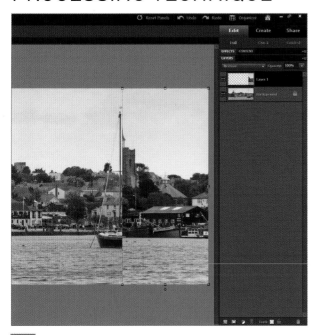

1 RESHAPE With the Crop tool, drag out a panoramic framing then click the tick. Now pick the Rectangular Marquee and drag a Selection over the left of the picture. Press Ctrl+C followed by Ctrl+V. Click Image>Rotate>Flip Layer Horizontal then use the Move tool to drag it over to the right edge.

2 HIDE THE JOIN Select the Eraser tool with a soft edge at 100% Opacity, and run it over the hard edge of the moved section to blend it in, then press Ctrl+E. Click Image>Resize>Image size. Untick Constrain Proportions and change both Width and Height to 2500 pixels. Click OK and your image will become square.

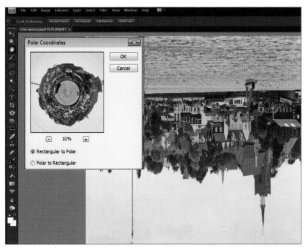

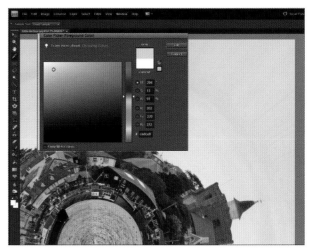

3 MAKE A PLANET Click Image>Rotate>180° to turn the image upside down and then click Filter>Distort>Polar Coordinates. Ensure Rectangular to Polar is ticked, then click OK. You should now have a perfectly formed planet but look closely at the corners and you'll notice some odd effects...

4 TIDY THE CORNERS Use the Eyedropper tool to sample a colour in the sky very close to the point where the image takes on the zoomed appearance. Now pick the Brush tool and, using a soft-edge, paint over the problem areas. Repeat this process for the other corners to complete the effect.

Conjure up a colourful and cool still life

Use a minimum of kit and everyday objects to make simple still lifes

WHAT YOU NEED
BOTTLE AND GLASS:
DSLR AND KIT LENS
A GLASSLESS PICTURE
FRAME
PACK OF COLOURED
TISSUE PAPER
LIGHTBOX AND
LIGHTING GELS –
OPTIONAL

WHITE PAPER:
DSLR AND KIT LENS
1 X A1 WHITE PAPER
6 X A4 OR A3 WHITE
PAPER
STAPLER
BLU-TACK

DIFFICULTY LEVEL
INTERMEDIATE/
ADVANCED

IF THERE'S A SPACE ON A WALL in your house that's crying out to be filled with some suitable artwork, then these simple techniques are ideal. Even if you've never taken a still life shot before, you'll finish up with some eye-catching images that will look great in a frame.

SHOOTING TECHNIQUE
WINE BOTTLE AND GLASS

There are two methods to achieve this shot – the first only needs some direct sunlight through a window, the second requires an old lightbox (or similar) to provide the necessary backlighting. Of course, you also need some bottles. Coloured glass bottles aren't too hard to come by if you hunt around car boot sales or simply hang onto a few empty wine bottles.

You'll also need some tissue paper or a similar transparent material. Ideally, the material you choose should have a texture to it as this adds to the overall appeal of the image. For the red-bottle-and-glass shot stretch some white tissue paper over a frame and tape it in place so that you can stand the frame upright on the table and make it much easier to place your props.

Place the bottle and wine glass, filled with Ribena, behind the frame and wait for the sun to come out. When it does,

the sun projects the shapes onto the tissue paper. Then you simply take a meter reading from the front of the tissue and allow for an extra stop of exposure compensation (+1), as there is a lot of white area within the frame that could fool the camera's meter. The mixture of sharper shadow area, lighter transparent colour, texture, and the slight distortion you get makes it an interesting image.

If you want to add a little more punch boost Contrast and Saturation fractionally in Photoshop. If you want to create some bright colours adjust the Hue slider to create a completely different look.

START

DIFFUSED Raise up the bottle and glass on a couple of old cook books and place as close as possible to the back of the tissue paper frame.

BACKLIGHTING Direct sunlight is all you need, so position your frame close to a window that gives you exactly that.

LENS CHOICE Any lens that allows you to compose tightly within the frame works fine. Your kit lens is probably ideal.

DELIBERATE DEFOCUS

The second method is to deliberately shoot the subject out of focus. This sounds like heresy to most photographers who go to great pains to make sure everything is pin-sharp and has plenty of depth-of-field to ensure that sharpness goes right through the image. But this is exactly what you can do for this alternative shot of the bottles. You can use the same sunlit backlighting as before or place an old slide film lightbox close behind the bottles to create the backlighting.

It gives a slightly more even lighting.

Defocusing works here because the shape is so familiar. To defocus successfully, switch your lens to manual focus. If you try to focus on the tissue paper in AF it'll keep trying to sharpen on the more familiar lines of the bottles.

Just arrange your composition normally, then use the focusing barrel on your lens to knock the bottles fractionally out of focus. Less is usually more, as all you are really trying

to do is take the sharp lines of the bottles back and bring the texture more to the front. If you have a range of coloured bottles, try a series of different colours next to each other, switching the tone of the tissue paper, too, to see what different effects you can get.

Incidentally, if you only have clear glass bottles you can create your colour by filling them with different coloured liquid.

FINISH

TIP

LIGHTING GELS

If you fancy something even more psychedelic then get yourself a set of lighting gels. They're a really useful photographic accessory and don't cost too much. By laying one over the other on a lightbox you can create all sorts of patterns of colour over which you can place a bottle. It's best to do this in the dark, so the strong colours come through. Not all the colour combinations will work but keep trying different gels and you'll find something that does. Shoot down from directly overhead and crop in tightly for a vibrant and remarkably simple still life.

SHOOTING TECHNIQUE
WHITE PAPER

You'd think that shooting a fine art image from a few sheets of white paper would challenge the most proficient photographer. But get it right and you'll create something very special. The key to success is window light – using shadows and highlights to give form to curved sheets of paper.

The technique itself is relatively simple, but setting up and packing away will take longer. Creating the curve out of six sheets of paper and stapling them together is fiddly, so get someone to help you. Once the paper background and curve are in place you may have to compose with an upside-down camera, which is tricky so this part takes a little longer than usual. With both subject and camera where they should be, it's time to shoot. Make sure you experiment with angle of paper and viewpoint, and shoot at different apertures to find the overall combination that creates the result you're looking for.

TURN OFF AUTOFOCUS Manually focus on the part of the paper you want to be sharp. Autofocus can really struggle with plain white subjects, so it's best to do it yourself.

KEEP IT STEADY A cable release makes shooting a lot easier, but if you don't have one use the camera's self-timer to avoid camera shake during long exposures.

CHANGE YOUR VIEW To get a low enough viewpoint you might have to put your tripod's centre column upside-down. This allows you to shoot from a very low angle while maintaining a steady camera.

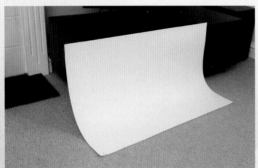

1 OPEN THE IMAGE Open your image and go to Window>Layers to open the Layers palette. Click on the half-black/half-white circle icon (Create new Fill or Adjustment Layer) and scroll along the drop-down menu to Curves. Select it to open the dialogue box. This box has a diagonal line running from the bottom left-hand corner to the top right-hand corner and it's this line you're going to use to manipulate each of the colour channels.

2 CREATE CURVES Place six sheets of plain white paper together and stagger them along their length. Staple both width edges to hold them in place. Now push the sheets up into a curve at the unstapled end. Once you're happy with the curved sheets, staple the paper to hold them in place then place the curve in front of the background.

3 CAMERA SETTINGS Set the camera to Aperture priority with ISO at 100. Choose the aperture you'd like – f/8 works well for a medium depth-of-field, while f/22 produces the most sharpness. Set your lens to manual focus and attach your DSLR to a tripod upside-down to shoot on the floor, or the right way up to shoot on a table.

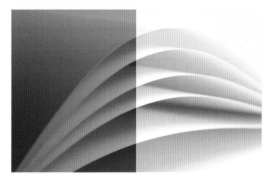

4 PERFECT EXPOSURE Working in Aperture priority and shooting a white subject guarantees exposure issues, so exposure compensation is the key to nailing this shot. For best results and pure white paper in the photo, dial in 2 stops of overexposure (+2). All DSLRs are different, so check the instruction manual if you're not sure how it's done.

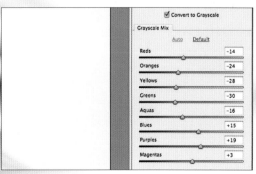

5 CONVERT TO MONO This photo is all about light, shadow and form and this just works better in mono because converting to black & white takes away unnecessary colour distraction and adds to the abstraction.

Shoot low for stunning landscapes

Get closer to ground level and capture some high-impact foreground deta

WHAT YOU NEED
DSLR
WIDE-ANGLE LENS
TRIPOD

DIFFICULTY LEVEL
EASY

WE'RE ALL VERY USED TO SEEING THE WORLD from a similar, head-height viewpoint and, because of this, you need to investigate new angles if you want to spice up your photography.

Shooting from low to the ground gives a unique angle of view that's not commonly seen – it's physically awkward to do in comparison to an eye-level snap so many photographers simply don't consider low-level shooting as an option. This is a real shame, though, as a low-angle viewpoint is as much of an asset as a shiny new lens or a flashy new camera, so the sooner you install it as part of your photographic approach, the better your pictures will be.

A low-angle viewpoint not only offers an interesting spin on the scene in front of you, it also helps make the most of the foreground interest that can really make your shot stand out. It's not just for classic landscapes either: a street scene with some leaves in the foreground can be as dramatic as a boulder on the beach or a fallen tree in a woodland landscape.

Above: Getting low makes it much easier to find foreground interest. Use a tripod and invert the centre column to get as low down as possible.

Left: Shooting the same scene from standing is OK, but doesn't have the impact of the low-angle shot.

Right: Using foreground detail close up to the lens adds impact and drama.

GET LOW WITH A TRIPOD

Just lying on the ground to get the shot is all well and good but, ideally, you'll need some form of support. Locking off your camera on a tripod, or similar support, will ensure your images are free from any blur caused by camera shake, as well as providing a stable platform from which to fine-tune your composition. This allows you complete control over your final image. There is a range of options to choose from.

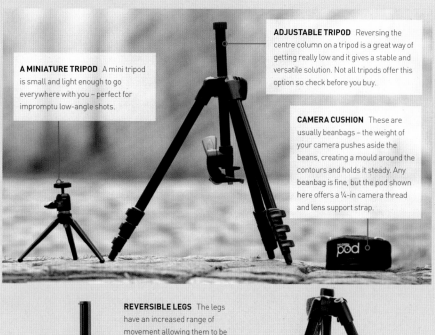

A MINIATURE TRIPOD A mini tripod is small and light enough to go everywhere with you – perfect for impromptu low-angle shots.

ADJUSTABLE TRIPOD Reversing the centre column on a tripod is a great way of getting really low and it gives a stable and versatile solution. Not all tripods offer this option so check before you buy.

CAMERA CUSHION These are usually beanbags – the weight of your camera pushes aside the beans, creating a mould around the contours and holds it steady. Any beanbag is fine, but the pod shown here offers a ¼-in camera thread and lens support strap.

GET DOWN LOW

If you've opted for a tripod you'll need to know how to increase its low-angle potential and get it into a low-shooting position. Not all tripods have these functions so make sure yours does before you start undoing knobs! Here are the most common methods found.

REVERSIBLE LEGS The legs have an increased range of movement allowing them to be pointed upwards. Once they're locked in place, this automatically gives an upside-down camera for low-angle shots.

REVERSIBLE CENTRE COLUMN Loosen the centre column and slide it out. Turn the column upside down and place it back through the collar from underneath. Your camera will mount upside-down.

HORIZONTAL CENTRE COLUMN Loosen the centre column and extend it all the way up, then angle it down 90° until it lies horizontally. With the collar still loosened, slide the column back through. The legs extend out almost flat allowing low-angle shooting without hanging your camera upside-down.

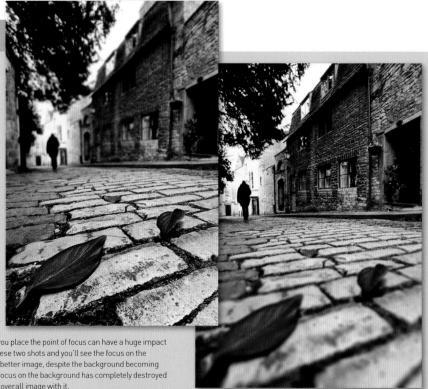

HOW TO FOCUS ON THE FOREGROUND

Since the foreground will be so close to your lens, and the background so far away, you'll struggle to keep everything sharp at the same time – even when setting the biggest depth-of-field you can muster. The most important part of the image is the foreground – if this is sharp, the rest will fall into place, so it doesn't matter much if the background goes soft, this won't change the overall mood of the image.

But if you focus on the background and let the foreground drop out of focus, the image looks messy. The strength of these low-level shots comes from the detail you can see in the foreground; if you let this blur out your image will suffer as a result.

The difference in where you place the point of focus can have a huge impact on a picture. Compare these two shots and you'll see the focus on the foreground is clearly the better image, despite the background becoming slightly soft. Placing the focus on the background has completely destroyed the foreground – and the overall image with it.

SHOOTING TECHNIQUE
HOW TO TAKE A LOW ANGLE SHOT

Getting down low is the key element here, but what else should you look out for? Is it as simple as just mounting your camera, lying on the floor and pressing the shutter? Well, almost. But you'll need to find some foreground interest first, and the good news is, it isn't as hard as you'd think. Grab your widest lens and get down close to the ground. You'll notice that the ground will appear very large in your frame in comparison with distant elements. This more unusual angle really draws attention to the textures on the ground and will give your image that low-angle signature look. It's also this large foreground that makes finding a focal point easy. Look for anything; it could be a leaf, a few interesting cobbles, a patch of moss or even the texture of the ground itself. Getting this low will allow even some of the smallest items to become your foreground interest for a shot. This will act as the starting point that grabs the viewer's attention and leads them through the image.

Since the ground is occupying such a sizeable portion of your frame, it deserves much of your attention but don't forget the background, and remember that the rules of composition still apply. Try placing a figure to add interest. Without something in the background to end up on, the foreground interest will take you straight out of the shot.

1 SETTING UP Grab your tripod, or whatever support option you choose, and set up as low down as you can. Spend time fine-tuning and making sure the composition is just as you want it. Once you're happy, lock off the tripod to ensure you don't get any camera shake blurring your images.

2 SETTING FOCUS Use Autofocus to focus on your foreground interest, about 0.5m or so in front of you. Once you've focused, switch the camera to Manual focus mode to prevent focus changing. Be careful not to knock the focus ring at the front of your lens or you'll spoil your shot.

3 SETTING SHOOTING MODE Switch over to Aperture priority mode, setting your aperture to f/22 to get as much sharpness around the point of focus as you can. In Aperture priority your shutter speed will take care of itself, so just set the ISO in your menu to the lowest setting (100 or 200), and engage the self-timer to avoid camera shake when you fire the shutter.

4 SHOOT AND CHECK When you've taken a shot, check the screen to make sure your composition is good. It can be quite difficult to spot wonky horizons when shooting low, especially if your tripod's legs are getting in your way. Once you've checked framing, zoom in tight to check the focus on your foreground interest. It may seem awkward, but it's better to do it now than find out it's not critically sharp when you get home.

TIP

ROTATE YOUR PICTURES

If you're using a tripod that requires your camera to be attached upside-down, this can cause landscape-oriented shots to display on your computer the wrong way up. Don't fret though, as this is easily fixed in Photoshop or Elements.
• Start by opening up the image then go to Image>Rotate>180° in Elements or Image>Image Rotation>180° in Photoshop. Your image will then be flipped around the right way up.
• To save, choose File>Save as... type in the new name for your image and select the JPEG option before hitting Save. When prompted, set the quality to 12 and hit OK.
• If you have access to Adobe Bridge you can rotate all your upside-down images at once. With bridge open, hold down Ctrl and click each picture you want to rotate. Go to Edit>Rotate 180°.

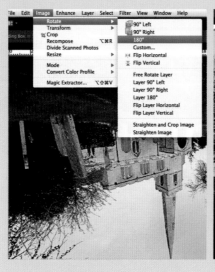

Bend light to your advantage

Use refraction in your photography for some exciting results...
and all in-camera

WHAT YOU NEED
DSLR AND KIT LENS
TRIPOD
FLASHGUN OR POP-UP
FLASH

DIFFICULTY LEVEL
EASY

CONTROLLING AND MANIPULATING LIGHT isn't only about using light modifiers with flashguns or studio lights. It can also include much more bizarre items such as glass bowls and drinking glasses full of water. This may sound completely mad, but getting back to the basic physics of light and using refraction in your photography can provide a wealth of amazingly creative opportunities.

Refraction appears to bend and magnify objects in water, like in this main shot of the magnified eye, although this is obviously just someone sitting behind the tank. Refraction occurs when light travels between mediums of different densities, such as air and water.

The change in the speed of the light makes the light change direction ever so slightly and objects in or near the water appear to bend. Think back to your days at school when you had to put a pencil in a glass of water for a science experiment...

Here you'll discover two techniques, using a fishbowl and a glass of water to magnify and bend light. The results are surreal and, most importantly, fun to achieve. Not to mention the fact that you won't need any more kit than a DSLR, kit lens, tripod, and a flashgun or pop-up flash. This really is one of those occasions where you have to pinch yourself because getting great results is so easy.

SHOOTING TECHNIQUE

Using a fishbowl or vase full of water is a great way to add a surreal twist to portraits. When planning your shot, consider the end result you'd like to achieve. A round fishbowl like ours produces massive magnification and works best for focusing on a single facial feature. The edges tend to distort what's behind too much, so it's important to keep the eye or other main feature behind the central region of the bowl. If you'd prefer a less distorted portrait, use a large cylindrical vase. With this you'll be able to include more of the subject's face in the shot.

Set up the shot with the goldfish bowl or vase near the edge of a table. It's best to half-fill the bowl at the sink, then fill it up to the top with a jug when it's in position. This avoids the danger of tripping over with a heavy glass object full of water! Once full, wipe away any smears or water droplets. Ask your subject to kneel down behind the table and place a cushion on the floor to make them more comfortable; you don't want a fidgety model. Kneeling down will position their head at roughly the same height as the fishbowl, so they won't have to stoop.

For best results use a flashgun bounced off the ceiling to illuminate the subject. This helps to reduce reflections from the room, but will also create its own reflections – it's a trade-off. If you have a flashgun, set it to TTL mode and aim it up at a 45-degree angle so it bounces off the ceiling. If you have a pop-up flash, use a small piece of white card to make it bounce upwards. Set the camera to ISO 400 in Aperture priority at f/4 or f/5.6. This will let in plenty of light and you only need a shallow depth-of-field.

With this technique, unless you shoot in a studio, reflections will be a problem. The only thing you can do is work with them, because there's little you can do about them. Here a reflector was used to block a distracting window reflection, but this also created reflection, albeit a less noticeable one.

The final thing to remember is the subject's distance from the fishbowl – too far away they won't be visible, too close and they'll squash their nose against the glass. You need to find a happy medium.

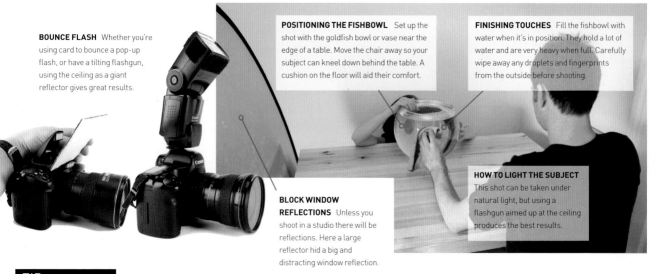

BOUNCE FLASH Whether you're using card to bounce a pop-up flash, or have a tilting flashgun, using the ceiling as a giant reflector gives great results.

POSITIONING THE FISHBOWL Set up the shot with the goldfish bowl or vase near the edge of a table. Move the chair away so your subject can kneel down behind the table. A cushion on the floor will aid their comfort.

FINISHING TOUCHES Fill the fishbowl with water when it's in position. They hold a lot of water and are very heavy when full. Carefully wipe away any droplets and fingerprints from the outside before shooting.

BLOCK WINDOW REFLECTIONS Unless you shoot in a studio there will be reflections. Here a large reflector hid a big and distracting window reflection.

HOW TO LIGHT THE SUBJECT This shot can be taken under natural light, but using a flashgun aimed up at the ceiling produces the best results.

TIP

HOW TO GET THE BEST MAGNIFIED PORTRAIT

As with all ideas, especially things you haven't tried before, they evolve as you go along and you need to be open to changes of direction. When shooting a highly reflective object that magnifies in a strange way, expect the unexpected. You'd expect a portrait to show the whole face – this didn't really work. You'd expect it to include both eyes – this didn't really work either, the fishbowl magnified them too much. So, the photographer tried focusing on one eye. This worked!

The next problem was the bright window reflection, which was cut out by a large reflector that caused a less distracting reflection on the fishbowl.

Having two eyes in the shot didn't really work, but even when the pose was correct, the shot was spoilt by the strong window reflection on the left of the bowl.

SHOOT A SIMPLE STILL LIFE

If you'd prefer to shoot a refraction photograph that's not a portrait here's a still life technique with eye-watering results, literally. Refraction is interesting to exploit photographically and, as well as producing a great photo, it'll also help you understand a little more about how light behaves. Since light is the raw ingredient of all photography, understanding it couldn't be any more important.

All you need for this technique is a highball glass full of water, and two pieces of diagonally striped black and white paper. The straight lines that pass behind the glass will take on a curved appearance, so contrasting strongly with the rest of the lines not behind the glass. It's a simple concept that works extremely well.

Reflections are easier to control with this technique than with the fishbowl portrait, but you still have to take care. The best way to do this is to shoot below a window with the curtains closed.

1 WHAT YOU NEED Set up under a window with the curtains closed using a makeshift workspace, such as a cardboard box with a sheet of mount board on top. You'll also need water, a highball glass, Blu-Tack and two pieces of black and white, diagonally-striped paper. Don't forget a tripod to keep the camera steady during the long exposure.

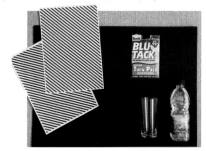

2 CAMERA SETTINGS Set your DSLR to Aperture priority at f/22 for a large depth-of-field, and set ISO to 100 because this will produce high-quality and noise-free images. Put your DSLR on a tripod to keep it steady, and zoom the kit lens out to the longest focal length. Then compose the shot so that the glass fills most of the frame.

3 GETTING THE SHOT Now manually focus on the front rim of the glass to ensure the shot is sharp from front to back. Autofocus might struggle with a shot like this, so it's best avoided. With everything ready, release the shutter with a cable release to avoid any camera movement during exposure. If you don't have one, use the camera's self-timer.

Pan to capture movement

Convey movement and drama in your photography with a slow shutter speed and some camera movement

WHAT YOU NEED
DSLR AND STANDARD
ZOOM

DIFFICULTY LEVEL
EASY

MOVING THE CAMERA DURING AN EXPOSURE is something all photographers work hard to avoid, but there are times when camera movement can actually be your friend. For example the panning shot, where you follow a fast-moving subject through the frame to keep it sharp while the background blurs.

All too often photographers get hung up on ultimate sharpness – they want to shoot a fast-moving subject, so start thinking about fast shutter speeds and forget all about the creativity that a slower shutter speed and a bit of camera movement can offer. Sharply frozen images are all well and good, but it's a panning shot that really shows the speed and energy of a fast-moving subject. In comparison a frozen subject just looks a bit dull and static. The aim of the panning shot is to get a relatively sharp subject speeding through a blurred background. To make this happen, all you have to do is move the camera at the same speed and direction as your subject; if you do this while you take a photo and use a slow enough shutter speed, you'll get great results.

Although this way of shooting may sound like a tricky skill to master, it's actually not hard at all and once you understand the basic principles, the rest is just down to a bit of practice with a willing subject.

FINISH

SHOOTING TECHNIQUE: HORIZONTAL PANNING

THE RIGHT STANCE

Panning can be done using any camera as long as you can manually set the shutter speed. You don't need any specialist equipment, tripods or flashes, just your trusty camera and a lens of your choice. It's worth remembering, though, that while the technique itself is straightforward, the results can vary greatly depending on your movement and that of the subject you're tracking. Results can be a bit hit or miss, but don't be put off if it takes a few tries to get a good shot – it's all part of the process.

Getting the right stance while panning is inherently a freeform technique with variable results. There are a few tips that will increase your success rate and getting a good firm grip on your DSLR is the right starting point. This will create a very stable base from which you can start panning.

Hold onto the camera with your right hand, index finger positioned over the shutter and use your left hand to support the lens (don't hold the focus ring though or you could end up changing what's sharp). Keep your elbows down and tucked into your sides to create as stable a position as possible; this will keep your upper body locked in place – the movement of the pan comes from a twisting motion through your hips.

Dialing in a slow shutter speed and tracking a moving subject will give stylish, dynamic action shots.

MOVE SMOOTHLY

With your grip sorted, you can now focus on the swing or pan itself. To get the smoothest pan you need to follow your subject's movement from the start to the end, not just from when the shutter opens and closes. With this in mind, place your feet shoulder-width apart and think about where your subject is going to be when you take the shot. You'll get the smoothest pan while rotating through to a forward-facing position so point your feet at where you're going to fire the shutter.

All the movement of your panning motion needs to come through your hips. Twisting from the hips rather than with the arms or shoulders will help to ensure a smoother and more consistent turn. During the pan, keep your subject placed in the same position in the viewfinder and, because the viewfinder will black out when the shutter fires, keep both eyes open so you can carry on following your subject. It's very important to remember to keep your swing smooth and to match the speed of your subject.

DIRECTION OF PAN

BEGIN PAN Keep your finger on the shutter button and track your subject as it approaches.

FIRE SHUTTER Don't break your movement, but hit the shutter to begin the shot.

BLACKOUT! As the mirror goes up, the viewfinder goes black, but keep panning.

SHOT ENDS As the shutter closes, don't stop – keep panning with it.

END PAN For a smooth pan keep following the subject after the shutter closes.

KEEP YOUR DISTANCE

Choosing a focal length is an important consideration when panning, because the distance you position yourself from your subject will affect how much camera movement you'll need to blur the background.

Shorter focal lengths, like those of wide-angle lenses, mean you'll need to be closer to your subject to fill the frame and will, therefore, have to move the camera more. But stand back from your subject and use a longer focal length

and you'll have less of an angle to swing your camera through, making it easier to achieve a smooth effect.

Imagine photographing a cyclist travelling fast along a straight road. If you stood next to the road with a wide-angle lens mounted on your camera body, following the cyclist through a pan will take a great deal of rapid movement. But move just 100m back and try the same thing again with a longer lens and

this time you'll find you have to move the camera far less.

So, using a longer lens makes it easier to achieve smooth results when panning, but you don't have to do it all the time. While it's harder to achieve good results in wide-angle panning shots, they do look really dramatic and are worth a try. Start out with a longer lens at first and progress to a wider one as you become more comfortable with the technique.

Shot with lens at 18mm – at wider angles you'll need to stand closer to your subject and move the camera more.

Shot with lens at 55mm – zoomed in, you'll need to move the camera much less to achieve background blur.

SHOOTING TECHNIQUE

1 SET EXPOSURE Switch your shooting mode to Shutter priority (S or Tv on the mode dial) and choose a shutter speed appropriate for your subject – see Expert Advice panel opposite. Set your camera's ISO sensitivity to its lowest setting, usually 100 or 200.

2 PREFOCUS If possible, get your subject to stand in the position they'll be in when you take the shot and frame up. Half-press the shutter button to focus on them, then switch over to Manual focus to lock it in place. Be sure not to knock the focus ring. If you can't rehearse your focus point, then pre-focus on where you think it'll be.

3 SHOOT THE ACTION Get into position and shout 'ready' to your subject (or wait for them to appear). Follow them as they move, keeping a nice fluid motion matching their speed through the viewfinder. Fire the shutter smoothly and keep following through the viewfinder blackout until well after the shutter has closed and the shot has been taken.

4 FINISH OFF Check the shot on your DSLR's screen. If it's much too blurred then increase the shutter speed a little. If, on the other hand, there's not enough blur and the subject looks frozen in place, try again – this time with a slower shutter speed. Remember, practice makes perfect!

TIP

HOW TO IMPROVE YOUR RESULTS

The streaks of blur within your shot can tell you a lot about your pan. So, when working out how to improve your image, look to your streaks.
• Streaks too short? Your shutter speed is too fast. Slow it down and try again.
• Diagonal streaks and a blurred subject? You aren't moving with your subject. Shoot again and try to only move in the direction your subject does.
• Curved or bumpy streaks? Your pan isn't smooth enough. Try again and keep as still as possible, only swivelling through your hips.

Smooth straight streaks in the background mean you are doing it right with a nice controlled pan.

If the subject is blurred and the streaks are bumpy or uneven, your pan needs smoother movement.

EXPERT ADVICE

WHAT SHUTTER SPEED?

The overall look of your pan depends greatly on the shutter speed you use – too fast and the action will be frozen, too slow and everything blurs – so which shutter speed should you choose? The appropriate shutter speed is closely linked to how fast the subject is moving: a slower subject requires a slower shutter speed.

1/25 SEC

1/40 SEC

1/100 SEC

1/250 SEC

SHOOTING TECHNIQUE
VERTICAL PANNING

Following moving objects isn't the only use for panning. Moving the camera at slow shutter speeds can be used to introduce background blur to any type of photograph. A vertical 'tilting' pan shot is a good example and all you need for this one is a bunch of trees. Your nearest woodland area shouldn't be too far away, so next time you get the chance, give this technique a try. It's a fun camera project that will only take a few minutes to shoot, and you'll be surprised how arty the results can be – especially if you bag a good one and are bold enough to have it made into a big, canvas print for the wall.

1 SET UP Set your camera's ISO sensitivity to its lowest setting (normally ISO 100 or 200) and set the exposure mode to Shutter priority (S or Tv). Dial in a value of 1/8sec – usually indicated by an 8 in the shutter speed display – not by 8" which is a long exposure of 8sec. Once you've done this your aperture will be set automatically.

2 SHOOT Start at the top of the trees and tilt the camera down in a smooth continuous motion, pressing the shutter down completely halfway through. Continue the smooth tilt after the shutter has closed so you don't get a wobbly finish. Keep doing this, varying your tilt speed and shutter timing until you get a good shot.

Shoot surreal multi-image portraits

Shoot a striking self-portrait that will have people asking 'how did you do that?'

WHAT YOU NEED
DSLR AND STANDARD
ZOOM
TRIPOD
PHOTOSHOP OR
ELEMENTS

DIFFICULTY LEVEL
ADVANCED

A PORTRAIT SHOT WITH MULTIPLE IMAGES of the same person can give some amazing and surreal results, and it's easier than you might think. Photographing yourself lying on the floor pretending to be doing something other than lying down, then rotating the image so it appears as if you are sitting upright will mess with the viewer's mind. You can give this a go anywhere, the more common and everyday the location the better. An office corridor is a good place for a staged shot that looks as if people are walking along the wall.

TIP

GETTING PERMISSION

If you plan to shoot in a public place, try to choose a quiet area free from crowds so people won't be tempted to ask what you're doing, thereby spoiling the shot. Also, remember that shopping centres and train stations are private property and you can't shoot in these kinds of places without permission from the owner or their agent.

SHOOTING TECHNIQUE

The first step is to find a suitable location. The final image will be turned through 90° so think about how the image will look after it's been rotated. You need to be able to lie down and hold on to something, or look as if you're falling, sitting on something or otherwise performing some form of activity that will look relatively 'normal' once the image is rotated.

When you've found a location, set up your camera on a tripod and lock it off to ensure that all the images line up, allowing you to

blend them together easily. When taking the shots it may also help to put a small marker in each position so you know where each figure will end to avoid problems with overlapping. Then just keep shooting until you've got a good selection of different poses and positions to choose from.

As you've only got one subject here that features multiple times in the image, you'll need to shoot multiple images to overlay in order for the technique to work. This requires

locking your camera off on a sturdy tripod so that all the Layers will line up, saving a lot of time and heartache later in Photoshop. You'll need to keep a consistent exposure and focus, too, otherwise the images won't match up when you try to combine them. The best way to do this is to use the Manual exposure mode on your DSLR.

1 SETTING UP Once you've found a location, gather your props and set up your tripod. To keep it stable and minimize movement extend the legs rather than the centre column, especially if you're shooting outside in the wind. The final image is going to be rotated by 90° so if you want a landscape shot you'll need to shoot in a portrait orientation, and vice versa.

2 FRAME UP With your position set you need to frame up the shot. Place your chair in the first position and put a marker where your head will need to go. Go back to the camera and make sure all this fits in the shot. It's also a good idea to put markers just outside the area of the shot to help you see the area you have available to work within.

3 EXPOSURE Focus on the chair in its first position then set focus to Manual. Set the camera to self-timer; it helps to set the timer delay to 10sec, or if you have a lot of distance between the camera and your furthest position then set the delay to 20sec. Switch to Manual exposure and set the aperture to f/11, or f/8 if you're struggling with light. Set the shutter speed to whatever it needs to be.

4 TAKE THE PHOTO Press the shutter release then quickly get back in position. Wait for the shutter to fire then check the image on the rear of the camera; repeat the process for each location you want to appear in. Keep trying different positions and locations until you're happy you have a few to work with. Be sure not to move the camera while you do this.

THE SHOTS THAT MAKE UP THE IMAGE

Combining the individually shot elements in Photoshop is the key to producing a believable composite image like this. Lock your camera off on a tripod to ensure it doesn't move between frames.

FINISH

PROCESSING TECHNIQUE

1 OPEN IMAGES   Open up all of the images in Photoshop or Elements. With the first image active, choose Select>All and Edit>Copy to copy it to the clipboard. Go to the second image and choose Edit>Paste to add the first image to the second as a new Layer. Bring the other images across as Layers of their own in the same way until you have one multi-Layer document.

2 MASK LAYERS TOGETHER   Start by hiding Layers two, three and four by clicking the eye icon next to the thumbnail. Next select Layer 1, go to Create Layer Mask. Use the Brush tool from the Toolbox set to soft 300px, Opacity 100% and Foreground Black. Paint over where the figure is in the Layer below. Repeat this for the other Layers, ensuring each one is visible before adding the Layer mask.

3 CLEAN UP BACKGROUND   Highlight the topmost Layer, head down to Create New Fill or Adjustment Layer, choose Hue/Saturation and drag the Saturation slider left to -100; your image will turn black and white. Choose the Brush tool and set a soft brush of 100px, Opacity 100% and a Foreground Colour of black. Paint over the areas of skin and the handles of the briefcases to bring the colour back.

4 FLATTEN IMAGE Head up to Layer>Flatten Image to merge all of your Layers. Right-click on the Background Layer and choose Duplicate Layer. You will now have two Layers in your Layers palette. Highlight the Background copy and go to Filter>RendeR>Lens Flare. Set to 105mm Prime and the Brightness to 140. Position the centre of the flare by dragging it onto the door at the end of the corridor. Hit OK.

5 MASK OFF LENS FLARE With the Background copy Layer selected, go to add Layer Mask then, using a soft 100px brush with Foreground Colour set to Black and Opacity to 50%, start to paint out the lens flare on the people in the shot. Remove less from each figure as you get closer to the source of the flare. You may need to go over the nearer figures a few times.

EXPERT ADVICE

TRY OTHER IDEAS

The great thing about this technique is that it has hundreds of variations to experiment with, and they're all really fun and easy to do. We've taken one in a field holding onto a signpost to look like an endless cliff, but why stop there? You could try street scenes, staircases or even at home in your living room. All you need is room to place your tripod and then you're free to experiment. Try some different positions, or use props and different camera angles.

Paint a scene with flash

How to illuminate night-time photography

WHAT YOU NEED
DSLR
TRIPOD
FLASHGUN
PHOTOSHOP

DIFFICULTY LEVEL
INTERMEDIATE

AS NIGHTS BEGIN TO DRAW IN they provide a great excuse to get out with your camera, but what if the location you want to shoot turns out not to be lit at night? To illuminate the whole scene would involve a huge lighting setup that just isn't feasible, but don't despair, simply grab a tripod and a flashgun and you'll be able to light the scene in stages. All it requires is for you to set a long exposure then walk around the scene lighting objects with your flashgun.

START IMAGES

FINISH

SHOOTING TECHNIQUE

You don't need a fancy flashgun for this technique, just one where you can fire the flash manually – any old flashgun should do this by pressing the Test or Pilot button and they can be picked up on auction sites for less than £10. However, it's vital that you use a tripod to prevent camera movement and ensure the images line up accurately. The less they line up, the harder they'll be to blend in Photoshop. You should also wear dark clothing so you don't show up on the images.

Using your camera's self-timer will allow you to get into position and maximize the amount of flashes you can fire off, but make sure you don't stand between the flash and the camera or you'll create a silhouette. Return to your camera and repeat the trick, flashing different objects in the scene. And remember – the more pictures you take, the more flexibility you'll have in Photoshop.

TECH TALK

EXPOSURE SETTINGS

Switch your camera to Manual mode (M), set aperture to f/14, shutter speed to 20sec and ISO to 100. Focus on your subject, then switch over to Manual focus so you don't need to refocus each time. Pick Self-timer mode, too; a 10sec delay will be fine. Finally set your flashgun to Manual mode and select full power (1/1).

FIRING THE FLASH

Take a test shot and if the sky is too dark, dial in a longer shutter speed. Now press the shutter button and, as the timer counts down, get into position in front of your first subject. As soon as the shutter opens you've got the length of the shutter to fire the flash, so start pressing the Test button on the back of your flash to fire it manually.

CHECKING THE RESULTS

Check the flash-lit exposure on the screen. If the flash isn't showing up enough, use more bursts or fire the gun closer to the subject. If the effect is too light, use fewer bursts or move further away. When you're happy, fire the shutter again and flash the next object within the scene. Repeat until all parts have been flashed.

PROCESSING TECHNIQUE

FLASH THE STEEPLE Of course, higher subjects like this will be more difficult to cover so, again, it may take several flashes to get a good enough exposure.

FLASH THE CHURCH Larger objects, like the side of the church, may need a few bursts to cover them, so keep flashing until the shutter closes.

FLASH THE GRAVESTONES Split the scene into sections to flash, then plan your route. Here, the photographer started at the gravestones and worked back to the church.

1 OPEN CHOSEN IMAGE Open your image(s) – three in this instance. Pick the first image, head up to Select>All then Edit>Copy. Bring up the second image and go Edit>Paste. The image will appear in your Layers palette (Window>Layers). Do the same with the third image, and paste it into the second. You'll end up with three Layers.

2 BLEND Click the Layer at the top of your Layers palette (Layer 2) then click where it says Normal and choose Lighten. You'll notice the Layer below now shows through. Do the same for the middle Layer in your Layers palette (Layer 1). You'll now be able to see all three images roughly blended together.

3 CLEAN UP Click on the topmost Layer again and choose the Eraser tool from the Toolbox. With a soft brush, Opacity 100% and Size 100px, paint over the sky and trees to remove them. Be careful not to remove any of the lit parts of that Layer, though. If you make a mistake, hold Ctrl and hit Z to step back and undo the error. Repeat the same process for the middle Layer (Layer 1).

4 SAVE Click on the top Layer, then click on the Adjustment Layer icon (half black/half white circle) and choose Levels. Drag the White point slider left to 230 and the Mid-point slider right to 0.95 then head up to Layer>Flatten Image. This will merge all the Layers into one. Head up to File>Save As… choose JPEG and give your file a name, then hit OK and you're done.

Unlock the potential of HDR photography

Capture the world as it really looks with high dynamic range imaging

WHAT YOU NEED
PHOTOSHOP OR
ELEMENTS
DSLR AND STANDARD
ZOOM
TRIPOD
REMOTE RELEASE

DIFFICULTY LEVEL
INTERMEDIATE

FINISH

HIGH DYNAMIC RANGE (HDR) IMAGING is a photographic technique where detail is captured throughout the shadow, midtone and highlight regions of a picture. This is achieved by shooting the same subject at different exposures, and then merging these shots together post-capture to arrive at a final image that contains detail throughout.

HDR photography is perhaps one of the most misunderstood and misused photographic techniques out there right now, and as a result it has become a real 'love it or hate it' technique – with few people doing it well. Most people say they only like it when it's done properly, but what exactly does that mean? Well, consider what it is that people dislike about HDR. Common gripes centre on over-processed images, where halos are visible around subjects, midtones are practically grey and detail has been over-emphasized. Successful HDR photos tend to display just the more favourable characteristics of the technique, such as detail in most areas of the image, increased mood and enhanced texture. The difference is that these effects are subtle, sometimes to the point where you can see the image has been processed but can't quite put your finger on what's been done. As soon as you're told that it's HDR everything makes sense. Aim for a movie-like quality that doesn't exhibit any of those negative effects.

SHOOTING TECHNIQUE

There's a common misconception that shooting HDR is cheating and it's for people who can't expose correctly. The reality is that it's actually more involved than taking a standard shot, because you have to take three or more exposures to blend together in image editing software. So, for a three-shot HDR image, one photo needs to be taken at the camera's standard reading, the second two stops underexposed and the third two stops overexposed. This ensures that between the three shots detail is captured in the shadows, midtones and highlights. If you shoot more exposures you'll need to shoot an odd number with the camera exposure always sitting in the middle. If you're feeling adventurous you could shoot nine exposures with 1 stop between each, but three will do a perfectly good job.

Since a number of images are merged together, subjects where there's minimal movement work best, so landscapes and cityscapes are perfect. Grimy and grungy-looking locations with tons of texture and detail work particularly well. When shooting for HDR you have to use a tripod to keep camera movement to a minimum between each shot. Editing software does align source images if there's been a tiny amount of movement, but it can't work miracles. With the camera firmly supported, minimize the number of times you have to touch it by firing it with a remote release or the camera's self timer. All you have to do is change the shutter speed for each shot; remember to be gentle.

START IMAGES

2 STOPS UNDEREXPOSED 1/250SEC | F/11 | ISO 100

CAMERA SETTINGS AND EXPOSURE

The best exposure mode in which to shoot HDR is Manual (M), since it gives you full control over shutter speeds and apertures and provides a clear exposure meter to ensure the right shots are taken. Set ISO 100 (or the lowest normal ISO your camera has) to ensure image quality is at its highest and set the aperture you need for the shot. For landscape shots an aperture of f/11 is a popular choice because this is often one of the sharpest lens apertures and also provides a large depth-of-field. Focus on your subject and switch the lens to Manual focus, so that focus remains the same for each shot. Make sure also that your aperture remains constant so that depth-of-field doesn't change. Achieve different exposures by changing shutter speed. Now take your three shots in one of these two ways:

'CORRECT' EXPOSURE: 1/60 SEC | F/11 | ISO 100

MANUAL BRACKETING

This is the best way to shoot for HDR because you remain in full control of each shot. The best way to check the meter reading is using the exposure scale on either your DSLR's top-plate or on the rear LCD screen. This eliminates the risk of knocking the camera when using the viewfinder. Adjust shutter speed until the meter says exposure is two stops underexposed (see LCD image) and take a shot.

Now change the shutter speed until your camera's meter indicates this is the correct exposure for the scene and take a second shot. Lastly change the shutter speed again until you are two stops over the correct exposure and shoot the final frame.

AUTOEXPOSURE BRACKETING

The other way to take your three bracketed exposures is to use a common DSLR function called autoexposure bracketing (AEB). All cameras are slightly different, so it's best to check the user manual to see exactly how AEB is done on your camera. AEB typically comes in two flavours: the first takes three successive shots at the desired exposure range when the shutter is released just once. The second requires you to release the shutter three times to take the three shots, but still re-calculates each individual exposure.

This latter AEB option is easier than the manual method. If you go down this route, set the camera's shooting mode to Aperture priority. This will ensure shutter speed is changed and the aperture remains fixed.

2 STOPS OVEREXPOSED 1/15SEC | F/11 | ISO 100

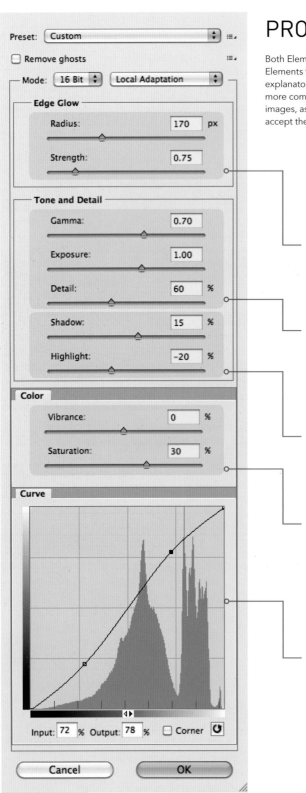

PROCESSING TECHNIQUE

Both Elements and Photoshop will let you process and create HDR images. Elements features a basic HDR option that's so easy to use it's almost self-explanatory. Photoshop, on the other hand, takes a fully manual approach that is more complicated – however, there is a 'one size fits all' recipe for creating HDR images, as explained here. This is a very good starting point before you either accept the results or experiment with the settings a bit more.

1 LOAD SOURCE IMAGES   In Photoshop open your three (or more) shots by going to File>Automate>Merge to HDR Pro and select your photos – these can be RAW files, JPEGs or TIFFs. Make sure Attempt to Automatically Align Source Images is ticked. When the Merge to HDR window opens you're presented with nine sliders. The logical step is to work through them one by one. The default Mode will be set to 16 Bit and Local Adaptation – this is ideal, so leave it as is.

2 SET RADIUS AND STRENGTH Zoom into the image so you're viewing it between 100–200% by pressing Ctrl and +. Set the Radius slider to 170px and the strength to 0.75. At this stage you won't see much happen, since it's the sliders below that will create the HDR look by compressing the tonal range.

3 COMPRESS THE TONAL RANGE Set Gamma to 0.70, which sets tone compression to a medium level that looks good. Initially set Exposure to 0.85 and increase or decrease as necessary depending on the overall brightness of the image. Contrast will be very low at this stage but you can deal with that later. Detail is set to 30% by default, which produces a realistic result. Boosting this setting to more than 50% really highlights texture and detail. Use with caution, though, as too much can ruin images. Less really is more.

4 CONTROL SHADOWS AND HIGHLIGHTS Shadows and highlights differ in every photo, and that includes HDR images. Initially set shadow to 15% and Highlights to -50 and experiment from here. Moving the shadow slider to the left darkens shadows, while moving it to the right lightens them. The same goes for the Highlight slider, but moving it too far to the left dulls highlights too much and makes contrast horribly low.

5 TWEAK COLOURS In the Color section there are two sliders – Vibrance and Saturation. Vibrance controls the intensity of more subtle colours without affecting stronger colours too much. Saturation, on the other hand, controls saturation of the entire image from black and white all the way up to double the original saturation. By default Vibrance is set to 0%, and saturation 20%. If colours in your image are looking a little dull increase these sliders for best effect.

6 CREATE AN S-CURVE TO ADD CONTRAST Now add a touch of contrast: open up the Curve by clicking the Curve tab next to Color. To increase contrast you'll need to create an S-shaped curve. Left-click near the top of the curve and drag the point upwards. Do the same near the bottom of the curve, but drag the point down. Fine tune the curve and click OK to open the HDR image in the normal Photoshop window.

CREATING THE SHOT
WITH NIK SOFTWARE HDR EFEX PRO 2

One of the best ways to create HDR images is with Nik Software HDR Efex Pro 2. This Photoshop plug-in makes the whole process easier than using just Photoshop, with some very impressive results and extremely useful pre-sets that can be used as a starting point for manual conversions. Like any software it takes a little getting used to, but the interface is extremely intuitive considering the power of the software. You can even put single images through the plug-in to give them a HDR effect – which is perfect for portraits as it's practically impossible to shoot three identical frames at different exposures.

HOLD THE SKY DETAIL An ND grad filter would hold the sky detail, but you wouldn't achieve the look of HDR, which is much more moody.

1 OPEN IMAGES In Photoshop go to File>Automate>Merge to HDR Efex Pro 2 to open the plug-in window. A second window will appear allowing you to choose your source files. You can use RAW files, JPEGs or TIFFs. Click on the Open button – it's hard to see but it's on the right – and choose your source images. Leave the Create Smart Object box unticked and click on Merge Dialogue.

SMOOTH TONES Smooth reflective tones, like car paintwork, can be a problem with HDR. This shot of an E-Type Jaguar looks great, but at some angles the blue reflective paintwork suffers from grey patches, which are reflected clouds.

2 CONTROL IMAGE MERGE Make sure Alignment is ticked as this ensures any minor camera movement between exposures can be fixed. Ghost Reduction helps to remove artefacts created when merging images. It's set to 100% by default, but if you see any strange blobs on the image reduce it one step at a time until things looks right. Chromatic Aberration removes colour fringes around objects if they're a visible problem. Click Create HDR.

4 SET TONE COMPRESSION The pre-set loads in all the settings to create an effect that can be kept or manually tweaked. It's impossible to say exactly how these should be changed because every image is different, as indeed is every photographer's taste. Try them one by one to see which settings look best. HDR Method is where the HDR effect comes to life and, with four distinct levels, it's easy to use.

3 CHOOSE A PRE-SET When the main HDR Efex window opens it looks quite daunting, but don't worry because it's very much a 'try it and see' sort of experience. First, go to the left-hand side of the window and find a pre-set that looks as close as possible to the effect you'd like to achieve. When you've chosen a pre-set simply left-click your mouse on the thumbnail to load the settings – 'Deep 1', for example.

5 CONTROL TONALITY AND COLOUR These controls take care of overall brightness, contrast and highlight and shadow detail. Go through them all to see whether you can improve on the pre-set or if the tonality is already perfect. The Structure slider is fantastic for bringing out texture and detail. At the right level it looks great, but too strong and it will ruin a great shot. When you're done, click on the OK button to open the image in Photoshop.

Shoot better firework pictures

Take firework shots to be proud of this year

WHAT YOU NEED
PHOTOSHOP
DSLR

DIFFICULTY LEVEL
INTERMEDIATE

IMAGES OF FIREWORKS, with their amazing colours briefly lighting up the night sky, often tend to disappoint. Their fleeting nature and the inherent low-light conditions when you shoot them present photographers with a challenge. But here's how you can increase your chances of capturing a successful image.

SHOOTING TECHNIQUE

You probably already know that you need a long exposure to capture both the fiery trail and the bloom of the fireworks, but it's not the best solution as you may end up over-exposing parts of the image and getting more fireworks than you want in the composition. Equally, you'll have to start the exposure without knowing when the fireworks will be launched, so there's a bit too much guesswork for comfort.

A better system, and one which goes back to the days of film, is to use Bulb mode and cover the lens with a piece of black card when you don't want the action recorded. This way

you'll only get the fireworks you want, while also judging the length of the exposure perfectly.

Set up on a tripod, frame the scene widely (you won't know exactly where the fireworks will be), then take a test exposure to assess roughly what camera settings you'll need – f/16 for 15secs at ISO 100, for example. If the general exposure looks good, then you're ready to go.

Now you know the length that the exposure needs to be (15sec), you can switch to Bulb mode (either via a B on the mode dial, or by scrolling past 30sec in shutter priority mode). Next, fire the shutter, then immediately cover the lens with your piece of card. As soon as the

fireworks go off, remove the card and start counting the seconds. When they explode and fade, replace the card and stop counting. If you're near the length of the test exposure, close the shutter and, if not, keep it open and repeat the process.

When activating the Bulb mode, it's best to use a cable release or remote control to avoid jogging the camera and, aesthetically, it's also worth remembering that – as with most low-light shots – some natural light in the sky will help the image enormously, as it contrasts with the blooms much better than the rather flat look of a jet black sky.

HOW TO SHOOT FIREWORKS IN BULB MODE

By shooting in Bulb mode (B) and using a black card to block the light when you don't want anything recorded you'll capture the fireworks only when you want them.

USE A 'FLAG' A black piece of card or a book is placed in front of the lens when you don't want light recorded.

USE A TRIPOD It's vital that your camera is kept still throughout the exposure so use a tripod and don't jog it while shooting.

PROCESSING TECHNIQUE

IMPROVE FIREWORK SHOTS IN PHOTOSHOP

These days there's no reason why you need to get everything right in a single exposure and with the power of Photoshop, and specifically the Layers palette, you can easily shoot the wider scene as a low-light landscape, and then the fireworks as individual blooms.

All that's required then is to import them into the same document and use the Lighten blending mode via the Layers palette to merge them. In this way you can even recompose the image, placing the blooms exactly where you want them in the wider scene.

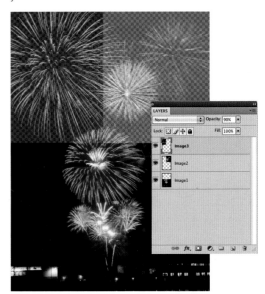

Raise your subject with floating portraits

Rise above conventional photos and try something a bit different

WHAT YOU NEED
A DSLR CAMERA
AND LENS
A TRIPOD
ADOBE PHOTOSHOP
OR ELEMENTSP

DIFFICULTY LEVEL
INTERMEDIATE

START IMAGES

HERE'S A CAMERA TRICK THAT'S SURE TO GIVE our people pictures a lift – a portrait in which your subject seems to float several feet above the floor. Done in the right way, it's a technique that always looks impressive and once you give it a go you'll discover it's much easier to achieve than it looks.

Making your subject appear to float involves shooting two separate pictures from an identical position then using Photoshop's Layers to merge them into a finished picture. In the first picture, your subject needs to stand on a ladder (or a chair) so they're raised above the floor. In the second, the scene should be empty.

When shooting, the camera's position, focus and exposure settings need to be kept identical, so that when the pictures are stacked as Layers in Photoshop the only difference between them is the subject and what they're standing on. With everything consistent you can erase the ladder from the upper Layer and let the empty background in the lower Layer show through, making it look like the ladder has disappeared.

If you're new to using Photoshop Layers, this might sound like a lot to tackle, but it's actually pretty simple, and a great way to learn about how Layers work.

EXPERT ADVICE

SHOOTING TECHNIQUE

To make this picture work, you need consistent framing, focus and lighting. Lock off your camera on a tripod, frame up and switch to Aperture priority mode (A or Av). Set the aperture you want, then check the resulting shutter speed. Switch to Manual (M) and dial in the same values. Using Manual mode will keep your exposure consistent between frames.

Once your camera's position, exposure settings, and focus are set, it's time to shoot the first picture – the one with the subject in it. Set your camera's Drive mode to Self-timer (to avoid camera shake at low shutter speeds) and fire off a few shots, getting your subject to vary their pose so you have plenty of options later. Review these images on screen, zooming in to check sharpness. Then, without changing the camera's position or settings, remove the subject and shoot the scene again.

LOCK FOCUS
With exposure set, autofocus on the subject. Once locked, switch to Manual focus and don't touch the focusing ring. This way your focus will be the same in both frames even when the subject has been removed.

POSE THE SUBJECT
Have your subject lean back on the ladder and point their toes, so it doesn't look as if they're standing on anything.

BACKGROUND SETTING
You can shoot this floating portrait camera trick anywhere, but putting the subject in an unusual setting looks great.

FINISH

By merging two identically framed pictures in Photoshop – one with the subject on a ladder and one empty, you can create a floating effect.

PROCESSING TECHNIQUE

By this point you'll have a selection of pictures, some with the subject in and some empty, so now it's time to combine them using Photoshop Layers. Open the two shots you want to use into Photoshop or Elements and combine them as a two-layer document. The quickest way of doing this is to select the entire canvas of one image (Select>All, or Ctrl-A), copy it to the clipboard (Edit>Copy, or Ctrl-C), and paste it onto the other image by clicking on its window and choosing Edit>Paste, or typing Ctrl-V.

Once you have a two-layered document it's worth renaming the layers so you stay organized. Do this by double clicking each layer's name and typing in the new name – 'Subject' and 'Background' for instance.

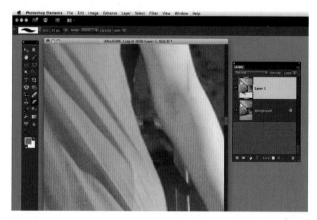

1 ERASE THE LADDER In the Layers palette choose the Subject layer. Next choose the Eraser tool from the Photoshop Toolbox. Choose a 300px soft-edged brush, set its Opacity to 100% and then run the Eraser tool over the bottom of the step ladder – it'll disappear. (Take a look in the Layers palette and you'll see a chequered effect, where the pixels have been deleted.)

2 KEEP ERASING Continue to erase the steps, but when you get near the subject's feet, choose a smaller, harder brush from the Brush presets. Run it closely around the subject's body, so only it remains visible and not the steps. If you erase some of the subject, press Ctrl+Z to Undo the mistake. Have a good look around the work you've done, making sure you haven't missed anything.

3 MAKE A SHADOW Now pick the Polygonal Lasso tool and quickly click and trace around the subject – you don't need to be precise. In the Layers palette, click on the Add New Layer icon, then go to Edit>Fill Selection, pick Black and hit OK. Go to Select>Deselect, then go to Edit>Free Transform (Ctrl+T). Hover the cursor just outside the bounding box and click-and-drag it to rotate it about 90°.

4 BLUR THE SHADOW Click and drag within the bounding box to position the shadow at the bottom-right of the frame, then click the tick. The shadow needs softening, so go to Filter>Blur>Gaussian blur, use a Radius of about 50px and hit OK. Now, in the Layers palette, click the Blending Mode pop-up menu (currently set to Normal) and choose Overlay. Now drag the shadow Layer's Opacity up to about 30%.

5 REFINE THE SHADOW Once it's blurred, refine the shape of the shadow by pressing Ctrl+T again, then holding Ctrl and dragging the corner handles to distort its shape. Click the tick or press enter to commit the change. Now go to Layer>New>Layer via copy and press Ctrl+T once more, distorting the second shadow over to the bottom left. Rotate it by 180° by choosing Edit>Transform>Rotate 180°.

7 MAKE A VIGNETTE Choose the Elliptical Marquee tool and drag it over the middle of the canvas. Invert the selection by choosing Select >Inverse and feather its edge by choosing Select>Refine Edge>Feather. A value of 250px is fine for a high resolution picture. Click OK, press Ctrl+J to create a new Layer from the selection and then Filter>Blur>Gaussian Blur. Input 10px and click OK. In the Layers palette, Ctrl-click on the Layer you've just made and click the Create New Adjustment Layer icon. Choose Levels and drag the middle slider to the right.

FINISHING TOUCHES

Once the basic floating illusion has been created, you might be tempted to simply leave the picture as it is. But just like any other image, it can be enhanced further with a few basic effects. You may want to remove some the more distracting parts of the scene, or create a vignette to concentrate attention to the middle of the picture.

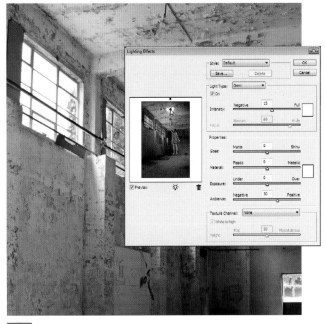

6 CLONE OUT DISTRACTIONS Press Ctrl+Shift+N to make a new Layer, then hold Alt and go to Layer>Merge Visible. This will create a single layer containing your new composite image. Use the Clone Stamp and Healing Brush tools to remove any distracting elements or parts of the scene that have been missed.

8 ADD A LIGHTING EFFECT Click OK, add a new blank layer as before, hold Alt and go to Layer>Merge Visible. Now go to Filter>Render >Lighting Effects... For Light Type choose Omni then drag the effect onto the image, in this case balloons, in the preview pane. Set the Intensity to 15 and the Ambience to 30, then hit OK. Finally change the Blending Mode of this layer by clicking Normal and choosing Lighten.

Fake a stunning studio shot

Create a new background and turn ordinary shots into glamorous ones

WHAT YOU NEED
PHOTOSHOP OR
ELEMENTS
FERRARI (OPTIONAL)

DIFFICULTY LEVEL
INTERMEDIATE

NOT MANY OF US HAVE ACCESS TO DRIVE-IN STUDIOS but you can transport your subject into a virtual studio environment, and it's easier than it looks.

If you don't have an appropriate car shot in your files you can shoot one specially – just remember to take a bucket of water, sponge and chamois leather to the car beforehand, and go for a classic three-quarter angle, as here. Shoot against a plain background as you'll be 'cutting out' the car.

Any car image can be used, so long as its outline is clear

START IMAGE

FINISH

PROCESSING TECHNIQUE

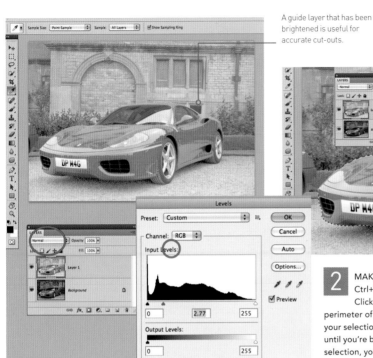

A guide layer that has been brightened is useful for accurate cut-outs.

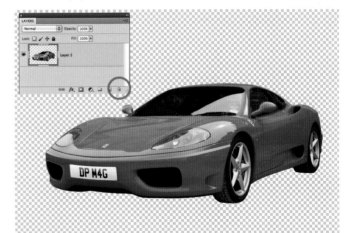

1 MAKE A GUIDE LAYER Use any car you like, so long as its outline is clear – if its shape is broken by people or other objects you'll have to cut around them, too. Open your car JPEG into Photoshop or Elements.

Look closely at the edge of the car. If there are shadow areas that are a little indistinct, as here, you'll need to make a brightened version to use as a guide in order to clearly see the outline to cut it out. Making 'guide' Layers is a brilliant way to make tricky Selection tasks easier. And once you're done, you simply bin them. To make one hit Ctrl+J to copy the picture into a new layer, and then open Levels (Ctrl+L) and move the middle slider to the left to brighten the mid-tones. You're not after a great picture – you just want to see the edge clearly. Click OK and then pick the Polygonal Lasso tool from the Toolbox by clicking and holding on the Lasso tool's icon and choosing it from the fly-out menu.

2 MAKE A MANUAL SELECTION Now zoom in tight on the car with Ctrl+Plus, and hold the Spacebar and scroll over to the outline. Click right on the edge and then carefully click around the perimeter of the car. Don't go too fast or you'll double-click and join up your selection. Slowly and steadily click right around the outline of the car until you're back at your starting point. When you've completed the selection, your car will be surrounded by 'marching ants' (see Tech Talk, page 142).

3 ISOLATE THE CAR You need to take the car from the original shot rather than the brightened reference version, so open the Layers palette (Window>Layers) and click on the background Layer. Now hit Ctrl+J and a new Layer 2 will appear above the background with just the car in it. You've now finished with the original background and the brightened Layer, so drag each to the trash icon at the bottom-right of the Layers palette and leave just the cut-out layer with the car floating on a transparency. Here, it's a little low in the frame, so pick up the Move tool (shortcut V) and drag it up and right a bit for a better composition.

TIP

SUBTLE LAYER SHIFTS

The Move tool is indispensable for repositioning layers in an image, but can be too heavy-handed for subtle shifts. For these, use the cursor (or arrow) keys on the keyboard. These will shift a Layer one pixel at a time in the direction indicated on the key. For bigger movements, hold down Shift and each keystroke will give a 10-pixel shift.

TECH TALK

SELECTIONS

When you make a selection in Photoshop or Elements, what you're doing is isolating part of the scene, so it can be adjusted or altered separately from the rest of the picture. A Selection can be made by using one of the Marquee or Lasso tools, where you manually 'fence off' part of the image, or it can be made using colour or tone with the Magic Wand or Quick Selection tool (or the Selection Brush in Elements). There are also options to select by Color Range in the Select menu, so you can choose just the darker tones (shadows), the lighter tones (highlights) or any of the individual colours in a scene.

Once a Selection is complete, the area chosen will be surrounded by flashing dotted lines known as 'marching ants'. You can then adjust the selection, or punch it into a new layer so it will float on its own above the rest of the image, ready for further editing.

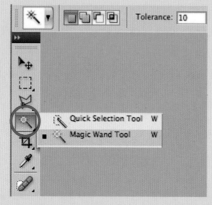

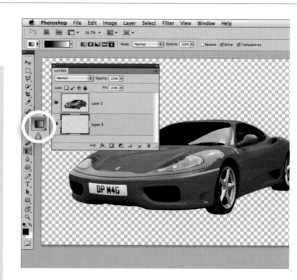

4 SET UP A GRADIENT Now the car is free of its messy background, it's time to create a more suitable environment. To create this classic studio look, you'll need a new layer that sits under the car. In the Layers palette, click on the Create a new Layer icon, and when a blank Layer appears above the car, click and drag it down to sit below in the palette. To get a nice, graduated background, hit G on the Keyboard to pick the Gradient tool. If you've got the Paint Bucket tool instead, click and hold, until the Gradient tool appears in the menu or hit Shift+G to get to it.

5 ADD A NEW BACKGROUND To pick some colours for the gradient, hit D to get the default Black and White, then click on the White colour swatch, and click directly on the image or choose a suitable tone from the Color picker. In this example a dark red from near the number plate was chosen. In the Options bar, check the Gradient is on Foreground to Background, and that you have the Linear Gradient option selected, then hold Shift and drag a line up from the bottom of the door to just above the roof, and watch the background appear. Use the Lasso tool to make an arched Selection around the top of the image, then click Refine Edge and move the Feather slider to 180px. Hit Ctrl+U to open Hue/Saturation and darken the area by moving Lightness to -50. Click OK and hit Ctrl+D to deselect.

Using black as the base colour avoids having to paint shadows under the car, but to darken the tyres, click the car Layer and select the Burn tool. In the Options bar, set Range to Shadows and Exposure to 6% then, with a 60px soft-edged brush, gently burn in the contact areas so the tyres don't look cut out. Use the square brackets to adjust Brush size and Shift plus the square brackets to adjust hardness.

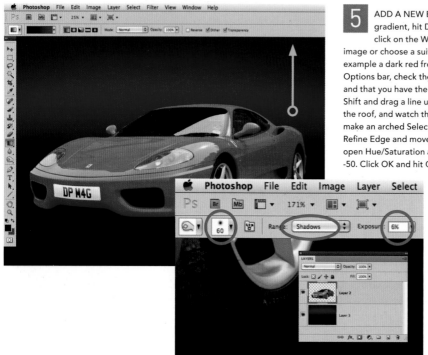

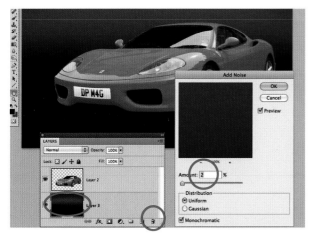

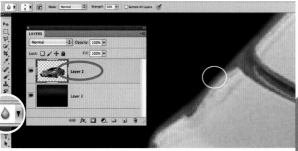

6 REFINE THE CUT-OUT EDGE If you zoom in really tight, you'll see that the absence of any Noise or grain structure in the gradient makes it look a bit unreal. To fix this, click on the Gradient Layer, then go to Filter>Noise>Add Noise and use a small amount of about 2%. Tick the Monochromatic box to keep the Noise free of coloured speckles. This will help the background match up nicely with the car in front. Click OK to confirm the Noise.

To further add realism, click on the car Layer and then pick up the Blur tool from the Toolbox (it's grouped with the Sharpen and Smudge tools). Use a small soft-edged brush of about 9px, and ensure that Sample All Layers is not ticked in the Options bar. Set strength to about 50%, and then carefully run round the edge of the car, sanding off the sharp edge.

When you're happy with the overall result, go to File>Save As... and use the Photoshop format if you want to keep all your Layers intact. If you want a more manageable file size when you've finished tweaking the image, save as a maximum-quality JPEG (Level 10 or more). This will flatten all the Layers into a single Background Layer, and provide an image that'll open in just about any software.

TIP

HOW TO DISGUISE BACKGROUND DETAIL

Here you can see some original background detail through the windows of the car. To disguise this, run the Burn tool over the dark parts of the car windows on the car Layer. In the Options bar, set Range to Shadows and Exposure to about 5%, and use a soft-edged brush of about 60px.

TECH TALK

GRADIENT TOOL

The Gradient tool is excellent when it comes to creating smooth, graduated effects. Most people only use the standard Linear Gradient option, which blends the set colours between the point where you click and the point where you release the mouse, but there are four other types of Gradient on offer in the options bar. The Radial, Angle, Reflected and Diamond gradient types are all worth experimenting with to see the effects they create. They all work in the same way – click on the image, drag the mouse and then release. Just remember to add a little Noise via Filter>Noise>Add Noise, as pure, Noiseless gradients won't match the more 'impure' image from a camera.

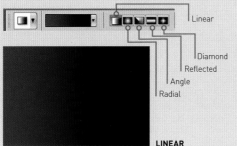

Linear
Diamond
Reflected
Angle
Radial

RADIAL

ANGLE

REFLECTED

DIAMOND

LINEAR

Turn your photos into pop art

Think bold and colourful for high-impact images that are sure to get you 15 minutes of fame

WHAT YOU NEED
PHOTOSHOP
OR ELEMENTSP

DIFFICULTY LEVEL
INTERMEDIATE

EVERYONE LOVES A GOOD SLICE OF POP ART, but creating a truly authentic rendition in Photoshop or Elements requires much more than just running a filter or two. To get a genuine pop-art look, a photograph must first be reduced to a black and white image (with no grey areas), before being coloured in a way that imitates the silk-screen printing process.

There are many ways to do this, but the method outlined here works well because you get a huge degree of contrast control over the black and white reduction, and get to add the colour manually. You can also build in as many 'errors' as you like, for a realistic look.

It's immensely enjoyable and technically challenging at the same time. You'll get a real sense of fun when undertaking the painting part, yet making the simplified reduction forces you to make demanding choices about which bits stay white and which bits go black. It's a whole new way of looking at your pictures – give it a try.

THE IMAGE This quick snap of a young girl was taken with the camera's built-in flash. Because pop art simplifies the subject into a two-tone, black or white image, your on-camera flash is all you need to keep the subject evenly lit and free from harsh shadows.

START IMAGE

CHOICE OF SUBJECT A simple, head and shoulders portrait with eye contact is the most popular option for pop art pics, and indeed that's what made the discipline most famous. But remember that anything which might be considered 'iconic' is suitable for the treatment, so a can of soup is just as valid as Marilyn Monroe. If in doubt, kids make perfect subjects and they'll love the effect just as much as you.

CHOICE OF BACKGROUND Provided the background contrasts with your subject's hair, you're safe to shoot, as any distracting elements will be painted out during the process. What you need to watch out for, though, is dark hair on a dark background or very light hair on a pale backdrop. This won't give you any separation when you create the black and white image, so reposition the subject to avoid this.

PROCESSING TECHNIQUE

1 **TURN THE PICTURE BLACK AND WHITE** Open up the image you want to use. Once it's up on screen in Photoshop or Elements, open the Layers palette (Window>Layers) and click on the Adjustment Layer icon at the bottom (half black/half white circle). Choose Threshold at the bottom of the drop-down list and the picture will turn into a very basic two-tone image, made solely of black and white, with no grey at all.

Leave the Threshold slider set to the default mid point of 128 and then, in early versions of the software, click OK (later versions don't have an OK button). Now click on the background Layer to make it active.

FINISH

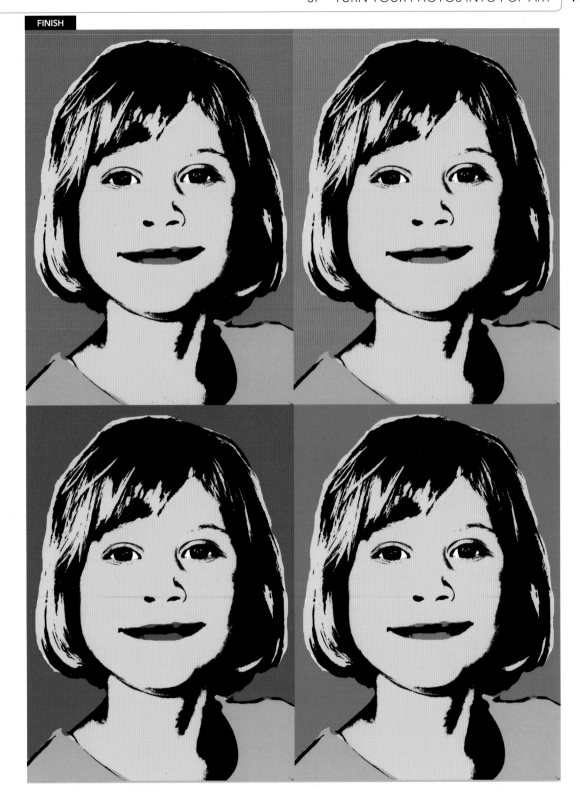

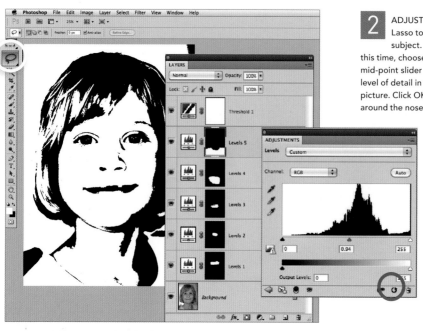

2 ADJUST CONTRAST TO BUILD UP EFFECT Pick up the Lasso tool, and make a Selection around the eyes of the subject. Now click the Adjustment Layer icon again and, this time, choose Levels from the list. In the palette, move the mid-point slider a little to the left and right until you get a nice level of detail in the eyes. The amount will vary from picture to picture. Click OK (early versions only) and then make a Selection around the nose. Make another Levels Adjustment Layer and tweak the middle slider to get a nicely defined nose without too much shadow.

Now the eyes and nose are sorted, select the mouth with the Lasso, and make another Levels Adjustment Layer, tweaking the mid-point slider to get the best definition. Now select the chin area, and tweak the Levels Adjustment Layer in the same way, and finally do the same for the neck and clothing at the bottom. You'll end up with a huge stack of Layers, but it's all pretty simple, and you'll have built up a nice graphic image of your subject, controlling exactly how you want the black and white tones all the way along.

TECH TALK

THRESHOLD

Threshold may well be a Photoshop command you've never heard of, and other than for simplifying images into their barest forms, it's not one that's often used in a creative way. What it consists of is a histogram – just like the Levels palette – but instead of giving you a way of adjusting tones to make them lighter or darker, you simply get a cut-off point that determines whether a particular brightness value is rendered as a white tone (anything beneath the Threshold) or a black tone (anything above it).

If you set the Threshold too low, you'll get too many white tones in the resulting image, and if you set it too high you'll force anything under the cut-off point to be black. Leave it around the mid-point, though, and you'll get a reasonable level of detail in the picture.

TOO LOW
Threshold too low at 90

TOO HIGH
Threshold too high at 160

JUST RIGHT
Threshold just right at 128

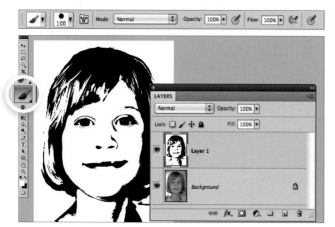

3 MERGE TO ONE LAYER Click on the top Threshold Layer and, while holding the Alt key, go to Layer>Merge Visible. Only release Alt when you've got the mouse on Merge Visible, and you'll see a new Layer appear that contains everything you've done so far. You can now get rid of all those Adjustment Layers to tidy up the Layers palette – hold down Shift and click on everything except the top and bottom Layers. Once they're all selected, go to Layer>Delete Layers, and your Layers palette will look much friendlier, with the original at the bottom and the black and white on top.

The next job is to clean up the black and white picture, so hit D then X to make white your foreground colour, then pick up the Brush tool (shortcut B). In the Options bar, pick a hard-edged brush and set the size to about 100px. Now clean up the image by painting white over any dark areas in the background, and also clean up any blemishes or shadows on the face that you don't want (see Project 13, page 52). Once you've done this, you'll have a nice clean image that's prepared and ready for colour.

To get the right look, don't be too careful with the edges. In genuine pop art pictures, the edges are far more obvious and unsubtle, so don't waste time being too meticulous!

4 ADD THE COLOURS In the Layers palette, click the Create a new Layer icon, and when the new Layer appears, click where it says Normal and set the Blending mode to Multiply. Open the Swatches palette (Window>Color Swatches in Elements, or Swatches in Photoshop), and choose a suitable skin tone – here it was Pastel Yellow Orange. With your brush, paint the face and neck, leaving the eyes white. Leave the teeth white, too, if they're visible.

You'll need some help from the original picture to help you paint the other areas, so in the Layers palette, switch off the black and white Layer with the 'eye' icon, and select a bright red from the swatches. Paint the lips and background with this, adjusting brush size as necessary with the square brackets keys. Don't worry about being too accurate as a less precise look actually gives a better result than a really careful piece of painting. Once you've completed the lips and background, select a hair colour (yellow here), and paint it in. All that's left now is the model's top, so pick a nice contrasting colour like a bright blue, and paint it in. The picture will look a bit odd, but not for long.

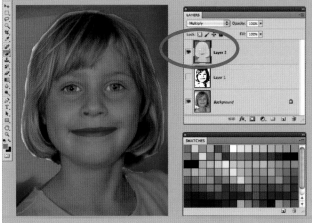

TECH TALK

If you go over a line or make any mistakes while painting, there's no need to worry. As all your colour paint work is on a separate Layer there's no chance of causing any damage to the image, so you can just Alt+click on the colour you need – directly on the image – and paint again to repair any problems.

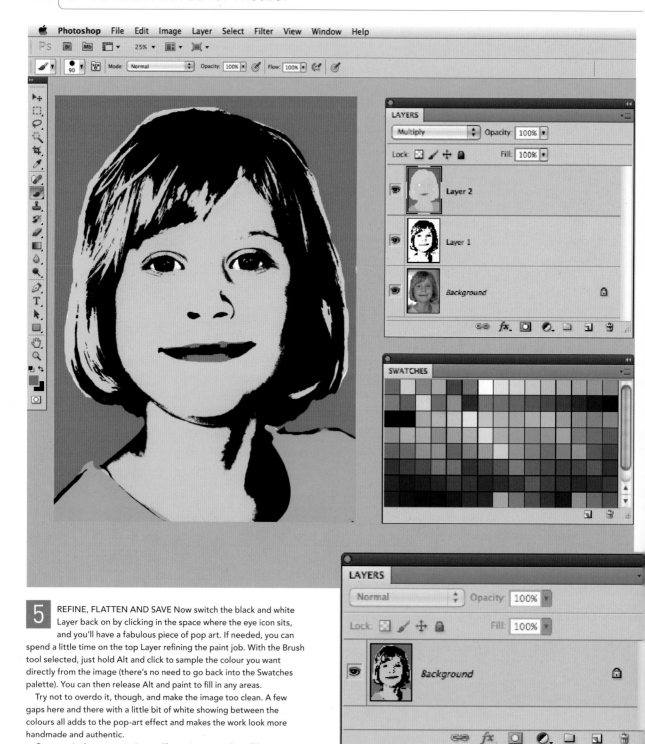

5 REFINE, FLATTEN AND SAVE Now switch the black and white Layer back on by clicking in the space where the eye icon sits, and you'll have a fabulous piece of pop art. If needed, you can spend a little time on the top Layer refining the paint job. With the Brush tool selected, just hold Alt and click to sample the colour you want directly from the image (there's no need to go back into the Swatches palette). You can then release Alt and paint to fill in any areas.

Try not to overdo it, though, and make the image too clean. A few gaps here and there with a little bit of white showing between the colours all adds to the pop-art effect and makes the work look more handmade and authentic.

Once you're happy, go to Layer>Flatten Image, and you'll have a great looking piece of pop art that will be loved by your subject – no matter what their age.

TURN YOUR POP ART INTO A GRID

This classic technique presents pop art as a panel of pictures, with one colour changed in each picture.

• Start with your flattened pop art image and then hit Ctrl+J to copy it. Click on the background Layer and go to Image>Resize>Canvas Size (Image>Canvas Size in Photoshop). Set the units to Percent, and type 200 in the both the Width and Height boxes. Make sure the Anchor box is set to the top-left. Click OK.

• Double-click the Hand tool to see the whole picture and click on Layer 1. Select the Move tool and drag the image to the top-right. Now hold Alt and drag it down to copy the Layer and position it at the bottom-right. Release Alt, then hold Alt again and repeat, dragging it to the left, so the next copy Layer sits at the bottom-left of the frame.

You'll now have a grid of four pictures, all of which are identical. To change the colours, click on the Layer that's positioned at the top-right (in the Layers palette), and then select the Magic Wand

tool. Make sure that Contiguous is not ticked in the Options bar at the top of the screen, and click once on the red of the background. This will select all pixels the same colour.

To change the colour, hit Ctrl+U and in the Hue/Saturation palette, move the Hue slider to wherever you like and click OK. Now select the Layer at the bottom right and select the same area with the Magic Wand in the same way. Pick another colour with Ctrl+U, and move the Hue slider to a different colour. Do the same with the Layer at the bottom-right and you'll have a great looking grid of images.

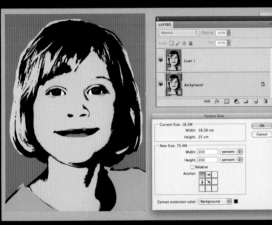

Above: Copy the image and then increase the Width and Height of the Canvas Size by 200 percent, and you'll make enough room for four identical images.

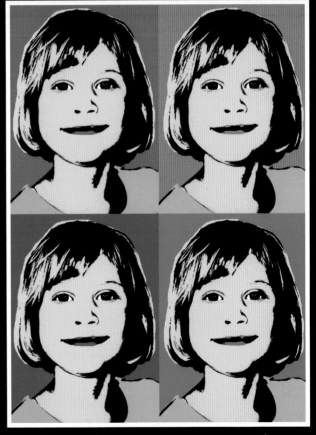

Above: The finished result

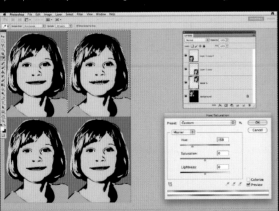

Above: After copying and positioning four images, you can select a colour to change and make it a different Hue using the Hue/Saturation palette.

Make a montage portrait

Add atmosphere to your portraits with this composite technique – who said three into one won't go?

WHAT YOU NEED
PHOTOSHOP OR
ELEMENTS

DIFFICULTY LEVEL
EASY

IF YOU ARE ONE OF THOSE PHOTOGRAPHERS who has a hard-drive creaking at the seams with portrait pictures you've never got around to doing anything with, here's something to try: take a simple portrait and some scenery then put them together to make a portrait montage that's much more than the sum of its parts. In this way you can make use of pictures that you'd otherwise have forgotten about, and the transformation is striking.

Putting the pictures together is done with Layers using Photoshop or Elements software, which gives you the freedom and flexibility to blend images in ways that would have taken years to master in the traditional darkroom. The technique involves exploring the Layers palette, Blending Modes and Eraser tool – all useful skills to learn that will come in handy for many other Photoshop or Elements projects.

FINISH

SHOOTING TEXTURES

Although you can shoot the pictures for this technique to order, the chances are you've got everything you need already in your image library. Have a look through, and don't discount those which may not have been a hit first time around because you'll be surprised at what can work once it's blended into a montage.

The one thing you may not have is a texture, but if you're serious about imaging, it's time to start building up a library. Keep a lookout for interesting examples, and shoot them with your lens at roughly 90 degrees to the surface. This will keep the texture flat, making it easier to use and also giving sharper results, as there's less chance of it falling out of focus when shooting with a wide aperture. Anything can be used for a texture – just take a few shots whenever you find a broken-up surface.

Technically, this portrait is ok, but shot on a cold and overcast winter's day it's definitely lacking some appeal. When looking for one of your own shots to try, choose images with a clean or defocused background. This will help the other images stand out once they're applied.

For the background scenery, it helps to pick a shot that's sharp from front to back (most landscapes will be), but you don't need a strong image in its own right. Areas of high contrast, like the silhouetted trees in this picture, will show up well in the final image.

Although not a vital addition to your montage, a layer of texture helps draw the different parts of the image together, and is a nice finishing touch. If you can find one that suits the colours found in the other pictures – earthy greens and browns in this case – then all the better.

PROCESSING TECHNIQUE

1 BUILD UP THE LAYERS The first thing to do is open the portrait you want to use into Photoshop or Elements. Do this from Bridge, by double-clicking in Windows or Mac OSX, or just going to File>Open, highlighting the file and clicking Open. Now open the scenery that you want to apply to the portrait in the same way. Once both images are open, you need to copy the scenery onto the portrait: make the landscape shot the active window and press Ctrl+A on the keyboard to make a Selection of the whole image before pressing Ctrl+C to copy it to the clipboard. Go to the portrait picture and type Ctrl+V to paste the landscape image onto it as a new Layer. You can now close down the scenery picture (Ctrl+W). The scenery will cover up the portrait for now, but go to Window>Layers and you'll see it's actually sitting above the original picture on a Layer called Layer 1, a bit like if you'd placed one photo on top of another in a pile.

2 MERGE THE TWO PICTURES The great thing about Photoshop or Elements is that you can control how the Layers in the pile, or 'stack' as it's properly called, interact with one another. First, do this by changing the Blending Mode of the top, landscape Layer: click on the drop-down menu in the Layers palette where it says Normal and choose Overlay from the list. Straight away, you'll notice that the two pictures blend into one – they're still separate but one shows through the other.

Now you can see through the scenery Layer you can resize and reposition it for a better fit. Press Ctrl+T and drag the corner handles until you are happy with your composition. If you don't want to manually resize the Layer with the corner handles you can input a new percentage Height and Width in the boxes in the Options bar.

BLENDING MODES

There are 27 Blending Modes in the recent versions of Photoshop. Each has a different effect and some are more useful than others. They work by comparing the active Layer with the ones below it. The Overlay Blending Mode was used here to blend the portrait with the trees, but it's worth going down the list to see the effect the others have too.

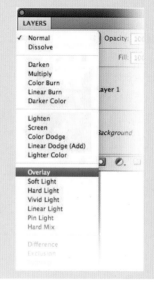

3 FINE-TUNE THE LOOK The image is taking shape, but parts of the scenery are cutting across the subject in a distracting way. To remedy this you can remove parts of the Layer they're on using the Eraser tool. Click it in the Toolbox (or press E), then click on the Brush Presets window in the Options bar and pick a soft-edged brush from the list. Set the Eraser's Size to about 700px and its Opacity to 100%. Finally, make sure Layer 1 is active by clicking on its thumbnail in the Layers palette. Run the Eraser tool over the subject's face to remove any parts of the scenery from there. If you delete too much, just press Ctrl+Z to undo (or step back in History in Photoshop) and try again.

TECH TALK

THE ERASER

If ever there was a tool which does exactly what it says on the tin, it's this one. The Eraser tool literally rubs out anything you use it on. On a regular photo (one with a single Background Layer) it'll just replace pixels with white (or whatever colour you've set as the background colour), but it's on layered pictures that it really comes into its own. Stack up a couple of Layers in your palette, then use the Eraser tool and you'll delete pixels on that Layer, letting the ones below show through and allowing you to accurately blend pictures. The Eraser tool can be controlled just like a brush, meaning you can set its size, shape and opacity – the only drawback to the Eraser tool is that you can't correct mistakes other than by stepping back through your document's history states using the Undo History or pressing Ctrl+Z.

4 ADD A LAYER OF TEXTURE Once the portrait and the scenery are working well, you may be pleased with the result and happy to leave it as it stands. If that's the case, great! But if you feel your picture needs something more to tie its elements into a whole, try adding a Layer of texture.

Open your texture image into Photoshop or Elements and then Copy and Paste it into the main image as before. Again, you'll need to change the Blending Mode: with the Layer highlighted in the Layers palette, click normal and this time choose Soft Light from the list, giving it a softer look than Overlay. Once again, use the Eraser tool to hold back the texture from the subject but, this time, lower the Opacity of the tool to remove the texture more gradually.

5 ADD A WASH OF COLOUR Lastly, apply a wash of colour which, like the texture, helps tie the various parts together. You can add this as a Layer, too, so it's controllable, just like the others. In the Layers palette, click the Adjustment Layer icon (half black half/white circle) and choose Solid Color. The Color Picker will appear and in here you can choose any colour you like for the overall tone of the image. Click on the Hue bar, then pick a precise shade in the main colour window: here it's a warm orange. Just click OK to exit the Picker. Go back into the Layers palette and change the Color Fill 1 Layer's Blending Mode to Soft Light, then click on the Opacity slider and lower it to about 60%. All that's left to do now is save the image, so go to File>Save as, give it a title and click Save.

Hand-colour your pictures

Two fun projects to bring colour to just part of your picture for dramatic emphasis

WHAT YOU NEED
PHOTOSHOP OR
ELEMENTS

DIFFICULTY LEVEL
INTERMEDIATE

FINISH

WAY BACK IN TIME, long before colour film had been invented, photographers would carefully paint onto their black and white images to create the impression of a colour photo. Of course, painted images will always lack the subtle range of colours that the real world lines up for us, but back in the day this was truly cutting-edge stuff.

Today, when we look at these hand-coloured images, there's an artistic charm that a modern colour photo doesn't always provide; things like the use of a muted palette and colours that have a slightly unreal feel about them can look fun and effective when it comes to hand-colouring.

Recreating the hand-coloured look on a modern digital image is easy and the technique itself very simple. What's really needed is patience as time spent accurately applying the colours will be rewarded with a better finished image.

Once you've given this easy technique a try, you'll see what a fun and rewarding way it is to add a creative look to your shots. And you don't need to stick to life-like colours – experiment with other hues and just have fun!

PICK A STRONG SUBJECT
Select a picture where the subject is nice and sharp, is not covered up by parts of the background, and has lots of different areas to colour. In this case the coat, scooter, skin tones and dress give you plenty of areas to work with.

WHAT IT WORKS ON
The vintage styling of the model is a good fit with this technique, but don't be put off from trying to hand-colour more modern subjects, too. If you have shots from a recent holiday or interesting locations, give them a go. Vehicles are also great subjects to try.

START IMAGE

PROCESSING TECHNIQUE

1 REMOVE COLOUR FROM IMAGE Before you can hand-colour anything you'll need to remove the existing colour. It's also a good idea to add a base tone to the photo and in this case we'll make it sepia. To do this, simply press Ctrl+U to open the Hue/Saturation palette and then click the Colorize box at the bottom. Moving the Hue slider sets the colour of the effect and Saturation its strength. For sepia, set Hue to 40 and Saturation to 15 for a nice-looking tone. Click OK to apply.

2 SELECT THE AREA TO COLOUR The best method of hand-colouring depends on what you're trying to colour. The scooter, for example, has nice clean lines so the best bet is to make a Selection of it before adding the colour. You can use any of Photoshop or Elements' Selection tools to do this, but the often overlooked Magnetic Lasso tool is ideal here. (Right-click on the normal Lasso tool and it will appear in a menu.) Zoom in for a close view and start your Selection by clicking on the edge of the scooter and slowly dragging around its edge. When you get to the edge of the screen, hold the Space bar to toggle the Hand tool and drag the on-screen image. Let go and the Magnetic Lasso will return. Keep going until you get back to the start and then double-click to finish the Selection.

3 ADD SOME COLOUR The colour needs to be added to a Layer, keeping it separate from the original. Go to Layer>New>Layer, give the new Layer a name and click OK. Now pick a colour and press Alt+Backspace to fill the Selection with the colour, here pink. The colour will be opaque but it just needs blending in. Go to Window>Layers and click Normal, then choose Color from the list of Blending Modes. You can now get rid of the Selection by pressing Ctrl+D and look for any areas that were missed by the Lasso. These can easily be painted in with the Brush tool and any overspill can be removed with the Eraser. Repeat Steps 1 and 2 for other elements in the picture.

4 HAND COLOUR THE SKIN Faces need a more gentle approach so, as before, add a new Layer, but instead of making a Selection, this time set the Foreground colour to a skin tone and use the Brush tool to paint in the colour. A small brush will help your accuracy here. The Blending Mode of this Layer should be set to Soft Light and you'll also find dropping the Opacity to about 50% helps on skin tones. For even more finesse, use the Eraser tool to remove colour from the eyes and lips, then paint it back in with the appropriate colours. The final touch is the hair, which is coloured in the same way as the other parts.

This picture is ideal for colour popping: it's not too cluttered and the sailboat makes a colourful subject in the sailboat.

COLOUR POPPING

Colour popping is a useful device used in advertising and editorial photography that makes a subject stand out from its surroundings. Back in the days of film it was created by making identical-sized colour and black & white prints of an image. The subject was then cut out from the colour print with a scalpel and pasted onto the mono version with Cow Cum glue (so if you've ever wondered where the term 'cut and paste' comes from, now you know).

Once assembled, the composite mash up of colour and mono was re-shot as a single colour negative. That was a lot of work; thankfully it's simpler these days.

This is an effect that everyone likes, in fact the popularity of the colour pop picture has made it a staple for wedding and social portrait photographers, as well as an ever-present style in advertising. This makes it an essential technique to learn for all photographers – before long someone will ask you if you can do it for them.

Colour popping in Photoshop needs no scalpels, prints or glue. Though there are many ways of doing it this method is the best way because it's straightforward, flexible and simple – just as digital retouching should be.
Pick an image with a bold subject that can be isolated from its surroundings to try this technique.

DETAIL IN THE BACKGROUND
You don't want the background to be too bland when it's converted to monochrome. If you use an old outdoor picture make sure there is some detail in the sky

COLOURFUL SUBJECT If you're going to pop colour make sure you have some colour to pop in the first place. Don't bother with subjects that contain subtle shades of grey or beige. You want bright bold colours – like the sails on the boat.

SIMPLE COMPOSITION You can sometimes get away with busier scenes (like yellow taxis in New York streets) but you'll probably have more success with more simple compositions that don't try too hard.

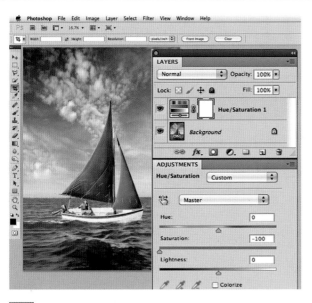

1 GOING MONO Before creating the effect the picture has to be turned black & white, but this must be done in a way that allows you to restore colour to selected parts of the picture afterwards. With this in mind, using a Black & White Adjustment Layer makes a lot of sense, as this gives a tremendous amount of flexibility.
Open up your image into Elements or Photoshop and make sure the Layers palette is showing (Window>Layers). Down at the bottom of the palette click on the Adjustment Layer icon and choose Hue/Saturation; to turn the image monochrome simply move the Saturation slider all the way to the left. This works in Elements and Photoshop, but in Photoshop from version CS3 onwards you can also choose the Black & White option, which is much better.

2 RESTORE COLOUR Adjustment Layers, such as the Hue/Saturation or Black & White one added in step 1, come with their own Layer Mask built in. This means that, to bring back colour in one part of the picture, all you have to do is paint black on the Adjustment Layer to mask off part of the black & white effect.
The Mask is the rectangle that sits alongside the Adjustment Layer thumbnail and is automatically selected for painting on. In the Toolbox choose the Brush Tool (or hit B) and black is the foreground colour (if it isn't, hit D to set black and white as the foreground and background colours, respectively).
Select a suitable Brush size with the square bracket keys and paint black onto the mask where you want to restore colour.

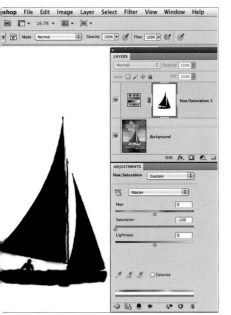

3 REFINE EFFECT AND CHECK MASK As you get closer to the edge of the subject you'll need to use a smaller brush to remain accurate. If you make a mistake then don't worry: hit X to swap the foreground colour over to white and paint over the error. Painting black stops the mask effect, allowing colour to show through; white allows the mask to show. By flicking back and forth between these two colours you can get a perfect result in minutes.
When the masking is complete, give it a check by holding down the Alt key and clicking on the Mask thumbnail in the Layers palette to see the Mask full screen – it's easy to miss a few bits. If there are any parts that are a bit sketchy, paint in any parts that are missing.
When you are happy save the image as a Photoshop file (PSD), which is a file format that preserves Layers intact.

TECH TALK
BLACK AND WHITE PHOTOSHOP

If you have access to the full version of Photoshop CS3 or later then there's a great mono option in the Adjustment Layers menu simply called Black & White. Select this and you'll find six sliders that allow you to mix up different effects for the mono reproduction.
If you have a particular colour in the scene, pulling the slider to the left will make it appear darker, and pushing it to the right will brighten it. Use this technique, if you can, as you'll get loads more control over your image.

Create a bright backlit picture

Try this simple lighting technique to add zest to your still lifes

WHAT YOU NEED
DSLR OR COMPACT
CAMERA
TRIPOD
HOUSEHOLD PROPS

DIFFICULTY LEVEL
EASY

BACKLIGHTING IS A GREAT WAY to reveal normally unseen detail in all sorts of subjects and it works well with any translucent item – think thinly-sliced fruit, dried leaves, glass or plastic.

In this project you'll see how you can create an effective backlighting set-up using props you probably already have in the house: a glass dish, a desk lamp, a tub of budget hair gel and some fruit. Hair gel is great for backlighting as it has thousands of tiny bubbles suspended in it that really respond to having light shone through them. The intricate structure of the thinly-sliced fruit will yield some nice effects, too!

Fill a glass dish with hair gel and get to work slicing some fruit very thinly. These are the ingredients for your shot.

SHOOTING TECHNIQUE

You don't need any special kit for this shoot, other than a tripod to support your camera. A couple of dining chairs are useful to suspend the glass dish over a desk lamp, but take care when setting this up, unless you want your floor covered in gloopy hair gel! And no matter how good it looks, don't be tempted to taste it!

Using an old desk lamp to backlight the subject from below reveals loads of intricate detail in the subject.

FINISH

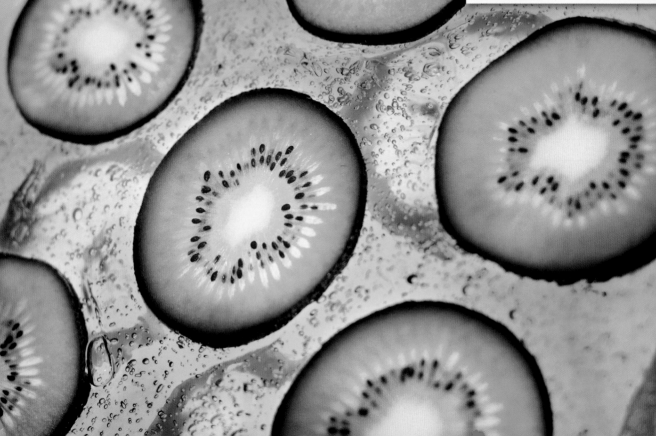

PREPARE THE SUBJECT Fill your glass dish with hair gel to a depth of about half an inch. Green gel will add a bit more colour. Then place slices of lemon in the bottom of the dish, submerged in the gloop, and position slices of kiwi fruit on top of the gel to create a nice layered effect.

BACKLIGHT THE SUBJECT Place the light source directly under your subject so it illuminates all those lovely bubbles and the intricate structure of the fruit.

USE A TRIPOD As you want to shoot at ISO 100 or 200 for the best quality, your shutter speed will fall and the chances are you won't be able to hand-hold the camera. Using a tripod will ensure there's no camera shake and it's also much easier to compose your image with the camera locked off.

1 SET UP YOUR CAMERA When you're ready to shoot, set your camera to Aperture priority mode (A or Av) and dial in an ISO setting of 100 or 200. It's important to leave the overhead lights on in the room to balance the backlighting otherwise you'll end up with a silhouetted picture, though you could use another desk lamp above the subject if necessary.

2 CONTROL THE LIGHTING Focus your camera on the central fruits and take a few test shots. If the backlighting is too strong it may still silhouette the fruit so, if that's the case, try placing a piece of baking paper (a quick home-made diffuser) over the light to soften the backlight effect and let you capture all the detail in the surface of the fruit.

3 CHECK THE RESULTS Remember to review your shots on the LCD screen, zooming in to check the sharpness and exposure. Experiment with different angles and aperture settings and try moving the light source to different locations. Finally, open your best images into Photoshop and use Levels to adjust the contrast so your shot really zings!

Shoot a time-lapse grid

A week in the life of a rose – tell the story in pictures with this technique

WHAT YOU NEED
DSLR
FLASHGUN
REFLECTOR
WHITE BACKGROUND
ROSE

DIFFICULTY LEVEL
EASY

IF YOU'VE ALWAYS BEEN INTRIGUED by time-lapse photography – a set of images taken in the same location but at different times of the day or year – then this project is for you. Often this kind of imagery is of a landscape view shot over the space of all four seasons, showing the progress of leaves emerging, dying and falling off trees, and capturing the ever-changing weather conditions the scene is exposed to. But it does involve you going out faithfully all year round to shoot your images.

This project takes that idea but makes it much more instantly achievable – in just seven days to be precise. In that time you'll be able to capture the beauty of a single flower at its peak of perfection and record its slow but inevitable disintegration and decay. Instead of capturing a single moment in time you'll capture several, telling the narrative of this part of the rose's life cycle. Sadly, one flower did suffer in the making of this image!

SHOOTING TECHNIQUE

The set-up for this couldn't be simpler. Buy your chosen bloom from a florist. The pink rose was chosen because it would stand out against a white background but also lose its colour as it died. Explain to the florist what you need the flower for – they may have some good tips or suggestions as to which type of flower is best for your purposes.

For example, if you're in a hurry and don't want the bloom to linger longer than necessary, keep it in a warm place and 'forget' to water it. It's also a good idea to keep it in a tight vase so that the stem keeps its shape and doesn't droop.

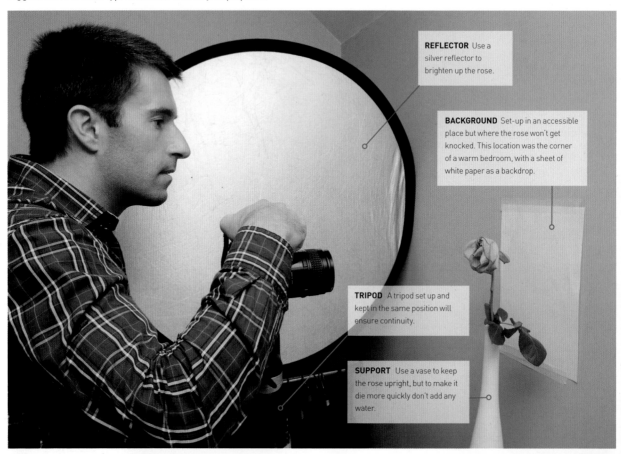

REFLECTOR Use a silver reflector to brighten up the rose.

BACKGROUND Set-up in an accessible place but where the rose won't get knocked. This location was the corner of a warm bedroom, with a sheet of white paper as a backdrop.

TRIPOD A tripod set up and kept in the same position will ensure continuity.

SUPPORT Use a vase to keep the rose upright, but to make it die more quickly don't add any water.

1 **POSITION THE ROSE** This set-up is simple. In the corner of a bedroom tape an A4 sheet of paper onto the wall to act as your clean background. Then, place a tall, thin vase in front of the sheet. Use this to keep the rose upright. Do not add any water to the vase unless you want to keep the rose alive for longer and extend your photo shoot time.

2 **FOCUS MANUALLY** If you want the first shot to show the rose at its most beautiful, indulge in a bit of gardening. Peel off any dead-looking petals from the bottom. Then place the rose in the vase, put your camera on a tripod and focus manually for exact spot-on focus.

3 BOUNCE THE FLASH This was shot using a 60mm macro lens in order to get really crisp shots close up. If you don't have a macro lens use your lens with the closest focus capability. With a standalone flashgun attached to the camera the flash was fired off to the side, using a silver reflector to bounce the crisp light back onto the flower.

4 REPEAT THE SAME SETTINGS Now it's just a case of revisiting the rose every day to see how the decaying process is going and photographing it. To keep all the images similar, make a note of all camera and flash settings and shoot on Manual mode to keep them the same each time.

EXPERT ADVICE

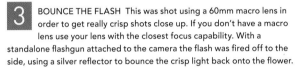

DISPLAY YOUR IMAGES AS A GRID

An excellent way to show the whole process of the rose decaying is as a grid. Displaying the images like this is just perfect for showing all the stages of the flower's demise – from the full bloom of a beautiful, vibrant flower, to the first signs of the bloom wilting away, then finally losing its colour, drying up and literally hanging its head.

It takes just a few simple steps to transform your individual shots into an arty collection of images. Once you've made your edits and decided how many images you want to appear, why not try a few different looks? The final image of the decaying rose quartet was left out to produce this triptych.

TIP

TRY THIS

If you don't want to rush things, experiment with shooting a rose that's in water or a cooler place. It allows you more time to shoot and means that you won't be forever checking up on progress, and you could shoot in more incremental stages, ending up with a whole panel of pictures.

FINISH

Play with projector-lit portraits

Using a side projector as a light source can inject a bit of fantasy into your portrait photos

WHAT YOU NEED
DSLR
PROJECTOR
IMAGES ON SLIDE FILM

DIFFICULTY LEVEL
INTERMEDIATE

IF YOU GREW UP IN THE GOOD OLD DAYS OF FILM you may have been forced to sit through a slideshow of family holiday snaps. That's not the slideshow you might be used to on your computer, but the old-school version: viewing slides on the projector with the living room curtains closed, the family squashed together on the sofa, and the distinctive smell and noise of the projector slowly heating up.

Occasionally someone would walk across in front of the screen, get lit up with the pattern of whatever image was being shown, and be shouted at by the rest of the family for getting in the way. And it's this that is the basis for the portrait lighting technique shown here. The effect can look like a double exposure, only with a more three-dimensional look to it. It works especially well if your subject is wearing white clothing.

From interesting graphic patterns to simple landscapes dominated by big skies, selecting the right slide to use for your portrait image is vital.

TOP TIPS FOR PROJECTOR PORTRAITS

1 Choose a simple image to project an abstract shape full of colour onto your model. **2** Distort your image by moving the projector around the room, making a once-boring slide into an interesting backdrop. **3** Don't worry about the noise you will get when shooting high ISO settings. It just adds to the arty creative result. **4** If your shutter speed dips under 1/30sec it may be a good idea to use a cable release to avoid camera shake. **5** As you're shooting in the dark you may find a torch useful to see what button you're pressing.

SHOOTING TECHNIQUE

The first step is choosing the image you're going to project on to your model. In many respects, 'the simpler the better' is a good rule of thumb here. Colourful repeating patterns work well, with bold colours and strong shapes. There are often light and dark spaces within the image being projected; position your model's face in one of the lighter areas and it will be lit up normally, while their body and the background will be covered in the pattern.

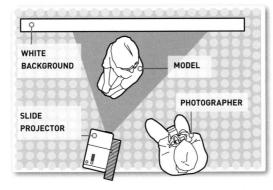

WHITE BACKGROUND

MODEL

PHOTOGRAPHER

SLIDE PROJECTOR

TRY SHOOTING A STILL LIFE

Why not try using this technique to shoot a starkly lit still life. The projector is a very portable light source so you can easily move it around for different effects. Still projecting an image onto a white backdrop, you can experiment with different coloured slides and choose a still life subject that works well with your projected image.

Left: Without projector

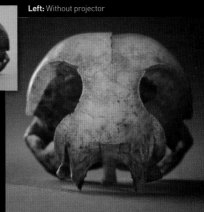

SET UP YOUR 'STUDIO'

Once you've chosen a suitable slide, set up the projector to shine onto a white surface such as a white wall in your living room. Then it's just a case of projecting the image onto your subject. If you don't have a proper projector stand an ironing board or small A-frame step ladder is ideal, since both allow some height adjustment so you can shoot your subject standing up and sitting down.

If you're lucky enough to have lots of room you can shoot directly over the projector ensuring you don't capture much of your model's shadow. Otherwise, it's a case of the closer you stand to the side of the projector, the smaller the shadow will be. Other creative effects can be achieved, such as moving the model further away from the backdrop so the projected image on the model is completely out of focus. And try moving the projector away from the backdrop for a larger projected image.

EXPOSURE

Even though the projector is your main light source it still won't cast a very bright light, especially if you are shooting with darker projected images. Get around this problem with a tripod, wide aperture, slow shutter speed and a boosted ISO setting. The camera settings that work best are very similar to those you might use at dusk or in low light. Shooting on manual mode allows you to alter the shutter speed and aperture to suit the lighting conditions, including how dark your subject's face should appear. Start with an aperture that's pretty wide – about f/5 – and don't worry about depth-of-field because there will be only a short distance between your mode and the background. With all this set, a shutter speed of about 1/30sec should do the job. That's too slow for hand-held photography, but fast enough to freeze any subject movement. A test shot should allow you to fine-tune ISO sensitivity to get a good result. Don't be frightened of a bit of noise – sometimes this can add to the image.

Above: Try getting closer to your model for a sense of drama.

Get creative with slow-sync flash

Get the best of both worlds by mixing a burst of flash with a long ambient-light exposure

WHAT YOU NEED
DSLR OR COMPACT CAMERA

DIFFICULTY LEVEL
EASY

THIS IS A TECHNIQUE THAT PRODUCES really impressive results and is a lot of fun, too. Put simply, slow-sync flash involves combining flash with a slow shutter speed on your camera. This allows you and/or your model to spin around, blurring the background while the flash freezes your foreground subject. The result is a creative and dynamic portrait shot.

Don't worry about needing any special kit either – you don't. Any camera with a pop-up flash will do nicely and it doesn't even need to be a DSLR; this technique will work with your trusty little compact too, so there's no excuse not to give it a go.

The key to getting the best shots lies in choosing the right location; it should be dim enough to set a slowish shutter speed but not completely dark – somewhere between the two extremes. Out on the street with some street lamps in the background is ideal, though you could just as easily use your front room at home. Any background that has a bit of detail is a good choice – a bare, featureless wall won't show the blur very well; you need plenty of detail present to form an interesting background.

The advantage of shooting outside is that there's plenty going on, with lights and colours that will create obvious trails and colourful streaks across the background of your image, really helping make the subject stand out against them. It's so easy to get some amazing images just by spinning around in a circle and using flash to freeze and light your subject.

Shooting outside at dusk ensures you'll be able to get the slow shutter speed you'll need to produce the blur and allows you to position your subject against some interesting and colourful backgrounds.

FINI

TECH TALK

EQUIPMENT

This technique doesn't rely on the latest and greatest technology – any DSLR or compact with a built-in flash is ideal. Most cameras these days come with some form of flash which is all you need to illuminate the subject but, if you have one, an external flashgun works well too. If you're planning on using a compact you'll need to make sure it has either a slow sync flash mode, or a night-time portrait scene mode.

If you're using a compact camera take a look at the scene modes in your menu system and then select the night portrait option.

If you're using a DSLR switch your Mode dial over to Shutter priority (that's S or Tv) and pop up the flash using the button on the camera body.

DSLR OR COMPACT WITH A BUILT-IN FLASH

Nikon

SCENE MODES

Scene Mode 1/2
Night Portrait
Portrait with night scenery. Hold t
Cancel   Select Set

MODE DIAL

SHOOTING TECHNIQUE
SPINNING

So, how does slow sync flash actually work? Well, it's really nothing more complicated than firing the flash during a long exposure. Thankfully, your camera will do most of the hard work for you!

Simply switch over to Shutter priority mode, pop up your flash and input the shutter speed; the camera will set the aperture based on the ambient light and then calculate the power of the flash for a balanced exposure.

The flash is vital for this effect because it lights the subject and freezes their motion. As you can see from the images illustrating this, without it you'd get a well-exposed picture but the slow shutter speed would blur everything.

Alternatively, if you were to pop-up the flash and leave it on auto or Aperture priority mode, the camera would automatically set the shutter speed, usually to a pre-set value of 1/60sec or faster. This is too quick to let the

ambient light in and you'll get a dark background. So you need the flash to light the subject while the longer shutter speed allows the ambient light of the background to register. All you need to do then is spin around with your subject and fire off a shot mid spin. The flash will freeze the subject as the shutter fires but it will remain open for the rest of the exposure resulting in a blurred background as you continue to spin around.

SLOW SYNC FLASH WHILE MOVING

NO FLASH

FLASH ON AUTO

SLOW SYNC FLASH

1 SETTING UP Switch your camera over to Shutter priority mode (S or Tv on the mode dial) and set the shutter speed to 1/2sec and the camera will set the aperture accordingly. Change the ISO sensitivity to its lowest setting, usually 100 or 200, then press the flash button to activate the pop-up flash. If the aperture value flashes or reads 'HI' then your scene is too light and you'll need to find a darker place.

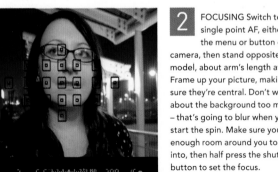

2 FOCUSING Switch to single point AF, either via the menu or button on the camera, then stand opposite your model, about arm's length away. Frame up your picture, making sure they're central. Don't worry about the background too much – that's going to blur when you start the spin. Make sure you have enough room around you to move into, then half press the shutter button to set the focus.

3 TAKE THE SHOT With focus and exposure now set, it's time to take the shot. Ask your subject to place their hands on your shoulders or to grip your wrists; This will ensure an even spin with nice uniform streaks. Count them in and start to rotate around each other, then fire the shutter button. You don't need to spin very fast; half a second is plenty of time to get some movement in the background.

4 CHECK THE RESULTS You'll never get the same photo twice with this freeform technique, so check the screen after each shot. If light-trails obscure the face, or there's a 'double' of them, try to keep their position more consistent in the spin, so they don't move from one part of the frame to another. And if the trails are too short, use a slower shutter speed. Keep shooting and you'll get some great shots.

USING SLOW SYNC FLASH FOR SELF PORTRAITS

If you fancy trying this technique out on yourself first, you can always give it a go indoors. Not only does this allow you to concentrate on the technique itself, rather than instructing your model and keeping them entertained, it can also be done regardless of the weather so it's a great way to practise the skills required to get the shot.

The technique is exactly the same: set your camera to Shutter priority on a DSLR, or night portrait mode if using a compact, and activate your flash. Set your focal length to a wide setting to ensure you get your whole face in. Now hold the camera at arm's length; for best results, take the shot with the camera raised slightly above your eye line as it makes for a more flattering pose (shooting from below can look a bit sinister). Once you're set up you can start to spin around in a circle. This can be done standing or using a swivelling office chair, which makes a fantastic aid.

Once the spin has started, fire the shutter to take the picture and continue to spin until the shutter closes. Check the back to see what you've got!

DIRECTION OF SPIN

SHUTTER OPENS | SHUTTER CLOSES

SLOW-SYNC FLASH AND SPORTS

Another scenario where slow-sync flash can come in handy is sports photography. Sports like mountain biking often take place in dark conditions so you can combine a short burst of flash with a longer shutter speed to get a pin-sharp photo of your subject and a terrific sense of movement in the background.

This technique is possible using both a pop-up flash or a detachable flashgun. A flashgun will produce more light and make it easier to get a successful result, but a pop-up flash can do a great job so long as the subject isn't too far away.

The best way to work is with the flash set to TTL (through the lens) mode, so the flash output and exposure are automatically calculated in camera. You'll still need to set the shooting mode to Shutter priority, choose a shutter speed and set ISO, but the camera and flash will take care of the rest. Remember, slow-sync flash works best in low light, so shoot indoors or at dusk for the best results.

SHOOTING TECHNIQUE
SPORTS ACTION

If you're shooting a static subject and moving the DSLR, set autofocus to single shot AF. If the subject is moving and you need to track it with the lens, set continuous AF.

1 ATTACH OR POP UP YOUR FLASH First of all attach your flashgun or open your pop-up flash. By default both will be set to TTL mode, which will make obtaining correct exposures easier. If you find yours is set to anything else, then change the mode back to TTL for the best results.

2 SWITCH TO SHUTTER PRIORITY It's essential that you control shutter speed. In Shutter priority mode you set the shutter speed and the camera chooses the aperture for you. With the flash set to TTL, flash power output will also be taken care of. Set a shutter speed of about 1/4sec so lots of blur can be captured.

3 SHUTTER CURTAIN SETTINGS Shutter curtain will make a difference to this effect. Front (first) curtain fires the flash first, then the slow shutter captures the movement, so the blur is in front of the subject. But here, for a more natural look, use rear (second) curtain flash so the subject is first blurred and then frozen by the flash.

Add drama with striking silhouettes

Turn the ordinary into the extraordinary by shooting into the light

WHAT YOU NEED
PHOTOSHOP
DSLR
CHESS SET
DESK LAMP
BAKING PAPER

DIFFICULTY LEVEL
EASY

FOR SUCH A STUNNING RESULT silhouettes are simple to create – one light source and, ideally, a dark location. The trick is to find a subject that is instantly recognizable. A silhouette of an orange could equally appear to be that of a tennis ball. The chess set knight is perfect.

FINISH

SHOOTING TECHNIQUE

To create a silhouette you simply need to place a light source behind your subject. Here an anglepoise desk lamp was used and, by using a sheet of baking paper over the front of the lamp, the light was diffused, creating a softer-looking background.

When using paper to diffuse your light, be sure to turn the lamp off between shots and never let the paper touch the bulb. Leave a good-sized gap between the lamp and the paper to avoid overheating as you don't want to melt anything or create a fire risk.

CAMERA A tripod is essential, not only to avoid camera shake if your shutter speed is quite slow but it also allows you to fine-tune the composition and get everything lined up more easily.

SET UP WITH CARE Your first step is to create an avenue of chess pieces, but it's important for them to line-up nicely in the shot. Aligning them against a ruler, position the pawns in rows, spacing them equally using the squares of the chessboard. Symmetry is the name of the game, so position the central piece midway down the avenue.

LIGHT SOURCE Place your desk lamp or a large torch so it points down the avenue of pawns towards the camera, lining it up to be as central as possible. Using your sheet of white baking or tracing paper, place one end under the light source and place the other end over the top. Be careful not to get the paper too close to the bulb, and regularly turn the lamp off to help it cool down.

1 SET FOCUS The central piece needs to be the sharpest part of the picture, so focus on it then switch to Manual focus to stop the AF 'hunting' when you shoot. Now decide whether you want a shallow depth-of-field, or for everything to be sharp. Here the photographer opted for a shallow depth-of-field, leaving just the knight in focus.

2 EXPOSE THE SCENE Turn off all the other lights in the room and pick Manual exposure mode (M). Dial in a low ISO sensitivity like 100 or 200 and, for the shallow depth-of-field desired, set a low f/number, like f/2.8 or f/4. Take a look on screen or through the viewfinder and you'll see an exposure bar – now adjust the shutter speed so this is near the middle.

3 TAKE THE SHOT Take the photo and check the picture on screen; if it's too bright then dial in a faster shutter speed, and if it's too dark dial in a slower one. Remember that your main subject should be as near to black as possible, while the light behind stays bright. Re-take the photo and keep fine-tuning the settings until it's spot on.

PROCESSING TECHNIQUE

1 OPEN FILE Open the raw file in Photoshop or Elements. In the RAW converter that appears, click on the basic tab and in the options provided drag the Temperature slider to 8400 and the Tint slider right to +39. Next, drag the Blacks slider to +6, Brightness should be set to +50, Contrast to +25 and Saturation to -8. All the other sliders should be set to 0.

2 SET GUIDE Click Open Image and head up to the View menu. Make sure the Grid option is ticked, then go to Edit>Preferences> Guides & Grid. Choose Percent in the drop-down menu on the right and then in the boxes provided set Gridline Every to 33.33%, with 1 entered into the Subdivisions box. Make sure Style is set to Lines. The guides are now set.

3 TRANSFORM TO FIX Now hit Ctrl+T to quickly enter Free Transform mode. Tick the Constrain Proportions box in the Options bar (Maintain Aspect Ratio in Photoshop), then click and drag out the top-right corner of your Transform bounding box until the pawns are equidistant from the grid lines. When done, click the tick.

4 CLEAN UP Pick the Clone tool from the toolbox, and set its Size to 50px with a hard edge. Check that Opacity is set to 100% and Mode is set to Normal. Now hold the Alt key on your keyboard and click in an area of white, then release the Alt key and paint out the reins to create a tidier and more iconic silhouette of the knight.

EXPERT ADVICE

TRY A DIFFERENT LIGHT SOURCE

This technique will work with a range of light sources, and it can be great fun playing with different types of illumination. This picture uses a very similar composition but instead of a desk lamp a window on a bright day provides the source of light.

- Start by taping some white baking paper to the window to diffuse the light and create a more even effect.
- Next, set up the pieces in an avenue-type arrangement as you did for the main technique image and set your camera on a tripod. Focus on the King.
- Finally, set your exposure; this time opting to keep more of the picture in focus, using an aperture of f/22 to get more of the pawns sharp.

Perform a vanishing act

Create a surreal portrait with your magic picture frame that turns things invisible

WHAT YOU NEED
DSLR OR COMPACT
CAMERA
TRIPOD
PICTURE FRAME
PHOTOSHOP OR
ELEMENTS

DIFFICULTY LEVEL
INTERMEDIATE

DIGITAL PHOTOGRAPHY HAS MADE THE WORLD of surreal photography available to everyone, rather than just master printers who spend hours in the darkroom perfecting images. With a considered approach to shooting, and a few basic editing skills, anyone can create their very own surrealist masterpiece. This photo technique is inspired by the work of artist René Magritte, who painted humorous images that challenged the viewer's perception of reality. The shoot is extremely simple, with the overall effect taking shape at the editing stage. The techniques

required are ideal for those new to Photoshop. There are basic processes for blending the two images together, then an Orton effect is added to give the shot a dream-like quality. The Orton effect is an old film-based technique developed by photographer Michael Orton. It can be replicated digitally and creates a sharp image with a small amount of blur and increased contrast. The overall technique is so easy, it'll feel as if you're cheating.

A surreal scene within a scene, where the person in the photo has disappeared from behind the frame. This photo packs a creative punch but is quite simple to shoot and edit.

SHOOTING TECHNIQUE

Location is absolutely everything for this shot and will require some forethought. The key element to look for is a strong connection between what will be around the picture frame and the area within it. Preserved railway lines are perfect locations because the tracks provide strong lines from the front of the shot that continue inside the frame. If you do go for this option, make sure you check that the trains aren't running and you aren't trespassing – this is against the law. Other locations such as paths and alleyways work equally well.

This technique can also be shot using black card instead of a picture frame, and making a selection at the editing stage to create an aperture to see through. But it's the use of a real picture frame, preferably with a mount, that produces the best results. Choosing a plain frame is the safest option because it'll work in a range of locations.

START IMAGES

Photoshop's Polygonal Lasso Tool and a Layer Mask were used to blend together these two pictures of a model holding the frame and the empty scene.

REFLECTOR If there's not quite enough light falling on the main subject use a reflector to bounce light back in. This could be especially important if the subject is wearing dark clothes, which absorb more light.

SAFETY Locations like these involve an element of danger. Make sure you don't put yourself at risk if shooting on a path, road, or on preserved railway lines – they're great locations but do take care.

FOCUS For this type of shot it's best to focus on the subject's hands and set ISO to f/11 or f/16. This will ensure the most prominent part of the shot is sharp and that depth-of-field is large enough to keep the background just about in focus.

SHOOTING TECHNIQUE

1 PICK A FRAME You can't beat a real picture frame with a mount to draw attention to the illusion. Plain frames are versatile but elaborate frames can also work in some situations. Alternatively, use black or white card and create differently shaped apertures in Photoshop for the background to show through.

2 SET UP YOUR CAMERA Getting the right crop requires a balance between working distance, tripod height and focal length. Kit lenses are ideal as they are short zooms offering versatility. Set the lowest ISO you can – one that allows you to shoot at about f/11 at no lower than 1/20sec. Shoot in Aperture priority so aperture and depth-of-field are fixed.

3 SET MANUAL FOCUS It's essential that focus is exactly the same in both shots to ensure consistency between the frames. Using autofocus is problematic, so set your lens to Manual and focus on the model's hands. With the aperture set to about f/11 the background will blur slightly, but objects and scenery will remain recognizable.

4 CONTROL THE LIGHT It's not always necessary to control light under natural conditions, but if parts of the shot are looking too dark, add more light using a reflector. When you come to shooting your two photos don't forget to take one shot of the model holding up the frame, and one of the empty scene itself – one without the other won't work.

PROCESSING TECHNIQUE

1 MAKE A SELECTION Open the 'frame' and 'scene' shots into Photoshop. Use the scene shot as the background image and drag the frame shot onto it to create a multi-Layer image. The frame Layer should be active at this point. Go to the Toolbar and choose the Polygonal Lasso tool. Zoom into the shot and place a point in each corner of the frame. When the path is completed it will become a selection.

2 BLEND THE IMAGES Press Ctrl+Shift+I to invert the selection made in Step 1. Press D to make black and white the foreground and background colours, respectively, and click on the Add Layer Mask icon at the bottom of the Layers palette – the rectangle with a circle. This will show the background in the frame. (If white was the foreground colour, everything around the frame would disappear.)

3 ADD DEPTH Hold down Ctrl+Shift+N to create a new empty Layer. Click and drag between the background Layer and frame Layer. Zoom into the frame by pressing Ctrl and +. Press B to activate the Brush tool, choose a soft-edged brush and paint lines along the inner edge of the frame. Lower the Opacity of the Layer to about 30% to lighten the vignette.

4 CREATE A LIGHT LAYER Click on Layer 1 to make it active and then press Ctrl+Alt+Shift+E to merge all the visible Layers into a new Layer. This should appear at the top of the Layer stack. Go to Image>Apply Image and set the Blending mode to Screen. This will make the photo lighter, but this is perfect. Click on OK to close the dialogue box.

5 DUPLICATE AND ADJUST You will need to duplicate the Layer created in the last step so press Ctrl+J to create a new Layer via copy. Go to Filter>Blur>Gaussian Blur. The Radius you need to set depends entirely on the photo, but as a guide an amount between 5 and 10 pixels is usually recommended. Once Radius is set, click OK.

6 GROUP AND REFINE The Orton effect was added in the previous steps, now it's time to refine the overall look. Layer 2 Copy should already be highlighted – so hold down the Ctrl key and left-click on Layer 2 so both are highlighted. Press Ctrl+G to group the Layers and then lower the opacity of the group to about 65%.

Succeed with stunning strobe

Use your flash to create a dramatic sequence of movements frozen in time

WHAT YOU NEED
PHOTOSHOP
DSLR
FLASHGUN
DARK ROOM
BLACK BACKGROUND

DIFFICULTY LEVEL
INTERMEDIATE

CAPTURING A SENSE OF MOVEMENT in a photo has always been a creative challenge for photographers, and with most camera techniques implying motion as a blur, you can't clearly show each movement of the subject. If, however, you want to freeze a series of movements and show each with clarity you need to create a sequential shot – and that's what's happening here. The principle behind this shot is simple; you need a dark room and a black background (like a black sheet) then, using a long exposure, you light your

moving subject with a series of quick flashes from your flashgun. The long exposure means the camera will record all the light that hits the sensor while the shutter is open, and because the room is dark and the only light is coming from these flashes, your camera will only record the subject during each flash duration – not any time in between. This gives you a sequence of frozen positions, rather than a long blurred trail of movement. Some flashguns have a 'stroboscopic' mode to automate the sequence of flashes (take a look in your manual) but

if yours doesn't, use the flash on Manual mode. Set the power to a low setting like 1/32 or 1/64 to ensure the flash recycles quickly enough to allow you to fire in quick succession. You won't be able to fire it as quickly as in an automated mode so you'll have fewer stages in the sequence. When you fire the shutter, press the flashgun's test or pilot button repeatedly, trying to keep equal timing between flashes. Whichever method you use, you should get some great results.

BACKGROUND TOO LIGHT It's important to shoot in very dark conditions for a good strobed action sequence. Shooting in daylight or against bright, detailed backgrounds will produce a ghostly image, where the background shows through and obscures the subject, making it difficult to see.

SHOOTING TECHNIQUE

Find a dark area to shoot your strobed sequence, picking a space where it's easy to block out light, like a garage. If you're struggling for room, you can also try it outside at night, as long as the background is sufficiently dark. Light backdrops won't work (see photo shown left). Next, decide how many stages (flashes) you want in your sequence shot – here there are 10 – and then work out how long the movement is going to last; a tennis swing may be 0.5sec or a dance sequence 2sec or more, but this fencer took roughly 1sec to complete his lunge.

This is all the information you need so enter it into the flashgun, setting the number of flashes and how fast they'll fire (the latter in Hz or cycles per second). 1Hz is equal to one flash per second, so divide the number of flashes you want by the duration of the subject's movement. In the case of the fencer that's 10 divided by one which gives you 10Hz, and ultimately a setting of 10 flashes in one second. Phew! That's the maths over.

1 SET UP YOUR FLASH Using the Menu button set Repeat or Multi flash mode. Next, using the Select or Set button, highlight the settings for the power, number of flashes and Hz, then input the values you need. Here 1/32 power and 10–10Hz, gives you 10 flashes in 1sec (but if you put 10–5hz, for example, you'd get 10 flashes in 2sec).

2 SET UP EXPOSURE Set your camera to Manual mode (M) and choose an aperture (f/5.6 in this case), and a shutter speed equal to or longer than the period of movement you've decided on. Remember, the flashes are all that will show in your picture, so err on the side of a longer exposure – here 2sec was set so that 10 flashes would comfortably fit into the exposure time.

3 SET FOCUS Now frame up and set your camera on a tripod. As it'll be very dark, your autofocus will struggle, so pre-focus on your subject then switch to Manual focus (MF). Be careful that your subject doesn't move closer or further away from the camera or you'll need to refocus. Next, set your Shooting mode to Self-timer at 10sec.

4 TEST SHOT Turn the lights off (it's a good idea to use a torch to see what you're doing) and start the Self-timer, moving to your flash position. As the shutter fires, get your subject to start moving and fire the flash with the test or pilot button. Check the results on screen and, if the subject is too bright, position the flash further from them. If they're too dark, step closer with the flash and try again.

5 TAKE THE PHOTO You can also control the brightness by altering the flash power (Step 1) or by using a higher or lower f/number. Here, closing the aperture from f/5.6 to f/8 would darken the subject. When you're confident you have a good exposure, fire the Self-timer again and, as before, get your subject to start their movement the moment they hear the shutter as you fire the flash.

6 CHECK YOUR RESULTS Go back to your camera and check the photo. If you think you need more or fewer flashes in the sequence, or if the flashes need to last for a longer or shorter period, adjust the settings on your flashgun as in Step 1. Also, check if the movement has worked or if the model moved too soon or too late, then just keep shooting until you're happy.

PROCESSING TECHNIQUE

Unless you are able to completely black-out your shooting area there will always be some cleaning up work to be done, but it's easy in Photoshop.

1 INCREASE CONTRAST Bring up the Levels palette (Ctrl+L) and in the window that appears, drag the white point slider under the histogram left to about 220. Next, drag the black point slider right to 10. This will lighten the highlights and darken the shadows to increase the overall contrast of the image. Try holding Alt as you drag for a clipping preview.

2 CLEAN UP BACKGROUND Now choose the Clone Stamp tool (S) from the Toolbox and set it to a 300px soft-edged brush at 100% opacity. Hold the Alt key and click on an area of black to sample it, then paint over the distractions to remove them from the shot. Keep re-sampling to ensure a natural look.

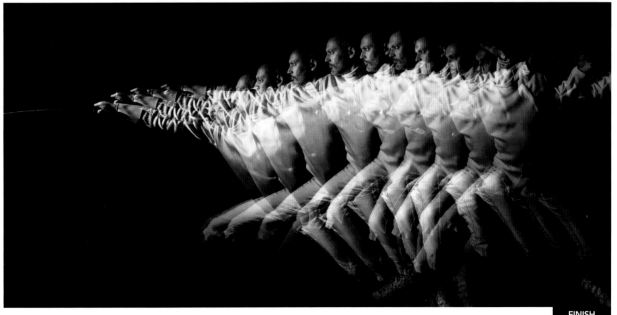

FINISH

Create light trails

Light trails are great for showing motion, and not just outdoors

WHAT YOU NEED
PHOTOSHOP OR
ELEMENTS
DSLR
TRIPOD
POINT LIGHT SOURCES
(TORCHES, FAIRY LIGHTS)

DIFFICULTY LEVEL
INTERMEDIATE

LIGHT TRAILS ARE GREAT FUN TO SHOOT, and produce a spectacular result, full of bright colour and bold shapes. The technique involves shooting a moving light source while the shutter is open; anything that moves during the timescale of the shutter speed you are shooting with will blur – in this case making a streak of colour across the frame.

Light trails are perhaps most often photographed in scenes containing traffic, but the same principle applies to portraits, action shots, still life and any other type of photography – as long as it contains moving lights. Let's look at two very different subjects that both rely on light trails to make a bold statement.

TRAFFIC TRAILS WITH A TWIST

Traffic trails – the streaks of light left by car headlights at night – are great fun to shoot, but the way they're captured using a long exposure means it's impossible to keep the cars sharp. Or is it? By shooting three images, all from the same position, it's possible to keep the car sharp while blurring the movement of its lights as it enters and leaves the frame.

The first picture is of the static car, and the second and third pictures record the trails of its lights. To give this a go yourself, find a quiet stretch of road and set up your camera in a safe position on the verge. After shooting the car standing still, set off another exposure and have your helper reverse slowly out of the frame to create the trails of light. Make sure you don't move the camera between exposures. Ask the driver to bend the path of the car which will give the trails a nice curve.

FINISH

SHOOTING TECHNIQUE

1 SET UP AND FOCUS After setting up your camera on a tripod compose the image so that the car is in the distance. Leave room for the trails, but make sure it's large enough to be clear in the picture. Focus on the car, then switch to Manual focus so the point of sharpness doesn't shift between frames. Now set Manual exposure mode (M), ISO 100 and an aperture of f/16.

2 FIRST EXPOSURE Next set the shutter speed to 20sec or 30sec, giving you enough time for the car to reverse out of the frame in subsequent shots. Switch the Drive mode to Self-timer (to avoid wobbling the camera) and take a picture. If it's too bright, close the aperture to f/22 or wait until the light dims a little. If it's too dark, open the aperture up to f/11 or f/8 and try again.

3 SECOND AND THIRD EXPOSURES Once you're happy with the exposure of the static car, fire the shutter again and have your helper reverse the car all the way out of the frame before the shutter closes, leaving a seamless trail. Get another shot of them driving back into the frame and stopping in the original position.

KEEP THE CAR SHARP What makes this shot different is the sharp subject, so the first image you need to shoot is of the car, stationary on the road. Use a marker so the driver knows where to reposition it (such as a tripod on the verge) and make sure its lights are on so that you can sync them up with the light trails from the later exposures

CAMERA POSITION By keeping the camera in a fixed position you can shoot separate pictures of the car and the light trails, then use a few simple tools in Photoshop to blend them together.

PROCESSING TECHNIQUE

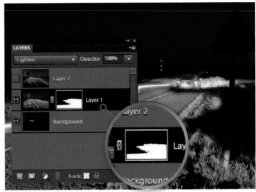

1 SET UP THE LAYERS Open your three images into Photoshop and go to Window>Images>Float All in Windows. With one of the trail images active pick the Move tool, hold down Shift, and drag and drop the image into the other trail's window. Do the same with the third shot, containing the static car, so that all three frames exist as different Layers in the same window. You can close the other windows now if you like. Rename the Layers as Trails1, Trails2 and Car and reorder them so the Car layer is on the bottom. Change the Blending mode of the Trails1 and Trails2 Layers to Lighten.

2 ADD A MASK Click the Layer Visibility icon next to the Trails2 Layer to hide it and then click on Trails1 before going to Layer>Layer Mask>Hide All. You'll now only be able to see the Car Layer. Pick the Brush tool, setting it to about 200px with a soft edge and its colour to White. Paint over the foreground of the picture to reveal the light trails.

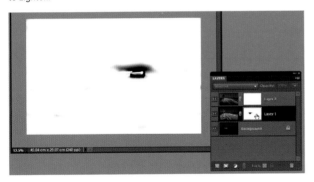

3 TIDY UP AND REVEAL THE MASK Zoom in, lower the Brush Size to about 30px and paint closer to the car. If you need to neaten things up, switch the Brush colour to Black and paint to erase the mask, ensuring the car is kept perfectly sharp. Now click on the Trails2 Layer, switch its visibility back on, and go to Layer>Layer Mask >Reveal All. Next hold Alt and click on the Mask next to Layer 1 to show it.

4 COPY THE MASK Go to Select>All and then Edit>Copy to copy the mask belonging to Trails1. Click on the Mask next to Trails2 and go to Edit>Paste to make this mask identical to it. Go to Select>Deselect and Alt-click on the Mask to hide it once more. You'll see the car remains sharp, but the light streaks of the Trails2 Layer are revealed. If you need to adapt the second mask, paint into it as before. When you are happy choose Layer>Flatten Image.

5 TILT FRAME Go to Select>All and press Ctrl+T to perform a Free Transform. Move your cursor just outside the bounding box then click and drag to rotate the picture – click the tick icon to confirm. Go to Select>Deselect, pick the Clone Stamp tool, and Alt-click on the sky to sample this part of the picture. Paint over any white areas revealed by the rotation and fill them in with copied sky. Press Ctrl+J to copy everything to a new Layer.

6 FINISH ZOOM BLUR Go to Filter>Blur>Radial Blur. Set the Amount to 5, the Blur Method to Zoom and the Quality to Best. Click in Blur Center to reposition the effect and click OK. Add a Layer Mask as before and paint Black over the car. Press Ctrl+J to copy the Layer, then Ctrl+Alt+F to reopen Radial Blur. Set the Amount to 10, click OK and paint round the car to graduate the effect.

Shoot daylight black-and-white portraits

Shoot great monochrome portraits with nothing more than a window and a few bits of card

WHAT YOU NEED
DSLR AND STANDARD
ZOOM
REFLECTOR
CARD FOR
BACKGROUNDS/
REFLECTORS

DIFFICULTY LEVEL
EASY

IF YOU'VE BEEN PUT OFF SHOOTING PORTRAITS because you think you need complicated lighting set-ups to get it right, or because you don't have access to a 20-something female model, then this technique is for you.

Using the simplest of equipment and shooting in your own home still means you can get great results. And who needs a 20-something anyway; a 60-something is infinitely more interesting to photograph!

Most family members aren't used to having their pictures taken other than at Christmas and family parties, but most will jump at the chance to have a photograph of them that's a bit more serious. When you photograph someone you know, it's often easier because you already have a relationship with them; you'll both be feeling comfortable. But you still need to balance this with the need to get the best from your model. That said, it's important to encourage, direct and continue to put them at ease as you shoot, whether you've known them for five minutes or 50 years.

When you photograph anyone – but especially a more mature model – it's essential that you think about the style that will best suit them. For middle-aged people a more contrasty, black and white treatment is the perfect way to bring out all the great character in their faces. This is definitely an approach that is better for men than women, though, as obviously it accentuates the lines in their faces. That's not to say you couldn't follow the exact same method of lighting and soften the effect slightly, just to make it a little more flattering!

So, if you can find yourself a member of your family who fits the black and white treatment, the only other things you need (apart from your DSLR) are a reflector, some black card and a window as the light source.

SHOOTING TECHNIQUE

Window light can be used to create a clean white background that looks as if it could belong in a studio and it's incredibly simple to do. You just need a window, because this technique involves harnessing the power of natural light and redirecting it to where it can create the effect you want. The window needs some clear space on the outside, in other words, if it looks out onto a neighbour's brick wall just a meter or so away, it won't work. Here, a downstairs window was used, through which the sun was shining but because it had a blind, the direct sunlight was diffused. If you don't have a blind, then avoid direct sunlight, just make sure the background is considerably brighter than the inside.

Stand (or sit) your model in front of the window facing into the room so the light is behind them. Obviously they will be in the shade but this doesn't matter because you're going to reflect the light back into their face with a reflector. Reflectors are about the most useful photo accessory you can have and don't cost a fortune.

As you're only shooting head-and-shoulder style, your subject can even hold the reflector themselves, although it's easier if you can recruit an assistant for this task. Here a silver reflector was used because the silver side helps to generate the contrast wanted, but a white reflector or card would certainly work OK. Now it's simply a case of bouncing some of the window light back onto your subject and taking a meter reading from the lighter area of their face. Make sure your DSLR is set to spot metering. This is really important because it will give you the most accurate reading, exposing the face well but blowing out the background for your clean, white look. The easiest way to work is to switch your camera to Aperture priority mode (Av) and set a wide aperture of f/4 or f/5.6. Dial in the shutter speed and aperture this gives you using Manual exposure mode. Left in Aperture priority the exposure would adjust itself every time the composition was changed.

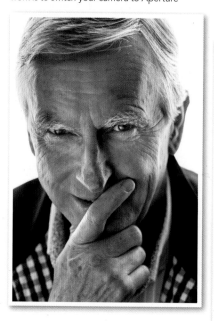

INTRODUCING BLACK CARD

A piece of black card to the right of the model helps cut out some of the light from the window on that side and gives a little more shadow to help accentuate the character in the model's face. It's like an 'anti-reflector'.

With all the elements in place – reflector, card, spot-metered exposure – it is then simply a case of keeping your subject amused while you snap away. Focus should always be on the leading eye (or eyes if you are square on to the subject) as this is the point in the frame that the viewer's gaze will be drawn to.

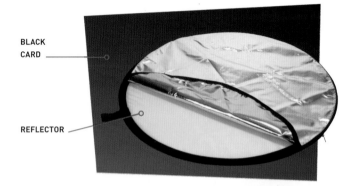

BLACK CARD

REFLECTOR

BLACK CARD This card (however old and tatty it is) will help to reduce the amount of window light spilling onto one side of your subject's face and create some interesting shadows.

LENS CHOICE A short telephoto or long end of your kit lens will be fine for portraits. In fact, you could use anything from 50mm upwards, depending on the space you have.

REFLECTOR A reflector is the simplest accessory going but it is also the most powerful tool you have to direct natural light where you want it. Here, the silver side was used.

THE DIFFERENCE A REFLECTOR MAKES

WITHOUT A REFLECTOR The background is still overexposed but there is not enough light on the subject's face or any catchlights in his eyes when shot without reflector or card.

WITH A SILVER REFLECTOR Adding a silver reflector instantly lights up the face and starts to bring out the character, although the totally even lighting isn't perfect.

WITH A REFLECTOR AND CARD With the reflector on one side and black card on the other the right look is starting to materialize – all that's needed is a good pose from your subject.

With black and white there's a tendency to always lean towards the mean and moody look! But you shouldn't ignore the fun and friendly side of your subject.

SWITCH TO A BLACK BACKGROUND

With a card full of clean white background shots it's easy to switch the background to dark, simply using the same back card you've been using. You don't need to change any of your camera settings, other than to check your spot-metered reading again to ensure the correct exposure. With the black background in place, take your reading from the side the reflector is mainly illuminating and use this new reading.

It's worth noting that with a black background like this you will probably find the effect of a silver reflector on the face too overpowering. To counter this, switch to a white reflector that bounces a softer light into the subject's face. You can see how the low-key look of this image dramatically changes the feel of the image – despite the fact that it was taken in exactly the same position as the others.

BLACK BACKGROUND You don't need anything expensive as a background – a piece of black card like this will be enough – it doesn't matter how tatty it is.

WINDOW LIGHT For this setup the window blind is drawn and a piece of black card is cutting out a lot of the light behind the subject.

WHITE REFLECTOR To dampen down the strength of the bounced light, for this style of image switch to a simple white reflector to redirect the natural light.

PROCESSING TECHNIQUE

1 BOOST CONTRAST Although your pictures will often already have a good amount of contrast, pushing this even further with the Contrast slider is usually worth doing. Try it with the image still in Color mode for now. Also add some extra black into the image, to darken the shadow areas further.

2 TWEAK CLARITY The finished image needs to be sharp and edgy so the next step is simply to increase the Clarity of the photograph. Normally you wouldn't push this slider too far but with this image try going to +15. The image will sharpen up, but it will also darken down a bit too, especially in the shadows.

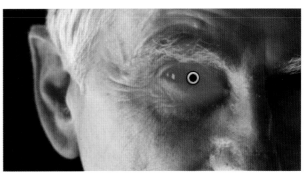

4 USE THE ADJUSTMENT BRUSH To make any small, localized adjustments the Adjustment Brush is the best Tool. You need to simply paint over the area you want to lighten or darken and then adjust the Exposure slider. But don't alter it so far that it is obvious in the final image, or it'll look a bit odd.

3 FINE-TUNE TONAL RANGE The Tone Curve allows both the highlights and shadows to be adjusted, so you can achieve the crispest shot possible. Push this further than you would if you were going to stay with colour, but you still want an S-curve that won't blow the highlights, so take care not to go too far.

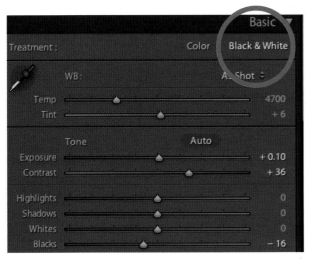

FINISH

5 HIT THE BLACK & WHITE TAB There's not much else to do unless you want to make a compositional change with the Crop Tool. Simply click the Black & White tab at the top of the palette and your images will go to monochrome. If this doesn't look right you can make more changes, toggling between Color and Black & White options as you process the photo.

Forecast changeable weather

Add some drama to your scenes with a modicum of mist, a ripple of rain or a soupçon of sno

WHAT YOU NEED
ELEMENTS
PHOTOSHOP

DIFFICULTY LEVEL
EASY

FINISH

HAVE YOU EVER GAZED THROUGH A WINDOW on a wet and rainy day and wished you could be out there shooting? Or thought how great those snowflakes would look. Well, next time, try this quick-and-easy technique instead! Using photos you've already taken it's simple to make pictures look as if they were shot in wet or cold weather – without leaving your dry, warm home.

This technique works with almost any image but the best type of pictures to use are those without large areas of white as the misty/snowy effect will stand out more strongly against dark areas in a photo. A landscape with a dark brooding sky would be perfect, so look through your image files to see if you have something which fits the bill.

This technique uses the Layers palette in Elements or Photoshop, so you'll also learn a lot about Layers.

PROCESSING TECHNIQUE
MISTY EFFECT

1 ADD BLUR Open your subject JPEG (in this case the mill) and press Ctrl+J to duplicate the layer (go to Window>Layers and you'll see it). Click Filter>Blur>Gaussian Blur and enter 15px, then hit OK. Pick the Eraser tool (E) from the toolbox and change its Mode from Brush to Pencil. Set the size to 300 pixels and rub a hole through the blur.

2 ADD SOME WATER ClickFilter>Blur>Gaussian Blur, apply a setting of 5px and click OK, then open your misty texture image (here a waterdrop effect, Start Image 1) and press Ctrl+A, followed by Ctrl+C to copy the image. Return to the main image and press Ctrl+V to paste it then, in the Layers palette, click Normal and choose Lighten. Finally click on Opacity and set it to 50%.

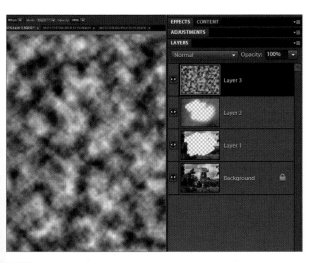

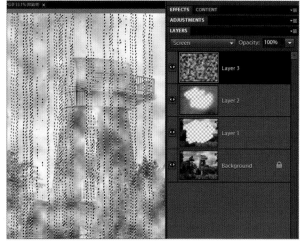

3 CLEAN THE WINDOW Pick the Eraser tool (E) again and change the Mode back to Brush, then erase another hole in the waterdrops, allowing the subject to show though. Press D to reset your colours and then go to Layer>New>Layer... and hit OK. Click Filter>Render>Clouds and then open your third JPEG (here Start Image 2).

4 ADD STREAKS Press Ctrl+V to paste the streaks (or whatever your image depicts) in, then pick the Magic Wand (W). Click on one of the streaks and go to Select>Similar then Layer>Delete>Layer and click Yes. Next, go to Edit>Cut, then click Normal and pick Screen, setting Opacity to 50%. Press Ctrl+X followed by Ctrl+D and then erase a hole as before.

PROCESSING TECHNIQUE
ADD SNOW

Photography and snow, what better combination? A good covering of fresh snow can transform a dreary landscape into a glistening world that's clean, and white. But it does throw up some challenges for photographers... is your camera weather-proof, camera settings, and how to avoid dull, flat lighting in falling snow. Much easier to make your own flurry of digital snowflakes! Layers to the rescue.

1 ADD SNOW Open your snow scene and go to Layer>New Layer. When prompted, name it 'Snow1' and click OK. Next, click Edit>Fill Layer (Edit>Fill in Photoshop), change the Contents to Black and click OK. Now click Filter>Noise>Add Noise, use an Amount of 15% and set the options to Gaussian and Monochromatic, then hit OK. Click Filter>Blur>Gaussian Blur, use 0.3px and press OK.

2 ADD MORE SNOW Go to Window>Layers and click where it says Normal, choosing Screen from the list. Make another new Layer by clicking Layer>New Layer and this time name it 'Snow2'. Go to Edit>Fill Layer, change the Contents to White and click OK. Now go to Filter>Pixelate>Pointillize, use a Cell Size of 5, then hit OK. Press Ctrl+Shift+U to desaturate the layer, then Ctrl+I to invert it.

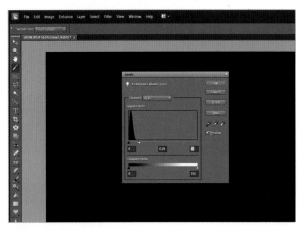

3 BLEND THE SNOW Go to Filter>Blur>Gaussian Blur and this time use 1px. Click OK and press Ctrl+L to open the Levels palette. Set the Black point slider to 0, Midtones to 0.2 and White point to 40. Change the Layer Blending Mode to Screen, then make a new Layer, naming it 'Snow3'. Go to Edit>Fill Layer, set the Contents to Black and click OK. Apply the Pointillize filter again, using a Cell Size of 10 and click OK.

4 INCREASE SNOW SIZE Desaturate this new Layer and invert the colour as before, then apply the same Levels, Gaussian Blur, and Blending Mode as in the previous step. Finally, press Ctrl+Alt+J and name this new Layer 'Snow4'. Now press Ctrl+T and, in the Options bar, increase the Width and Height to 500%, then click the tick. Go to Layer>Flatten Image and you're done!

TIP

ERASER TOOL

For an even better result, use the Eraser tool (E) to selectively remove a few patches of snow from the top three layers.

FINISH

Get creative with blur

Give a new lease of life to those old night-time snaps

WHAT YOU NEED
PHOTOSHOP OR
ELEMENTS

DIFFICULTY LEVEL
EASY

IT'S ALL TOO EASY TO THROW AWAY PICTURES that don't measure up to our exacting standards, but sometimes some blur or camera shake isn't the end of the world. In fact it can be the basis for a great photograph.

This night shot of Hamburg was taken from a boat on the River Elbe. It was just a snap at the time and, since a shutter speed of 0.5sec was the fastest possible, the movement of the boat has introduced some camera shake. But the Photoshop technique explained here will give this low-light shot a new lease of life. The end result is an arty effect that's easy to create.

CHOOSING AN IMAGE

This image was taken from a moving boat and some camera shake has spoiled sharpness, but it has great composition, bold colours and dynamic shapes. Look for similar things in your pictures. High contrast helps, too – bright highlights will blur well against darker parts of the image.

START IMAGE

FINISH

1 SET UP YOUR LAYERS You'll make good use of the Layers palette with this technique so, once you've opened your image into Photoshop or Elements, ensure Layers option in the Window menu is ticked. Inside the Layers palette you'll see the Background Layer – you need to make some copies of this to apply your filter effects to.

There are various ways of duplicating a Layer, but the quickest by far is a nifty keyboard shortcut; just hit Ctrl+J and you'll see Layer 1 appear above the Background in the Layers stack. This is an exact copy of the Background Layer. Hit Ctrl+J a second time, and you'll see Layer 1 copy appear above that. You should now have three identical Layers.

To stay organised, give the Layers names. Double click on the words 'Layer 1' and they'll be highlighted. Type in 'Vertical Blur' as the new name. Do the same for 'Layer 1 copy' calling it 'Horizontal Blur'.

Next change the Blending Mode of the Horizontal Blur Layer to Lighten using the pop-up menu in the Layers palette (you'll see this is set to Normal by default). Do the same for the Vertical Blur Layer. You won't see any difference in the image yet as you're just setting up your Layers for the next stage.

2 ADD BLUR With the Vertical Blur Layer active, choose Filter>Blur>Motion Blur. In the Motion Blur dialog box set the Angle to 90° and the Distance to 280px. This will create a streaky, blurred effect in the up-down direction. If you switch off the eye icons on the other two Layers, you'll be able to see it in isolation. It looks a mess on its own, so switch them back on again!

Next. click the Horizontal Blur Layer to make it active. Go to Filter>Blur>Motion Blur again and, in the dialog box, leave the Distance set to 280px, but set the Angle to 0°. This will give a side-to-side blur effect 280 pixels in length.

TRACK PROGRESS

Using the visibility icon (the 'eye') in the Layers palette to switch Layers on and off may sound like a strange thing to do, but it's actually a brilliant way of keeping track of your progress and trying different effects. By keeping these effects in different Layers, you can check the 'before' and 'after' views quickly and easily, which makes it simple to see what is and isn't working when you're creating an image.

3 CHECK THE BLUR EFFECTS Switch off the 'eye' icon on the Background Layer and you'll see the two blur effects working together producing a criss-cross effect – almost like a painter's brush stroke. If you really like the impressionist look and feel then jump straight to Step 5 and add a bit of extra contrast to finish off. Or, to get the intended effect here, carry on with a little more editing.

Switch the Background Layer back on and you'll see the Layers working together again. The result is pretty good, but the Motion Blur Layers need a bit of a kick to make them stand out more strongly.

TECH TALK

USING THE LEVELS PALETTE

The Levels palette is one of the most important in Photoshop and gives you a graphical representation of your image. The graph – known as a Histogram – shows all the pixels of a particular value stacked up on top of each other, with the darkest tones on the left and the brightest tones on the right.

The three sliders under the Histogram allow you to control the black point, mid point and white point. By moving these, you change the contrast. Moving the black point to the right tells Photoshop to make the pixels to the left of the slider pure black, while moving the white point to the left makes the pixels above this point pure white. The mid-point slider controls how bright or dark mid-tones appear: sliding it to the left will brighten them, and moving it right will make them darker.

TIP

HOW TO CHANGE THE BLUR STREAKS

With a camera you simply pan from side to side while releasing the shutter to create blurred streaks and a sense of movement. The length of the streaks is governed by the length of the shutter speed and how fast you're moving. Photoshop's Motion Blur filter emulates the effect of moving the camera during an exposure. You change the length of the Motion Blur streaks by adjusting the Distance slider.

For example, if you go for, say, 200 pixels, then the streak will blur by 100 pixels on either side of the subject. The angle of the movement is set in degrees in the Angle box. For a dead-flat pan, set the Angle to 0 degrees, and for a vertical tilt, set it to 90 degrees. Here, both these settings are used in the same pic – something you could never do in one single shot with a camera.

4 BRIGHTEN UP THE BLUR With the Horizontal Blur Layer active, open the Levels palette with the shortcut Ctrl+L and move the white point slider to the left to brighten the highlights. How much you move the slider will depend on your image.

Once you're happy with the brightness of the highlights, click OK and select the Vertical Blur Layer. Apply the Levels command again (hit Ctrl+L once more). Use the same white point setting on this Layer, and click OK. Don't worry if the highlights blow out – it's all part of the artistic effect.

5 **ADJUST CONTRAST ACROSS THE IMAGE** The Lighten Blending Mode has knocked out some of the overall contrast and made the image look a little washed out. To counteract this apply a Levels adjustment to the whole image. To do this, click the Adjustment Layer icon (the half black/half white circle at the foot of the Layers palette) and select Levels from the pop-up menu. Move the black point slider inwards to darken the shadows and really add some impact. Try adjusting the mid-point slider as well; moving it to the right will darken the mid-tones and give the image a moodier feel.

6 **BOOST THE COLOURS** A colour boost will enrich the shot and is really quick and easy to do. Click on the Adjustment Layer icon again and choose Hue/Saturation. In the Adjustments palette the Saturation slider will increase or decrease the intensity of the colour in the scene. Crank it up to +20 (or so) to give the colours in your picture a real lift.

All you need to do now is save your edited image. If you want to keep all the Layers as they are, save in Photoshop format (PSD), but if you just want the finished result, a JPEG will be fine and will take up less space on your hard drive. To do either of these things go to File>Save as… and pick the format you want along with a new name for the image.

TIP

TRY THIS: DAYTIME CROSS BLUR

FINISH

You've seen how cross blur was used to great effect on a night-time shot but the great thing about this technique is that it works with all kinds of images – you'll be pleasantly surprised.

Twinkly lights help but all you really need are some bright highlights. Who'd have thought this simple meadow shot would have yielded such an eye-catching result?

START IMAGE

Add grain for dramatic effect

A sprinkling of Noise can add texture and a certain old-fashioned appeal to your images

WHAT YOU NEED
PHOTOSHOP

DIFFICULTY LEVEL
INTERMEDIATE

FINISH

ALTHOUGH PHOTOGRAPHERS ARE GENERALLY inclined to remove digital noise and interference from their images, there are many times when it can be useful or even attractive. Working in black & white is one of those times.

You'll often discover that the 'lumpy' texture of a traditional fast-film grain effect can give your shots both a worthy documentary style and add pleasing antique appeal.

There are options to add film grain via the Filter>Artistic>Film grain but, like many Filters in Photoshop and Elements, this isn't necessarily the best way to go, because adding a grain effect manually will give you much more flexibility.

PROCESSING TECHNIQUE

The best way to add a 'fast film' effect to your mono shots is by using Layers. Adding the Noise to a separate Layer will let you control the intensity of the effect, how it interacts with the original photo, even how lumpy it is. and best of all, if your Noise is on a separate Layer to the picture and you make a mistake, you can delete it and start again without damaging the original.

Layers make all this simple and remember, once you've made a film grain effect you like, you can save it as a separate image and then use it on other pictures. Just open your film grain image and use the Move tool to drag it into another photo.

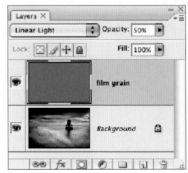

The power of the Layers palette makes it easy to control how your film grain effect is applied to the image on the Layer beneath, using Opacity and Blending Modes.

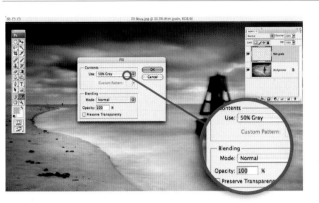

2 MAKE SOME NOISE Now go to Filter>Noise>Add Noise. In the palette, set the Amount to about 10%, the Distribution to Gaussian, finally, make sure that the Monochromatic box at the foot of the palette is ticked (you don't want colour noise in a mono image). Click OK and, in the Layers palette, click where it says Normal and change the film grain layer's Blending Mode to Linear light.

1 ADD A LAYER Open your selected image and then bring the Layers palette up on screen (Window>Layers). Now go to Layer>New> Layer... call it 'film grain' and press OK. Now you need to fill the layer with a midtone colour, so go to Edit>Fill. Under Contents, pick 50% Gray from the list, leaving the Blending Options at Normal and 100%. Now press OK. they're very near the ground you'll practically have to lie on the ground to get the shot!

3 SOFTEN THE NOISE Again, using the Layers palette, change the Opacity of the film grain Layer to about 50%. This will tone down the effect and it's worth trying a few values to see what works on your chosen pic. Now go to Filter>Blur> Gaussian blur, and use an amount of about 0.5px to just soften the hard digital Noise into something more organic looking. Press OK when you've finished.

4 MAKE IT LUMPY If the effect isn't strong enough, go back to step 2 and increase the Amount of Noise. Alternatively, with the grain Layer still active in the Layers palette, press Ctrl+T and, either holding Shift on the keyboard, or making sure the Constrain Proportions box is ticked, click and drag the corner handles outwards to about 150%. Press Return and then go to Layer>Flatten image.

3 WAYS TO FIND THE RIGHT GRAIN EFFECT

Experiment until you find the right film grain effect for your image. What worked for the buoy image won't necessarily work for other pictures, it's always worth varying the settings to see if they help improve the look and feel of your mono work. Here three different effects have been used, twice changing the Blending Mode of the film grain Layer to get a look that's subtly different from the Linear Light mode, and, finally, enlarging the film grain Layer even more.

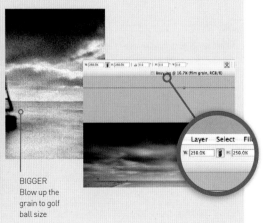

SOFTER
Use the Overlay Blending Mode

GRITTIER
Use the Hard Light Blending Mode

BIGGER
Blow up the grain to golf ball size

Relive those holiday memories

Winter – the perfect time to do something creative with your holiday snaps

YOU'VE PROBABLY GOT LOADS OF PHOTOS stashed away on your hard drive gathering dust and waiting for their time to shine – shots that just haven't hit the mark or need others to tell the story of that particular event. These images may feature some great scenes or inspire some happy memories but, unfortunately, that's not always enough to make a great photo.

Thankfully, software packages can save the day, letting you shoot your great view and add the interest in later, or simply present several existing images in a new and exciting way.

PROCESSING TECHNIQUE
BLENDING IMAGES

A landscape image will probably fall flat if it doesn't contain a distinct focal point that will engage the viewer and hold their attention. The pic of the pyramids at Giza isn't a bad image but it's not particularly inspiring so a shot of some camel riders taken at a similar location on the same day has been used to add some vital interest.

START IMAGES

PYRAMIDS This shot of the pyramids at Giza is OK but really needs something to lead the viewer's eye in and add a sense of scale. Without it, the foreground is flat and empty.

CAMELS Here's the perfect answer – a group of camel riders, taken in roughly the same light at the same location, which can be flipped and positioned exactly where you want it.

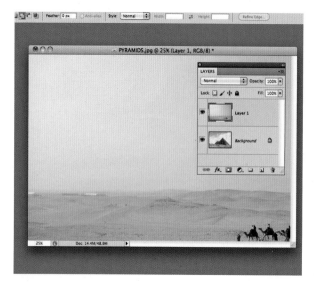

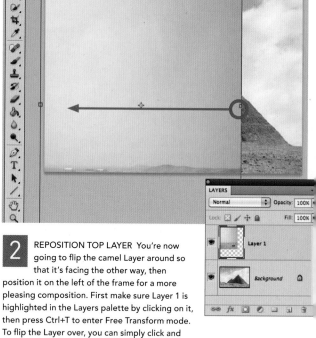

1 BUILD UP LAYERS Before you get cracking, you need to bring the two images into the same document. In Photoshop or Elements, go to File>Open, then navigate to your Image 1, in this case of the pyramids and press Open. You'll now be able to see the image on screen with a single Layer visible in your Layers palette (if you can't see your Layers palette head up to Window>Layers). You now need to open the second image, following the same method, so go to File>Open and load your equivalent to the camels here. You now have both images open, but you need to combine them into the same image. So, on 'camels', press Ctrl+A to select the whole image, then Ctrl+C to copy it into memory. Next, bring up 'pyramids' and press Ctrl+V to paste the camels in. Both images should now be visible in the Layers palette, with the camels pic (Layer 1) sitting above the pyramids (the Background Layer).

2 REPOSITION TOP LAYER You're now going to flip the camel Layer around so that it's facing the other way, then position it on the left of the frame for a more pleasing composition. First make sure Layer 1 is highlighted in the Layers palette by clicking on it, then press Ctrl+T to enter Free Transform mode. To flip the Layer over, you can simply click and drag the side handles in opposite directions, turning it over like you would with a piece of paper. Just make sure that the Width (W) box in the options bar reads100%, or you'll distort it. Hit return to confirm the change. An alternative route is to go to Edit>Transform>Flip Horizontal (or Image>Rotate>Flip Layer Horizontal in Elements).

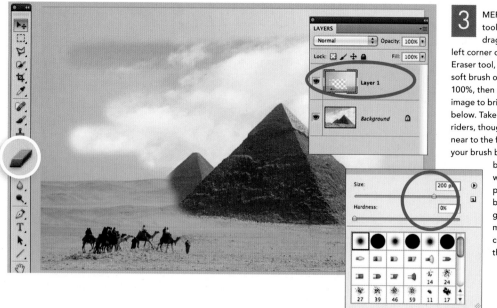

3 MERGE LAYERS Pick the Move tool (V) from the Toolbox and drag the camels to the bottom-left corner of the scene. Next, choose the Eraser tool, and in the Options bar, pick a soft brush of 200px and set Opacity to 100%, then start to delete areas of the image to bring through the pyramids below. Take care not to delete the camel riders, though! When you start getting near to the figures, reduce the size of your brush by hitting the left square brackets key, and carry on working until you've erased practically all of the background. Keep a bit of ground below their feet to make the composite look more convincing and to help blend the two images together.

4 OPEN LEVELS TO BLEND COLOURS It's starting to take shape now, but you'll notice the ground under the camels doesn't quite fit with the rest. To fix this and match up the shades, you're going to make a Levels adjustment. With Layer 1 still active (it should be highlighted in the Layers palette) press Ctrl+L to open Levels. Click on the Black point slider and move it right to 26, then grab the Middle slider and move it right to 0.75. Finally, click on the White point slider and take it left to 227. Click OK and the two Layers will now match up. As you're trying this technique on your own shots these precise values won't apply, but just move the sliders in a similar way until you get a match. If you make a mistake and want to start again, hold Alt and click Reset.

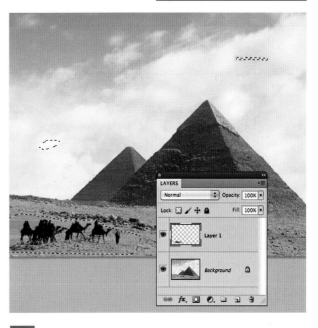

TECH TALK

LAYER MASKS

If using Photoshop and the newer versions of Elements, you'll have access to a powerful feature called Layer Masks. They function in a similar way to the Eraser tool, but instead of deleting areas of an image, a Mask will just hide it from view. This allows you to bring areas back later, if you want to. To do this, highlight Layer 1 in your Layers palette and at the bottom click on the Add Layer Mask icon (it looks like a grey box with a white circle inside). This will bring up a white box next to your image thumbnail. To hide areas of your image, follow the directions as if you were using the Eraser tool, but instead use the Brush tool with your Foreground colour set to Black. if you make a mistake, switch the foreground colour to White and paint back over it to remove it.

5 CLEAN UP WITH ERASER TOOL The last step is to double-check you haven't missed any areas in your erasing. Have a good look around the image for any parts of the top Layer you may have missed with the Eraser tool first time round. To help, hold the Ctrl key and click on the thumbnail of Layer 1 in your Layers palette. This will select any pixels on that Layer, so if there are any islands of marching ants within your image you've missed a bit! Press Ctrl+D to deselect, then choose the Eraser tool again, setting it to a soft brush of 100px and its Opacity to 100%, then paint over the parts you've missed. Finally, go to Layer>Flatten Image to complete your picture, but make sure you don't save over the original! Go to File>Save As... and give it a new name, then click ok.

EXPERT ADVICE

USING THE TRANSFORM COMMAND

The Transform command is a really powerful tool for this technique as it can be used to resize, rotate or flip an image to better fit in with the background pic. If you are enlarging with the Transform command, try not to go over about 150% of its original size or you'll start to lose clarity and sharpness as Photoshop uses interpolation to create the new pixels.

The key to making this technique a success lies in choosing the right images to work with. These may be photos you've shot with the specific idea of blending together later, or ones you've had stashed away on your hard drive – what's important is that they're shot in similar lighting and with a similar focusing set up.

When visualising how the shots will blend, think about where you want the added subject to go and how the lighting looks; if the shadows in each picture are going in different directions, it's always going to look fake. Similarly with the focus; if you put a sharp subject in an area surrounded by blur, people will instantly know that everything is not as it seems. And don't feel limited to using just two images – if they're consistent in lighting and focus you can use as many different ones as you like.

Don't enlarge your pics too much or you'll lose quality.

PROCESSING TECHNIQUE
MAKING A COLLAGE

Collages are quick and easy with Adobe Lightroom and a great way to present your holiday pics. Lightroom is so much more than just a RAW converter. There's a veritable smörgåsbord of pre-sets and templates to make your post-processing life so much easier and it has the perfect solution to sorting those holiday snaps in the shape of the often overlooked Print module.

As its name suggests, this is where you ready images for printing, but it's capable of a whole lot more. Using its page templates, you can create greeting cards, contact sheets and triptychs in seconds, and even make your own templates using a wealth of custom settings. As always, this module can be as simple or as complicated to use as you like, so to get started try this basic pre-set and a few simple drag-and-drop operations.

TO THIS

FROM THIS

TIP

HOW TO CHOOSE THE RIGHT IMAGES

Chances are you've returned from your hols with hundreds of shots – portraits, views, group shots and so on. Try to choose a variety of images that tell a story, and think about which way faces are pointing when you lay them out in your chosen Lightroom template.

1 IMPORT IMAGES Edit and save the images you'd like to include in your collage – it doesn't matter whether they're edited in Photoshop or Elements, as you can import JPEGs into Lightroom. Group them together in a folder and import into Lightroom by selecting the Library module and clicking the Import button. To whittled your selection down further rate the images by how you think they'll work best as part of a set.

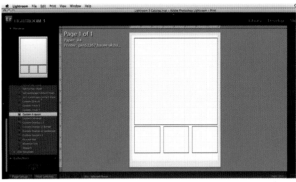

2 SELECT PRINT MODULE In the top right-hand corner of Lightroom's main interface you'll find five modules – Library, Develop, Slideshow, Print and Web (plus Map and Book modules if you have Lightroom 4). Select the Print option. You should now see a sheet of A4 paper in the centre of the interface and a number of options on the left-hand side, including Template Browser and Collections.

3 CHOOSE A TEMPLATE Click on the arrow next to Template Browser and again on the one next to Lightroom Templates. This will open a lengthy list of pre-sets. Take a minute to scroll through them – here the 'Custom 4 square' template was used, but choose whichever template suits your needs. The sheet of A4 paper will change according to which template you click on.

4 DRAG AND DROP IMAGES Once you've chosen your template, simply drag and drop your images onto the blank squares or rectangles on the A4 sheet. The images will instantly 'snap' into place. If you've chosen a template with square insets and your images are rectangular, you'll need to fine-tune their placement. Hold down the Cmd key (the cursor will turn into a hand) and drag the image left, right, up or down as needed.

5 ADD PHOTO BORDER If you're happy with your layout, simply hit Print in the bottom right-hand corner. If you'd like to add a classy border effect, tick the Photo Border box in the top right-hand corner and drag the Width slider to the right to increase the gap between image and stroke (the thin black border). Note that this will affect all images. Here the photographer chose to keep the original borders.

6 CHANGE BACKGROUND COLOUR You can also change the colour of the page to complement your images. Tick the Page Background Color box in the right-hand menu and click on the small swatch box to open the colour picker window. Drag the right-hand slider up and down to change the colours and tones to suit. Again, this is very much a question of taste. Clean, crisp and white worked well for the background here.

Essential Accessories

IF THERE'S ONE ESSENTIAL TRUISM that all photographers should learn early on, it's the fact that you don't need lots of expensive kit to take great photographs. In the right hands, even the most basic DSLR and lens combination can be used to take a thoughtful, emotive, high-impact image. Look at examples of great photography in art galleries the world over and you'll realize that it's the idea behind the picture, and its successful execution, that really count.

However, there is a slight proviso to all this. While your DSLR can be considered the main workhorse in putting your ideas into practice, there are certain accessories that will help. Think of them as photographic allies, making it easier to communicate your great ideas.

Some accessories, such as tripods and filters, will help you refine your picture taking technique to get better results. Others, such as camera bags, memory cards and sensor-cleaning kit, help you care for your DSLR and maintain it. Others still, such as computers, monitors, software and printers, help you create a "digital darkroom" at home centring on your personal computer, where you can edit your images and present them for others to enjoy.

The main thing to remember is that you don't need all these accessories straightaway. Most of the items featured in this chapter should be acquired over time, as and when your budget allows. It's better to avoid making false economies buying the cheapest "beginner-designated" accessories; invest in those which will stand the test of time, and accommodate your growth as a photographer.

Tripods

Keep the camera steady with a tripod for pin-sharp results

IF THERE'S ONE ITEM OF PHOTOGRAPHIC GEAR that always seems to get neglected, it's the tripod. You can have the best gear in the world – the latest DSLR and a bag full of pro lenses – but it's all going to be a big waste of time and money if your shots keeping coming out slightly blurred. The main culprit is camera shake, which we'll deal with in greater depth in the next chapter. Suffice it to say here that the best and most reliable way to counter camera shake is to use a tripod to help steady the camera.

Although most DSLRs these days offer some form of image stabilization technology, this can only do so much to stop camera shake. What's more, as you become more ambitious and creative with your photography, you will find a tripod is often indispensible – especially for long exposures, night-time shooting and for many remote flash set ups. Best of all, a tripod slows you down and makes you consider the image before you take it. If a shot's worth taking, it's worth getting the tripod out.

Though it's true that "the best tripod is the one you've got with you", there's actually a huge difference between tripods costing £30 and those costing £200. The shortcomings of budget tripods really aren't worth enduring if you love your photography and intend to stick at it.

A budget tripod will get you started in longer exposures, more considered composition and creative effects that demand a locked-off camera, and it'll be nice and light to carry. But it'll also have leg-locks that will eventually fail, components that will flex under pressure, critical parts that will snap off when you clonk them against rocks, and delicate threads that will eventually strip when you over-tighten them. The end result is you'll be splashing out on another tripod sooner than you think.

Buy a pro tripod and though it'll be bigger and heavier, it'll also be designed to avoid all those problems and compromises mentioned above. It'll offer more adaptability too – you're not always going to be shooting at eye-level, and a pro spec model can be positioned at various angles, both vertically and horizontally.

Though most tripods are made of aluminium, the best pro spec tripods are made of lightweight but super-strong carbon fibre, offering a high strength-to-weight ratio. Another lightweight material used for tripods is basalt rock: crushed and then melted at high temperatures, basalt fibres offer a 20% lighter alternative to aluminium. The luxury of owning a lightweight tripod like this comes at a premium; if you're serious about switching from alloy to carbon you'll need to spend an extra £100 or so for the privilege.

It may seem that a pro tripod is a pricey option, but look after it and it'll last a lifetime, unlike cheaper models that'll need to be replaced time and time again.

EXPERT ADVICE

CHOOSING A TRIPOD HEAD

ONCE YOU'VE PICKED OUT YOUR TRIPOD, next you've got to start thinking about which type of head you want to go with it, as the camera doesn't sit directly on the tripod legs.

Although it might seem expensive to buy a pro tripod with a separate head, it's actually a bonus, as it means you can choose the right head to suit your photography. There are several types of head to choose from:

■ **Ball and socket.** Landscape photographers swear by these as they allow complete manoeuvrability in all directions and normally feature a single locking mechanism. This makes a ball head very quick to use out in the field. They're also quite compact – ideal if you're going to carry the tripod around all day. The downside is that they're not suited to panning and precise adjustments.

■ **Pan and tilt/three-way.** As the name suggests, these have three adjustments for vertical, horizontal and side-to-side control.

These are slower to use than a ball and socket heads, but the three individual controls offer plenty of precision, as each one can be locked off independently, making it ideal for subjects such as macro and still life and also for panning shots. Whereas a ball head is compact, a three-way, with its handles, is more cumbersome.

■ **Panoramic.** Specialist professional tripod head designed for shooting smooth panoramic sequences. These tripod heads allow you to position the lens's "nodal point" above the axis of rotation, helping the sequence of images to align correctly.

■ **Quick-release plate.** If you're taking your camera on and off the tripod a fair bit, a quick-release plate is very handy. Rather than having to screw the camera back onto the tripod every time you want to use it, simply screw the quick-release plate to the camera's bottom and it'll snap on and off the tripod as and when you need it.

WHAT TO LOOK FOR... TRIPODS

CONSTRUCTION
Most tripods are aluminium construction, though carbon fibre and basalt models are available.

STANDARD OR WIDE SPREAD
As well as having a standard leg angle of around 30°, there should also be options for wider spreads for ultra low-angle shooting.

CENTRE COLUMN
For added shooting flexibility, the centre column should be able to be shortened, reversed and positioned horizontally, too.

$^3/_8$IN STUD
$^3/_8$in is the standard thread for a pro tripod head. If the tripod has a $^1/_4$in stud (as on the base of a camera), it's an amateur tripod and will be limited in scope.

LEG LOCKS
Most tripods extend by three or four telescopic sections. The leg locks should be quick and easy to operate and, once locked, should not slip under load.

CLOSED LENGTH
A compact closed length is always an advantage, whether it's for storage, comfortable carrying or stowing away in the boot of your car.

LEG WARMERS
These pad your shoulder to add comfort when carrying the tripod, and if it's really chilly, also protect your hands from the cold aluminium.

SEALED LOWER LEGS
You'll often need to stand the lower leg sections in water, so look for sealed lower legs that won't hold water then leak it all over your car boot later.

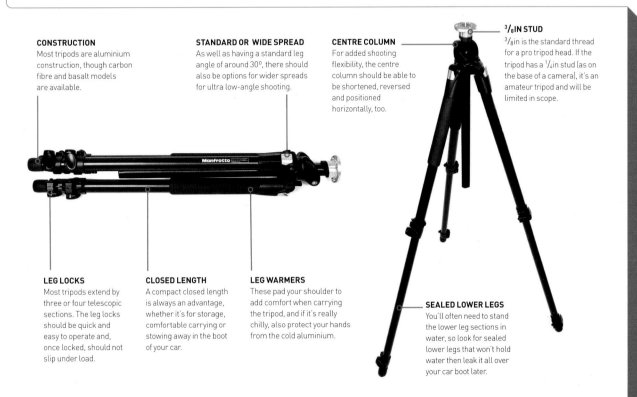

Filters

Use filters to control exposure

WHAT YOU'LL LEARN
CONTROL EXPOSURES
WITH AN ND GRAD;
BOOST COLOURS
WITH A POLARIZER

THE NEUTRAL DENSITY GRAD OR ND GRAD is a useful tool for balancing landscape exposures where the sky is much paler or brighter than the land below. The filters come in a range of strengths, commonly reducing the light from the sky by one, two or three stops, to suit different lighting conditions. The most useful is the 2-stop grad, especially at sunrise or sunset.

When choosing between ND grads, you can opt for either hard or soft-edged filters. This refers to the type of graduation between the dark and clear areas (see comparison, right). ND grads come in different strengths, but different manufacturers use different numbering systems. The chart (shown right) compares the Cokin and Lee filters systems.

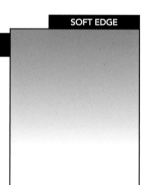

SOFT EDGE

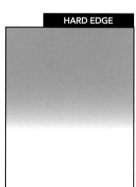

HARD EDGE

Light reduction	Cokin	Lee
1-stop	ND2	0.3
2-stop	ND4	0.6
3-stop	ND8	0.9

A 1-stop ND grad is good for reducing the contrast between sky and land, when brightness is only just beyond the capability of the camera. The 2-stop ND grad is more versatile as an all-rounder.

GET THE GRAD EFFECT, DIGITALLY

EVEN IF YOU DON'T HAVE ANY ND GRAD FILTERS, it's possible to get a similar effect in one exposure by shooting RAW images. Because these files contain more highlight and shadow detail than JPEGs, you can adjust the exposure when you process them, creating two images (one at 1 stop under, the other at 1 stop over, see below) then combining them again to create a final image with more detail in the sky.

As you only shoot one image, you don't risk encountering any subject movement between exposures.

Combining two images from the same RAW file has the advantage of allowing you to mask specific areas. This means you can deal with complicated and intricate detail separately. The downside is that all this image manipulation takes more time than simply slipping a filter over the lens.

1 STOP UNDER

+

1 STOP OVER

=

RETAIN SKY WITH AN ND GRAD

ND graduated filters are half grey and half clear – the darker half cuts down the amount of light reaching the sensor, while the clear half allows all the light through. Simply by positioning the dark half of the filter over the brightest part of the scene (usually the sky), you can retain extra detail in your landscapes.

The effect of a soft-edged grad is less obvious than a hard-edged one, making it better for scenes where objects such as trees, mountains or buildings cross the horizon. A hard-edged grad is better suited to subjects where the horizon is clearly defined, such as seascapes.

WITHOUT ND GRAD

WITH ND GRAD

1 ATTACH THE HOLDER Almost all ND grads are square and can be slotted into a special holder (shown above). This fits over the front of the lens via an adapter, rather than screwing directly into the lens. Most filter holders have two or more slots, allowing you to use several filters at the same time, but you should always use the slot nearest the lens for your ND grad. Getting the filter as close to the lens as possible ensures that the filter effect remains out of focus, so makes it less likely that you'll be able to see the transition between the dark and clear areas of the filter.

2 ASSESS EXPOSURE Do this before you fit the ND grad into the holder. The most reliable and accurate way of getting the exposure right is to set the camera to manual exposure mode, and then point the camera down so that the foreground fills the frame. Set the desired aperture, then take your meter reading and select the shutter speed according to the conditions.

Once you have set the exposure you can then re-frame the image and place the camera on a tripod, but keep the same shutter speed and aperture settings.

3 ALIGN THE FILTER This is where it becomes clear why most ND grad filters are the square, slot-in design. Unlike a round screw-in filter, using a filter holder allows you to gently slide the filter up and down so that the transition between the dark and clear areas of the filter are correctly aligned with your subject. For many landscapes this transition will need to be positioned along the horizon. It can be tricky to see the position of the transition, so take a little time and slowly move the filter down so that the dark area just covers the sky, but doesn't mask any of the land or water below the horizon.

4 TILT THE FILTER Although the transition is usually positioned horizontally along the horizon of your image, sometimes the change between the light and darker areas is at a different angle. The most common example of this is when mountains, cliffs or trees obscure the horizon, but it can also occur when a large area of the image is in shadow, while the rest is in bright sunlight. In these situations you may need to tilt the filter holder to align with this change between the light and dark areas of the image. Using the same technique as before, slide the filter down to position it correctly.

Flashguns

Moving on from pop-up flash

WHAT YOU'LL LEARN
TYPES OF FLASH;
GUIDE NUMBERS;
FLASH ACCESSORIES
AND TRIGGERS

LIGHT IS PHOTOGRAPHY'S MOST ESSENTIAL INGREDIENT, so if there's not enough natural illumination for a shot you'll need to generate it artificially. One of the most useful and versatile ways to do this is with flash and it comes in several guises, from the neat little pop-up devices built in to your camera to accessory flashguns and studio flash units.

Pop-up flash can be a really powerful tool and a great introduction to the world of artificial light. Units are small, compact, portable and always attached to your DSLR just in case you need a quick blip of additional "fill-in" light. Because they are built into the camera, they're compatible with the camera's own automatic exposure metering system and you can access all manner of useful flash techniques – there's more about this in the next chapter.

However, if you want to take things further in terms of power, features and functionality, you'll need to buy an accessory flashgun – a great compromise between the ease of pop-up flash and studio flash heads, which are often simply too big and cumbersome for convenient everyday use.

Accessory flashguns represent a step-up in performance over pop-up flash, offering quicker recycle times and a greater number of continuous flash bursts. They also offer more versatility because they can be used either attached to your camera via the hotshoe, fired off-camera via a flash-sync cord, or triggered remotely by radio or infrared signal (see opposite page). The advantage of using off-camera flash, instead of keeping the flashgun mounted direct on top of your camera, is that it gives you more control over the way light falls on your subject, with the strength and spread of the light modifiable using a wide selection of diffusers or softboxes, available to buy separately.

Plus, unlike the fixed position of a pop-up flash, the burst of light from a flashgun can be directed up or down or side-to-side, thanks to their "bounce" and "swivel" design.

The main advantage flashguns offer over pop-up flash is greater power, described in terms of a "Guide Number". The greater the number, the more powerful the flash.

CHOOSING A FLASHGUN

Top-of-the-range flashguns can cost as much as a decent fast lens, but most people like to keep a reasonable lid on their flashgun budget, and it's entirely possible to get a great, versatile flashgun for half the price of the top spec models.

First thing to consider is that a flashgun has to be compatible with your camera system. So, just like lenses, a Nikon flash won't work on a Canon camera. This is because each camera's unique metering system needs to work in tandem with the flashgun, to set the correct flash exposure. You do have some choice between own-brand and third-party options however – many of them offering a viable alternative to your manufacturer's own flashgun, full automatic metering compatibility, plus a number of remote triggering options too.

WHAT TO LOOK FOR... FLASHGUNS

WIDEANGLE DIFFUSER
Pulls out and sits over the flash head to disperse the burst of light when shooting with wideangle lenses.

AF ASSIST BEAM
Emits a beam of light to help your camera focus in low-light conditions.

BOUNCE AND SWIVEL
Angle the flash light away from the subject for more natural results.

LCD SCREEN
Navigate the menus and change flash mode or power settings using the LCD screen on the rear.

HOTSHOE FOOT
Metal ones are more durable than plastic ones and the lock will ensure the flashgun is secure on the hotshoe.

FLASHGUN ACCESSORIES

Most flashgun accessories are designed to mimic the effects achievable with professional studio flash, only on a smaller scale. Many of the pitfalls of using on-camera flash – harsh, directional, frontal lighting that casts a stark black shadow on nearby backdrops – can be avoided by using bounce flash or diffusing accessories. The other more complex accessories – snoots, barndoors, honeycomb grids – are chiefly designed to modify the flash burst by channelling and directing it for more sculptural, three-dimensional effects.

It's worth noting however that flash accessories can reduce the amount of light reaching the subject, so it's best to conduct a test shoot first to check your camera's automatic metering sustem takes account of the drop in light or compensate by adding +1-2 stops exposure accordingly.

REMOTE TRIGGERS

Off-camera flash or "strobism" has become hugely popular in portrait and action photography. Here, vivid colours, bold shadows and theatrical lighting effects are achieved through the use of multiple flashguns or "strobes" placed carefully around a subject, allowing the photographer to take total control of the lighting.

Supporting, positioning and triggering the flash once it's off the camera present a number of dilemmas – tripod-style stands are available with flash hotshoe connectors, but when it comes to triggering your remote flash there are five main ways to do it:

1 **Flash sync cord.** This fits directly into your camera's hotshoe at one end and, via a length of coiled cable, provides a mount for your flashgun at the other end. This system can support multiple flashes but will need a host of cables, adapters and splitters to do so. TTL (Through the Lens) metering is preserved and no batteries are required, but your working range is restricted by the length of the cable.

2 **Optical or "slave" trigger.** Small and simple to operate, an optical flash trigger works by sensing the increase in light intensity caused by a flash or other light source as it fires and, in turn, responds by triggering the flash it is attached to. Often comprising a combined shoe mount and tripod thread block, with a hotshoe mount, these handy little items are often not a lot bigger than a sugar cube. The main downside here is that the flash response can be erratic in bright outdoor conditions, and can be triggered by the pulse of light emitted by your main flashgun when assessing exposure.

3 **Manufacturer's own wireless systems.** Most mid- to higher-end DSLRs have a built-in system to fire flashes off-camera using a "commander" flash unit. The majority of systems work using an infrared signal sent from either the camera's pop-up flash or the commander unit. You'll usually get full control of the flashes, including power adjustment, but you'll be limited to using flashes manufactured for your specific system.

4 **eBay-style trigger/receiver kits.** These are widely available from numerous online retailers and come in a variety of shapes, sizes and brand names. These are inexpensive, compact and compatible with a huge range of cameras. The price and compatibility of these kits makes them an attractive option, along with the ability to mix and match flashguns.

5 **Pro-style trigger/receiver kits.** Pocket Wizards, Radiopoppers and Elinchrom Skyports systems allow a high level of control, and some even support wireless TTL and power control from the DSLR's own commander unit. Pop the transmitter into your camera's hotshoe, attach the receiver to the flashgun, and you're ready to go. Controlling the flash may require a bit of trial-and-error if working manually. As a cost-effective approach, use cheap, secondhand flashguns and work in Manual mode.

EXPERT ADVICE

MODIFY YOUR FLASH

A wide range of accessories exists to help modify the burst of light from your flashgun.

■ **Softboxes:** these are fabric boxes which enfold the flashgun, with a layer of diffusing fabric between light source and subject to soften and spread the light more evenly.

■ **Diffusers:** usually of plastic or fabric construction, these soften harsh shadows and reduce "hot spot" flash highlights.

■ **Filter gels:** can be fixed over the front of the flashgun to light a scene or backdrop in colour.

Left: LumiQuest's Soft Screen – a diffuser for DSLR's own built in pop-up flash.

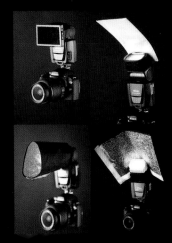

■ **Bounce cards:** these help bounce light from your flashgun, avoiding harsh and unflattering effects of directional on-camera flash and creating a softer and more even illumination.

■ **Barndors, snoots, honeycomb grids:** all designed to help channel the flash into a tighter beam, ideal for lighting backdrops. low key and fill-in effects

■ **Beauty dishes:** these will diffuse the flashgun's burst for soft, even lighting.

Left: a selection of Interfit's Strobie flashgun accessories.

Image storage and monitors

Accessories to store and view images

WITH DIGITAL CAMERAS OFFERING EVER-INCREASING resolution, there's a corresponding increase in the size of image files and electronic data to store. It's not so long ago that standard PC hard drives were around 10GB in capacity; you can now capture that amount of data in a few days' shooting. Add to that any other data you want to store and before long, even large-capacity hard drives will clog up.

A portable external hard drive allows you to store all your electronic data away from the internal hard drive, freeing up valuable space so software programs such as Photoshop can run more smoothly. They also have the added flexibility of allowing you to transport precious digital files around and accessing or modifying them wherever you are.

> **WHAT YOU'LL LEARN**
> STORING IMAGES ON A PORTABLE HARDDRIVE

PORTABLE EXTERNAL HARD DRIVES
There are plenty of good reasons why a portable external hard drive is an essential piece of kit: its smart design and technology means it'll hold incredible amounts of data so you'll be able to store all your files in a small, slick unit that takes up a tiny amount of desk or shelf space. And, because a portable drive draws power from your computer's USB port – not the mains – there are no bulky cables or power supply units to carry around, either.

It's never a good idea to move a hard drive while the disk is spinning as it's like playing Russian roulette with your data, but some portable drives offer features such as shock absorbers and armoured shells to provide extra protection. This is ideal if you work across multiple computers; perhaps a laptop on location and a desktop at home, because you'll really improve your digital workflow by having the same saved version of your images with you at all times.

BACKING-UP FILES
Portable hard drives are a cost effective and efficient way of backing-up your image files, too. Bearing in mind the relative fragility of electronic equipment, it's prudent to have at least two copies of irreplaceable images. Splashing out on two external hard drives may seem like a bit of an extravagance, but it really is a sensible back-up solution if one hard drive fails. Back-up software solutions, which save a copy of your entire system into compressed data files, will often come bundled with external hard drives. While these are great for creating a restore point in case your whole computer fails, when it comes to backing up image files we recommend ignoring the back-up software and just manually saving your images over at least two drives.

FORMATTING AND PARTITIONS
Many portable drives are pre-formatted "plug and play" devices that you connect up and start using, but some may need formatting. Formatting wipes all the data and sets what file structure the drive uses to store data. The most common file structures are currently FAT32 (File Allocation Table 32), NTFS (NT File System) or HFS+ (Hierarchical File System). If you're running Windows then format using the NTFS file structure. This is more secure for PCs but doesn't work fully on Apple Macs. Apple has developed HFS+ for Macs but it doesn't work on PCs, so if you need to share your portable hard drive across platforms, opt for FAT32 that works on both. FAT32 is limited to 32GB if formatted through Windows but you can create disk partitions to split the drive into several 32GB sections or use the Disk Utility on a Mac and select the MS–DOS File System that creates a single FAT32 partition.

BUYING ADVICE
HARD DRIVES

LOWER CAPACITY OPTION
If you think 500GB of storage is more than you'll ever need, it might make more sense to invest in a couple of smaller drives. Most models on the market come in a variety of smaller sizes and lower capacities.

MEGA CAPACITY OPTION
Mammoth 2TB (that's 2000GB) mirror drives provide plenty of space to save duplicate copies of your image files and back-up your entire computer. What's more, they'll automatically create a mirror copy of data to a partition, too.

ULTRA DURABLE OPTION
Body armour will protect the outer shell of your portable hard drive against serious bumps and knocks. If you think you'll give the drive some serious hard knocks, consider ultra-durable hard drives such as Lacie's "Rugged" design.

MONITORS

Your monitor is the most important component in your "digital darkroom" home printing set-up. If you want to produce the best results from your images, a good monitor is crucial. Conversely, a bad monitor will hamper you at every turn, because the poor colours, lack of detail and flat tonal range will lead to making poor decisions when you're editing your pictures.

Advancements in technology mean the old-style Cathode Ray Tube (CRT) monitors are fast disappearing in favour of Liquid Crystal Display (LCD) screens. The latter don't have a bulky cathode ray tube to accommodate, so you can have a much larger screen without taking up all the desk space behind it. LCD monitors are also easier on the eyes, leading to less fatigue if you're working on an image for some hours.

Colour calibration of your monitor is also less of an issue with modern LCD screens, the best of which will often represent colours faithfully straight out of the box, without having to download profiles or buy extra calibration tools.

Screen sizes are measured like a TV screen – diagonally. Widescreen monitors are popular as they allow plenty of room for your images, plus space for creative palettes when editing.

MONITOR JARGON BUSTER

VGA (VIDEO GRAPHICS ARRAY)
Also referred to as D-SUB or RGB, this was the common way of connecting Cathode Ray Tubes (CRTs). Less popular with LCDs as it only carries a lower quality analogue signal.

DVI (DIGITAL VISUAL INTERFACE)
Monitors connected via DVI require no compression to the digital signal sent by the computer and therefore the quality of the image is superior to VGA.

HDMI (HIGH DEFINITION MULTIMEDIA INTERFACE)
An alternative to DVI for sending an uncompressed digital signal. Not yet standard, but some graphics cards now include HDMI.

GRAPHICS CARD
A piece of PC hardware that sends the signal to your screen. Graphics cards can have a range of sockets including VGA, DVI and HDMI.

NATIVE RESOLUTION
The recommended optimum resolution setting. LCDs cannot scale images as well as CRTs and attempting to run one at a non-native resolution can lead to blurring around images.

PIXEL PITCH
Also known as Dot Pitch, it is the distance between colour elements in adjacent pixels. Generally, the smaller the Dot Pitch, the sharper the image.

RESPONSE TIME
How quickly a monitor reacts to changes, measured by how long it takes for pixels to change from white to black and back again. Less important for static pics, but crucial for smooth video.

CONTRAST RATIO
The variance between black and white pixels in the display. In theory, the higher the contrast ratio the wider the tonal range, but there are varying ways to measure this and environmental factors such as reflected light can lower the quoted ratio.

STANDARD RATIO

WIDESCREEN RATIO

HDMI cables carry an uncompressed digital signal for audio and video.

A DVI cable is currently a common way of connecting LCD monitors.

A VGA cable transmits an analogue signal mainly used on CRT monitors.

With widescreen LCDs, use a 16:10 aspect ratio resolution, such as 1920 x 1200, to avoid problems with distorted images.

Optional extras

More handy little gadgets

THERE ARE HUNDREDS, PERHAPS THOUSANDS of gadgets and gizmos for photographers to use – from basic things like photographers' fingerless gloves, raincovers and kneeling mats to sophisticated flash triggers, GPS recording devices and radio remote control camera handsets. Step into any major camera shop and you'll be amazed at the ingenuity of manufacturers in helping us part with our hard-earned cash!

Some of the most useful devices are those which will protect and maintain your DSLR, and provide back-up image storage and battery power. Gadgets such as sensor-cleaning wands, lens wipes, memory cards, spare batteries and/or a spare charged battery are worth keeping in your camera bag at all times and are worth their weight in gold.

Also useful are a chamois leather (for wiping rain or salt sea spray off your lens) and a large black plastic bin liner (for lying down on or putting your bag on in muddy conditions). If you're holidaying abroad, a travel adapter plug will be invaluable too, plus your battery-recharging equipment. It has often been said that it's worth taking two of everything in case one of them breaks, but this is taking caution to the extreme. At some point you just have to take pot luck.

Beyond the core essentials, it's the little things that successful photographers often swear by: a hotshoe-mounted spirit level to keep horizons straight; a foldaway reflector to bounce sunlight onto a shaded foreground subject; an 18% grey card to help take exposure readings in tricky lighting conditions. Rootle around in a professional photographer's camera bag and you may be surprised by the unconventional and sometimes homemade gizmos that lie within: bull-dog clips, duck tape, rubber bands, petroleum jelly. We've even heard of photographers making flash accessories out of drinking straws! Of course, we haven't been able to feature all these gadgets here, but this is a small selection of the most useful "unsung heros" to keep in your gadget bag.

MACRO FLASHGUN
Macro flashguns like this are ideal for photographing small subjects in fine detail, providing a bright but shadowless light from dual flash tubes, one either side of the lens (not to be confused with ring flash). With this Sigma model you can also set the flash tubes to fire separately, so the subject casts a shadow and looks three-dimensional.

CIRCULAR POLARIZER
Attach a polarizing filter to your lens and rotate it against the plane-polarized light to cut through non-metallic reflections and glare off sky, water, glass and foliage. Its effect is to darken blue skies against white clouds and make colours look more richly saturated. Works best when orientating the filter at 90° to the sun's axis. Be sure to buy a filter with the correct filter thread (diameter) for your lens.

SPIRIT LEVEL
Fitting a spirit level into the camera's hotshoe before you shoot a landscape or seascape is the surest way to guard against a wonky horizon, thus saving you precious time straightening your horizons in Photoshop. This digital spirit level by Seculine fits just above the viewfinder, and literally gives you a green light as soon as the view is all straight and perpendicular.

GPS MODULE
Nikon's Global Positioning System unit attaches to compatible Nikon DSLR cameras in the camera's accessory sh[...] on the top plate, recording location information in the image data EXIF file. Data such as latitude, longitude, altitud[...] and time are automatically recorded – a[...] powered direct by the camera body. Th[...] is a huge boon to travel photographers when captioning images by location.

SPARE BATTERIES
It's always helpful to have more power to hand by keeping a ready-charged spare battery in your camera bag. Keep a spare battery charger in your luggage when you travel too, complete with travel adapter compatible with overseas plug sockets.

SPARE MEMORY CARD
It pays to keep a few spare memory cards to hand when holidaying abroad or out shooting on location. There are lots of different types and makes – CompactFlash (CF), Secure Digital (SD/SDHC), Mini and Micro SD, Memory Stick, Smart Media and xD cards. They offer different amounts of storage capacity, measured in gigabytes (GB).

SUN COMPASS
When making a reconnaissance trip on location, it can be hard to visualize where the sun will be at sunrise and sunset, and thus work out the best time of day to return. This sun compass from Flight Logistics gives all sunrise and sunset positions throughout the year – a huge help for travel and landscape subjects.

SENSOR-CLEANING WAND
Dust and dirt on your camera's sensor lead to marks and smudges on your images that can be a real nuisance to remove in Photoshop. It's a good idea to invest in a sensor-cleaning brush such as the Arctic Butterfly. Simply give it a whizz to generate static on the filaments then switch off before giving the sensor a gentle wipe over.

REMOTE CONTROL HANDSET

Invest in the correct remote control handset for your camera and you'll be able to take self-portraits and include yourself in group shots, triggering the camera from the posing position instead of from beside or behind the camera. Used in conjunction with the Mirror Lock-Up function on your DSLR, a remote control handset such as this Sigma device can also reduce the possibility of camera shake.

UNDERWATER HOUSING

Shooting underwater is an exciting proposition – not least for the sense of thrill you get as you gently submerge your precious DSLR under the waves... Make sure you invest in a guaranteed water-tight housing like this one from Ewa-Marine that's especially designed for your camera and gives you full control over its functions. Check the depth you can take the housing to, as well as which lenses and flashgun will fit.

POCKET WIZARD

This handy Pocket Wizard radio-controlled system from enables wireless flash triggering for off-camera TTL flash or manual remote control of flash zones. Slip the radio transmitter into the camera's hotshoe and attach the receiver(s) to your remote flashguns – the system will even work round corners. (See page 41 for more).

SILVER AND GOLD REFLECTORS

These are useful for adding warmth to outdoor portraits, bouncing the available light onto a shaded part of the subject. Look for a large fabric reflector design that can be folded away neatly. Silver reflectors provide a bright "zing" of light in dull conditions, while gold reflectors will warm up the light.

TRAVEL TRIPOD

When luggage space and weight are restricted on overseas flights, a small but sturdy tripod alternative such as the Joby Gorillapod proves a useful ally in combating camera shake on holiday. Its flexible bendy legs allow you to wrap the tripod around railings, chair backs and benches to secure a higher viewpoint – very helpful for night and other low-light scenes.

10-STOP ND FILTER

Landscape photographers are always using Neutral Density grads of various strengths (see page 34) to help balance exposures between land and sky. This type of ND filter works in a slightly different way – deliberately reducing the amount of light entering the lens in order to achieve long exposures even in broad daylight. For instance it can blur waves to mist or make people "disappear" in a busy street scene.

COLOUR CHECKER

Specifically designed for digital photographers, this colour calibration tool will help you keep your colours true. Take a test shot of the checker in the same shooting conditions as your subject and you can then check and compare the digital reproduction of the real scene and maintain a neutral colour balance, even in mixed lighting.

EXPERT ADVICE

LENSBABY

A Lensbaby is a creative optical device that fits onto the camera like a conventional lens, but which can be manipulated to alter the focusing point and depth of field. In principle it works in the same way that a specialist tilt and shift lens or bellows attachment might be used, twisting and angling the front element independently from the camera's focal plane (where the sensor sits). Such manipulations are impossible with conventional lenses because they have a rigid lens barrel, rather than the flexible one here. When the front element is angled away from the focal plane you can isolate the focus on one specific plane or "sweet spot", with blurred areas graduating away from it.

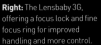

Right: The Lensbaby 3G, offering a focus lock and fine focus ring for improved handling and more control.

CORE CAMERA SKILLS

ONCE YOU'VE SET YOURSELF up with a basic DSLR and standard zoom lens, it's time to learn how to use them. Although in theory you could simply switch the camera's exposure mode dial to "Auto" and start snapping away, it's actually far more rewarding to fully understand what's going on inside the camera – in fact, it's the only way you'll ever progress as a creative photographer. Chiefly you need to know how through-the-lens (TTL) light readings are made, what sort of errors can occur and why, what the aperture and shutter speed do in order to make exposures, and how they relate to things like ISO speed, image sharpness and subject movement. You also need to be able to recognize the tell-tale signs of under- and over-exposure, and understand how to correct the problem.

Armed with just a modicum of knowledge about the first principles of photography you will soon be making correct exposures and assessing them on your camera's LCD screen, working out how to improve composition and heighten visual impact.

Of course, the great thing about digital cameras is that you can experiment with exposure and composition to your heart's content, without spending any money on processing those images that don't work. Instant image playback on your LCD screen allows you to review images just seconds after taking them, so you're still in the right place to shoot the scene again and correct any mistakes as you go.

Master the basics

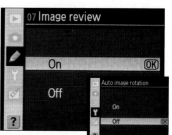

Learn how to set up the camera

DELVE INTO THE MENU OF ANY DSLR and you'll uncover a bewildering array of options and settings to choose between. From the ISO speed setting to white balance and in-camera colour saturation, it can all sound a bit daunting. But don't let this first impression put you off – we'll be learning about all these settings in detail later in this chapter. First, let's take a look at some of the basic settings to help you get started. Don't worry if they don't look exactly like the menus below – every camera differs in menu layout, but the settings work in exactly the same way.

WHAT YOU'LL LEARN
USEFUL SETTINGS TO
GET YOU STARTED

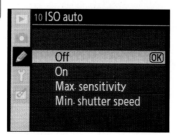

ISO SPEED
This controls how sensitive the camera is to light. The higher the ISO setting, the more sensitive it is, so the less light you need to take photos. Some DSLRs default to an automatic ISO setting, which you'll need to turn off if you're going to start taking full control of your camera. On most models, selecting one of the ISO values such as 100 or 200 is all you need to do. On some cameras you can also disable the automatic setting in the Custom Function menu.

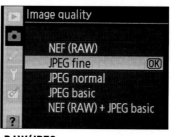

RAW/JPEG
To practise most of the techniques and projects in this chapter you should set the camera to record in JPEG mode. This means that all of the changes that you make on your camera will be applied directly to the images you produce. To set your camera to JPEG mode, go to the Image Quality setting and choose the highest quality JPEG option available. We'll cover the advantages and disadvantages of RAW and JPEG files on page 86.

IMAGE REVIEW
The ability to see your results instantly on the back of the camera is one of the most useful features of your DSLR. Of the options available, there are two main set-ups you will find useful:
• If you want the image to be displayed immediately after you take every shot, select Image review – on and Auto image rotation – off.
• If you want to playback the images when you've finished shooting instead, select Image review – off and Auto image rotation – on.

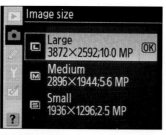

IMAGE SIZE
Many cameras give you the option of recording images at various resolutions to save space on your memory card. Although you can use the lower resolution settings to practise some of the techniques in this chapter, you'll find it better to use the highest resolution offered by the camera to help assess the quality, sharpness and ultimately the success of the results that you get.

IMAGE ADJUSTMENTS
The default setting on most DSLRs will automatically make adjustments to sharpening, saturation and tone. While this is great for general shooting, these automatic adjustments are not good when you're learning how the different settings work. So, in the Custom Function menu, change these functions so they're on the normal or unadjusted settings rather than Automatic.

BEEP
This is an audible signal to confirm your autofocus has locked onto the subject. It can also indicate other camera functions are in progress. But when you're practising your photographic skills you'll find that the continual beeping of the camera is more of an irritating distraction than a help. Turn it off by finding the relevant part of the Custom menu and selecting the Off option.

HOLD YOUR DSLR THE RIGHT WAY

It's surprising how few people know how to hold their cameras properly. Technology such as image stabilization will help you achieve sharper shots, but it's no excuse for poor technique. To learn to handle your camera like a pro, use the following checklist:

- Hold the camera in your right hand with three fingers on the handgrip, placing your index finger on the shutter button and your thumb pressed against the rear.

- With the palm of your left hand, cup the camera from underneath, freeing your index finger and thumb to control the lens's zoom and focus rings.

- Tuck in your elbows and rest them against your midriff to support your camera from below.

- Hold your breath for a second while squeezing the shutter gently, rather than jabbing at the shutter button aggressively which will jog the camera.

CORRECT HANDLING: HORIZONTAL SHOTS
By holding your DSLR like this you'll really reduce the chance of the camera moving as you press the shutter button.

CORRECT HANDLING: VERTICAL SHOTS
Hold the camera in the same way but use the "overhand" grip with your right hand at the top and left hand supporting from underneath.

INCORRECT HANDLING
You really don't want to be holding your DSLR like this because such a fragile grip on the camera body and lens is an invitation to camera shake.

LEAN ON SOMETHING
When handholding the camera (working without a tripod), look out for props that might offer extra stability. Leaning against walls or trees will help stabilize you, and railings or fences can be used to support your camera directly. Any of these options will help to give sharper pics, so before shooting, see if there's a support nearby.

USE A TRIPOD
The age-old and perfect way to prevent camera shake is to use your three-legged friend! A sturdy tripod may feel awkward as a constant companion, but stick with it and it'll soon become second nature. If you don't have one yet, invest in a pro-quality model – it'll last you a lifetime if you look after it.

Using the mode dial

Get to grips with the semi-automatic exposure modes

THE LARGE CIRCULAR MODE DIAL on top of your camera is one of the first controls you'll notice. The dial lies at the very heart of the creative options of your DSLR, and it's here that you can start to take control over key aspects of picture taking, such as the aperture and shutter speed settings, when making exposures.

Selecting new settings can be pretty daunting at first, but with a little practice you'll find that this one dial will open up a whole new realm of photographic skills.

So, if you've never ventured off the fully automatic settings before, here's what each letter means and how you can use them for better picture taking.

WHAT YOU'LL LEARN HOW THE MODE DIAL WORKS; AUTO MODES TO AVOID

MANUAL MODE

With this mode you have to set both aperture and shutter speed yourself. Because of this it's probably best to leave this mode until you've mastered the controls in the semi-automatic modes.

APERTURE-PRIORITY

Usually indicated by A or Av (Aperture value), this semi-automatic mode allows you to select the aperture manually, but tells the camera to automatically select the appropriate shutter speed to make a correct exposure. This gives you control over the amount of the image that will be in sharp focus, known as depth of field.

SHUTTER-PRIORITY

Usually indicated by T or Tv (Time value), this semi-automatic mode allows you to select the shutter speed manually but tells the camera to automatically select the correct aperture. This gives you control over how subject movement is recorded – whether frozen sharp or allowed to blur. It also helps you to avoid camera shake.

PROGRAM MODE

This mode is similar to Full Auto mode, in that it sets the shutter speed and aperture automatically, but does allow you a little more creative control. On most cameras you have control over settings such as exposure compensation and autofocus, plus you also have limited control over the combination of shutter speed and aperture the camera will use. Although this gives you some control, it's still not ideal when you're learning about photography.

SCENE MODES

These fully automatic modes are normally indicated on the mode dial by small icons showing different photo subjects (here we've got sport, macro, landscapes and portraits in daylight and at night-time). They're popular with many DSLR users as they offer the most foolproof way of getting appropriate settings for a whole range of subjects, without having to think about it. Instead, using these modes instructs the camera to select subject-specific values for shutter speed and aperture etc, according to how the manufacturer has programmed the camera. If you want to learn more about photography, it's best to avoid them.

FULL AUTO MODE

This mode is usually indicated by the word Auto or A on the dial, or a setting highlighted in green. In this mode the camera takes control of most of the exposure settings for you, so you can't direct proceedings. Some models also lock settings such as the autofocus, ISO and exposure compensation. Although the mode is great for happy snaps, if you want to learn how to control exposure it's best to avoid using Auto mode from now on.

APERTURE-PRIORITY

This is probably the most useful semi-automatic mode to master when you're learning how exposure settings affect your images. This mode gives you control over the size of aperture used to take your images, which has a major effect on the amount of the image that is in sharp focus from near to far away. This is known as controlling the depth of field – one of the key skills that will make your images more creative and eyecatching.

Move the mode dial to the A or Av position and point your DSLR at a subject. Press the shutter release button halfway down until the display illuminates in the viewfinder and the autofocus lens brings the subject into pin-sharp focus. Turn the aperture input dial (usually found on the right-hand grip), while looking through the viewfinder or at the LCD. As you turn the input dial you'll see the f-numbers change. These are your aperture settings, given in increments known as f/stops.

In this mode the correct corresponding shutter speed is automatically selected according to the aperture you select, so with the metering switched on you'll also notice the shutter speed changes as you turn the dial, too.

Thanks to the semi-automatic nature of this mode, you can avoid under- and over-exposure, so try taking two pictures of the same subject at apertures f/2.8 and f/22, then compare the results.

SHUTTER-PRIORITY

After experimenting with aperture-priority, you'll find that shutter-priority (Tv) works in a similar way. The main difference is that in this mode you're controlling the shutter speed, while the camera automatically sets the correct corresponding aperture. The length of time the shutter remains open will affect how moving subjects are recorded in your image. Remember that the shutter speed also determines whether you will be able to hold the camera steady enough to get a sharp image, or whether you'll need to steady it using a tripod.

Turn the mode dial to the S or Tv setting and this time use the input dial to alter the shutter speed. Shutter speeds are given in seconds and fractions of a second, and you can see them changing as you turn the input dial. As you change the shutter speed you will also notice that the correct corresponding apertures are set automatically by the camera.

When you scroll through all of the shutter speeds on your camera you'll see that the aperture display will change at some settings. At the faster and slower shutter speeds the aperture display will either read "Hi", "Lo" or the number will flash. This is because the range of shutter speeds is much greater than the number of apertures available on most lenses. When this happens you won't be able to use this shutter speed in the available light conditions, so you will need to select a faster or slower shutter speed.

SHALLOW DEPTH OF FIELD
With the camera set to aperture-priority, a wide aperture such as f/2.8 has the effect of minimizing depth of field and rendering only a small section of the image sharp (here, just the heather). Thanks to the semi-automatic nature of the mode, the camera will set the correct shutter speed (here, 1/160sec at ISO 100).

GREAT DEPTH OF FIELD
This time, with the camera still set to aperture-priority, selecting a narrow aperture such as f/20 has maximized depth of field. Note how the zone of sharpness extends all the way from the heather to the tree and horizon beyond. The camera simultaneously set the shutter speed to 1/15sec at ISO 100 to avoid under-exposure.

SLOW SHUTTER SPEED
With the camera set to shutter-priority you can set the shutter speed to a slow setting such as 20 seconds, to turn moving water into a soft blur. Here the camera automatically set the aperture to f/22 at ISO 100.

FAST SHUTTER SPEED
In shutter-priority mode you can select a fast, action-freezing shutter speed such as 1/250sec, while the camera sets the aperture automatically (here, f/9 at ISO 100).

Aperture, shutter speed and ISO

Understand how to make and control exposures in any situation

THE CORE COMPONENTS OF ANY EXPOSURE are light and time. These two variables are governed by the camera's aperture and shutter speed, but also by the sensitivity setting in use, the ISO setting.

It's the aperture window, located inside your lens, that controls the amount of light that reaches the camera's sensor. By varying the size of the aperture, we can also creatively control the depth of field of the shot.

The shutter curtain meanwhile, located inside the camera body just in front of its sensor, controls the length of the exposure. It opens up for a specific number of seconds (or fractions of seconds) as you press the shutter release button, controlling the amount of time the sensor is exposed to the image-forming light.

The amount of light available changes according to the brightness of each scene and the aperture in use, so the shutter speed you select will need to vary accordingly. Match the correct shutter speed with the aperture you're using, and you'll make a correct exposure.

If your shutter speed is too fast for the aperture, your image will be under-exposed as you're not allowing enough time for the light to be recorded properly by the sensor. Conversely, if your shutter speed is too slow, too much light will get through to the sensor and your shot will be over-exposed, blowing out the highlight detail.

If you wish, you can control both the aperture and shutter speed via the Manual mode on your DSLR. This gives you complete control over the exposure, but being in charge of both light and time can be a bit daunting if you're just getting into photography. So, along with a full Manual mode, every single DSLR (and some compacts) offer aperture-priority and shutter-priority modes. As we saw on the previous pages, these are semi-automatic exposure modes. In aperture-priority mode (A or Av on the mode dial), you can set the aperture to your desired value, and the camera will automatically work out and set the correct shutter speed for you. In shutter-priority mode (S or Tv) – you set the shutter speed and the camera will select the aperture value required to achieve the correct exposure.

WHICH "PRIORITY"?

Speak to most photographers and they'll say they use aperture-priority far more than shutter-priority, and there's a good reason for this. Though there will always be a few exceptions, your main decision after composing a shot will be how much of the scene do you want to record in sharp focus – how much depth of field do you want?

Since depth of field is determined by the aperture setting, aperture-priority is the best mode to use. And, as the range of shutter speed options is always much greater than the range of apertures available on your lens, it's the apertures that usually dictate your exposure settings.

In truth, there will be plenty of times when there just isn't an aperture value to be paired with the shutter speed you've

SHUTTER SPEED COMPARISON
Here's some typical shots and their corresponding shutter speeds.

FAST SHUTTER SPEED

1/2000SEC

1/500SEC

1/250SEC

1/125SEC

selected. In the viewfinder, this will result in a "Hi" or "Lo" warning and you won't get a picture. This is never the case when you work in aperture-priority mode, because, apart from some very extreme situations when it's impossibly bright or dark, you'll always be able to find a shutter speed to match your aperture and take the shot.

This isn't to say that shutter-priority is entirely worthless however. If you're into sports or wildlife photography, your main worry may well be securing a shutter speed of 1/500sec to freeze the action, though you may need a fast lens (with a wide maximum aperture) to achieve it. But for most general shooting scenarios, aperture-priority offers the most convenient and fastest route to finding the combination of light and time that you want.

SHUTTER SPEEDS AND THEIR EFFECTS

We've explained how shutter speed is used to complement a selected aperture to make a correct exposure, but understanding the creative effects shutter speed can bring to an image is just as important as knowing how aperture controls depth of field (see the sequence of images, below).

Most DSLRs offer a range of shutter speeds from slow (30 seconds) to fast (1/4000sec, and in some cases even as fast as 1/8000sec). This range goes up in a neat, calibrated sequence of increments that are called "stops". For example, an increase from 1/125sec to 1/250sec is a one stop increase, as is 1/1000sec to 1/2000sec. Increasing the shutter speed by one stop halves the amount of light reaching the sensor.

Sometimes you want to be even more precise in your exposure-making, so modern DSLRs allow you to increase the shutter speed by a half or a third of a stop, too. Most cameras incorporate shutter speeds in third-stop increments simply because they offer more control.

If it's an incredibly bright day and you've selected a wide aperture, you'll need a very fast shutter speed to avoid over-exposing the shot, owing to the vast amount of light coming through the lens. The key benefit of using a fast shutter speed is that it allows you to freeze the action, stopping even fast-moving subjects in their tracks. This happens because the sensor is exposed so quickly, there's no chance to record any motion at all.

As you select slower shutter speeds, more and more subject movement will be recorded, because the shutter is open for longer. When you reduce the shutter speed down to 1 second or longer, any movement that's recorded will appear as a blur. (Note that it's essential to support the camera during such long exposures, so that at least some of the scene records sharp.)

Long exposures have some excellent creative merits: subject blur adds a sense of movement to a shot. Use a long exposure for landscapes which have some form of movement in, such as running water or reeds blowing in the breeze, and these elements will be blurred nicely against their static surroundings, adding some real mystery and intrigue to the image.

SENSITIVITY

There will be occasions when the available light prevents you from securing a fast enough shutter speed to freeze the action and/or avoid camera shake. Even with your aperture wide open, your shutter speed may still be too slow. Without resorting to flash or a faster lens you're stuck.

Fortunately, there is a third variable that we can control along with light (aperture) and time (shutter speed), and it's how sensitive the camera's sensor chip is to light. This sensitivity, commonly known as the ISO setting, is adjustable too and we'll be looking at that aspect shortly.

Using a fast shutter speed such as 1/4000sec will freeze even the fastest-moving subjects.

A slow shutter speed such as 1 second (shown here as 1") will turn anything moving into a blur. It's crucial to use a tripod for best results.

SLOW SHUTTER SPEED

1/60SEC

1/8SEC

8 SECONDS

16 SECONDS

APERTURES AND F-STOPS

We have already seen how apertures control the amount of image-forming light reaching the camera's sensor. The aperture itself is an adjustable "window" that can be opened or closed to let a maximum or minimum amount of light through.

In the past, aperture was controlled mechanically by rotating a ring on the lens, but nowadays the f-number is selected by an input dial on the camera. The f-number in use is displayed in the viewfinder along with the shutter speed, and both can be found on the top-plate LCD if your camera has one. Inside the lens, aperture size is varied by a number of blades making up the diaphragm and these move in and out to create the size of the window in the middle.

Just like shutter speeds, the range of aperture settings on a lens is calibrated in a regular sequence of increments that are called "f-stops". Depending on how wide your lens's maximum aperture is, the standard full f-stop sequence goes: f/1.4, f/2, f/2.8, f/4, f/5.6, f/8, f/11, f/16, f/22, f/32.

Half and third-stop increments will also show on most DSLR displays – which is why you'll encounter settings such as f/3.5 and f/6.3, too. This is not something to worry about, even though it may seem confusing at first. Suffice it to say that as you move the input dial to make the aperture smaller by one full f-stop (according to the standard sequence above), you are exactly halving the amount of light reaching the sensor. For example, stopping down the lens from f/5.6 to f/8 is a one

stop decrease in light, reducing the amount of image-forming light by exactly half.

The fact that altering your shutter speed and aperture can be done in neat, measured f-stop increments to halve and double the light in turn is no accident. The relationship between shutter speed and aperture settings is "reciprocal" – open up the aperture one stop and increase the shutter speed one stop and you keep the same, correct exposure.

Another thing that often confuses photographers is the fact that the larger the f-number (eg f/22), the smaller the aperture becomes, when it would seem more logical the other way around. Sadly this is just something you'll have to remember: hopefully the pictures opposite will help.

MAXIMUM APERTURE

Of the full aperture sequence offered by your lenses, there's one aperture in particular that's more significant than the others. This is the lens's maximum aperture, which is always etched on the barrel itself. This could be anything in the region of f/5.6, f/4, f/2.8, f/2 or f/1.4 – what you need to remember is the lower the f-number, the larger the maximum aperture, and the more light the lens can let in. In turn, this affects how fast your lens is, and how easy you will find it to freeze action in low-light (see the panel on fast lenses on page 21).

The maximum aperture of a lens is always etched on its barrel, and shows how "fast" the lens is. Here, the 1:1.4 marking on the barrel tells us the lens has a maximum aperture of f/1.4.

APERTURES & DEPTH OF FIELD

Here we've set up a really simple shot you can try for yourself out in the garden, or in an open space, that lets you experiment with apertures, shutter speeds and ISO settings.

1 SET UP THE SHOT Set up your camera on a tripod using a standard zoom lens and place a still life subject, such as a flower, about 30cm (12in) in front of the camera. Zoom out to around 18mm then frame up the flower with the camera in the vertical, portrait format so the subject fills the bottom half of the frame. Now switch over to Manual Focus and focus on the flower in the foreground.

2 SET THE APERTURE Set the exposure mode to aperture-priority (A or Av on most cameras) using the mode dial on the top plate. Now set the ISO sensitivity to the lowest value (normally 100) and make sure your camera's metering mode is on its multi-segment setting. Now set the aperture to the maximum value, usually f/3.5 on a standard zoom lens. Gently press the shutter and take the shot.

3 TAKE SECOND SHOT Next, stop down the aperture value to the minimum possible, usually f/22, and take the shot again. Later on, when you've downloaded the images to your computer, zoom in to 100% and you'll notice how in the first shot, where we've used a wide aperture, the background is out of focus compared to the sharp background in the second shot. This shows how aperture affects depth of field

F-STOPS

APERTURE: F/1.4

APERTURE: F/2

APERTURE: F/2.8

APERTURE: F/4

APERTURE: F/5.6

APERTURE: F/8

APERTURE: F/11

APERTURE: F/16

ISO AND SENSITIVITY

The ISO setting on your camera governs the sensitivity of the camera's sensor to light. The term ISO refers to "International Standards Organization" – the governing body that created a standard for film sensitivity back in the days when photographers used film to record their images.

Rather than all film types having the same degree of light-sensitivity, different film "speeds" were developed which had improved levels of sensitivity to light. The higher the film speed, the more sensitive it was to light, allowing you to use faster shutter speeds in lower light conditions. ISO 100 became the baseline speed, though ISO 50 was very popular too. ISO 200 was twice as sensitive as 100, ISO 400 twice as sensitive as 200, and so on.

What has this to do with digital photography? ISO is still the term used when referring to the sensitivity of the recording medium – in the case of DSLR photography, the image sensor inside the camera. Just as before, low ISO settings (ISO 100 and 200) are best for fine resolution and optimum image quality, while faster ISOs (ISO 400, 800, 1600) are great if your maximum aperture is too slow and you're stuck for a faster shutter speed to use in low-light.

For instance, if you need an exposure of 1/125sec at f/5.6 for a scene at ISO 100, setting the camera to ISO 200 instead will halve your exposure time – thanks to its extra sensitivity – allowing you to increase your shutter speed to 1/250sec and maintain the same aperture. What's more, ISO changes can be made from one frame to the next.

ISO 100 1/30sec

ISO 3200 1/1000sec

NOISE COMPARISON AT HIGH ISO
For all the shots here we used an aperture of f/11. As the ISO was increased, the shutter speed reduced to compensate. When enlarging the tower section to compare results (right) you can see the high ISO picture (taken at ISO 3200) shows more "noise", in the form of errant colour pixels.

White balance

Recognize the colour temperatures of different types of lighting

WHAT YOU'LL LEARN
COLOUR TEMPERATURE;
COLOUR BALANCE;
SETTING WHITE BALANCE

THOUGH OUR EYES SELDOM NOTICE IT, different light sources produce different-coloured light. Some produce cool blue light while others are much warmer-looking, more red or yellow. Daylight itself can produce different colours at different times of day. Human vision adjusts automatically to see only a neutral output from most types of light. We only tend to notice the colour when the light source quickly changes from one to another, or there are two different light sources visible at the same time. When it comes to photography, however, the light source you use to illuminate a subject can make a huge difference to your results.

COLOUR TEMPERATURE
These differences in the colour of light are expressed on what's known as the colour temperature scale, in degrees Kelvin (abbreviated to K). The lower the colour temperature,

the more red light is present and the warmer the light will appear. The higher the value, the more blue light is present, making the light look cooler. Typically you'll find that the colour temperature ranges from around 1000K for candlelight to 10,000K for shady conditions, lit only by a clear blue sky.

PRE-SET OR CUSTOM WHITE BALANCE
Along with the other automatic and manual settings, DSLRs also allow you to customize your white balance setting to get very accurate colours. This involves taking a picture of a white or grey subject filling the frame that's in the same lighting as your main subject. This neutral image can then be used to calculate the pre-set white balance and, so long as the lighting doesn't change, you'll get more accurate colours in every shot.

CANDLELIGHT: 1000K

Candlelight occupies the very warm, red end of the colour temperature scale. Here you can see how the camera's Auto White Balance setting has corrected any colour casts for a more naturalistic skin tone.

SUNSET: 2000–3000K

Sunset registers at around the 2000–3000K mark on the Kelvin scale, and can present a problem if your camera is set to its automatic white balance default... To keep the warm orange colour of the light, set to the white balance to the Daylight preset option instead.

MIDDAY SUNLIGHT: 5400K

With a mixture of light from the sun and blue sky, daylight lies at around the middle of the Kelvin scale. While many cameras will give good results on the automatic white balance setting in these conditions, using the manual daylight setting can give more consistent results.

COLOUR TEMPERATURE SCALE

Candlelight
1000K

Sunrise or sunset
2000–3000K

Household light bulb
3000–3500K

Studio photo flood
bulbs 3200–4000K

Early morning or late evening
sunlight 3500–4000K

HOW TO CUSTOMIZE WHITE BALANCE

1 SHOOT A NEUTRAL SUBJECT Place a white or grey object, such as a piece of paper or an 18% grey card, in the same light as the subject you want to shoot, then fill the frame with this neutral object. Switch to manual focus if the AF on your camera struggles to focus on a plain subject filling the viewfinder.

2 MEASURE THE WHITE BALANCE In the custom settings menu, find the pre-set or custom white balance option, then scroll through to find the option where you can use the image you've just shot to update the white balance. Some cameras can take a white balance direct from the paper, so check your manual.

3 APPLY THE CUSTOM WHITE BALANCE With the custom setting loaded into your camera's memory, you now need to tell the camera to use your image as the new white balance setting. Go to the list of pre-sets and select the custom setting. Now, so long as the light stays the same, you can be confident you'll get accurate colours in this new location.

CLOUDY: 6000–7000K

The cooler-coloured light present in cloudy conditions like this can produce very unflattering results if you use a Daylight white balance setting. Instead, try setting a cooler colour temperature around 6000K.

WHICH SETTING?

WHITE BALANCE is the system cameras use to compensate for the different colour temperatures. This system can be set to work in several different ways, depending on the effect you're after and the prevailing lighting conditions.

AUTOMATIC WHITE BALANCE

The default white balance on most DSLRs is the automatic setting where the camera analyses the colour of the image and sets the appropriate colour temperature. This setting is good in many lighting conditions but, like all automatic systems, some lighting conditions or subjects can cause it to give inconsistent or incorrect results.

For instance, the automatic white balance system can struggle to differentiate between the colour of the light falling on the subject and the colour of the subject itself. This is especially difficult if the subject has a strong single colour, as this can fool the camera into adjusting the white balance to compensate for what it assumes is a colour cast.

MANUAL WHITE BALANCE

To simplify the task of matching the white balance setting to the lighting conditions, most cameras have a range of preset options for the most common light sources. While they aren't the most accurate way of setting the white balance, they are sufficient for most lighting conditions and will give a more predictable result than using the automatic option.

The exact white balance settings vary between different cameras and manufacturers, but here are some typical options to help you out.

■ **Incandescent** Use this option for shooting interiors lit by household light bulbs with a colour temperature of around 3000K.

■ **Fluorescent** Although fluorescent lights don't have a precise colour temperature, this setting uses a colour temperature of around 4000K to correct for most types of strip light.

■ **Direct Sunlight** The digital equivalent to daylight film, this setting uses a colour temperature of around 5500K.

■ **Flash** Although electronic flash has almost the same colour temperature as daylight, some cameras have a separate setting with a colour temperature of around 6000K to compensate for the slightly cooler light given out by many flash units.

■ **Cloudy** For shooting under cloudy skies, set a colour temperature of around 6000K.

■ **Shade** To compensate for the blue cast created when shooting in light shade, the camera sets a colour temperature of around 7000K.

| Midday sunlight 5400K | Electronic flash 5500–6000K | Cloudy or overcast 6000–7000K | Open shade 7000–8000K |

Using flash

Easy techniques to start with

WHAT YOU'LL LEARN
FLASH SYNC SPEED;
GUIDE NUMBERS; FILL
IN AND SLOW SYNC
WITH POP-UP FLASH

FLASH IS AN INCREDIBLY VERSATILE TOOL. An artificial source of light specially designed for photographers, it allows you to control the light quality, quantity and direction whatever the conditions, indoors and out. It can be used as a source of fill-in illumination to boost portraits outdoors (see right); it can create a twinkling catchlight in a model's eyes, bringing a portrait alive; it can be used to help freeze action and isolate a subject from its setting – the creative possibilities are almost endless.

It's never been easier, either. One of the problems with flash in the past was that you never knew if you'd got the exposure right until you got your film back. With digital photography, we're now able to quickly assess whether we've got our exposure spot-on thanks to the LCD on the back of the camera. The way the camera communicates with the flash has improved dramatically too, resulting in ever-more sophisticated flash meters that make our lives so much easier.

WITH FILL-IN FLASH

WITH NO FLASH

Using a touch of fill-in flash has lightened the subject nicely, and added a pleasing catchlight to the eyes.

FLASH SYNC SPEED

Often taken for granted, a key part of using flash is your camera's shutter. DSLRs have what's known as a focal plane shutter, comprising two curtains. As you take a shot, the first curtain of the shutter starts to travel across the sensor, followed by the second curtain. For short exposures, the two curtains allow a travelling slit of light to reach the sensor; for longer exposures there'll be a period when the entire sensor is fully exposed to the incoming light before the second curtain starts to follow the first, to curtail the exposure.

As such, a DSLR has what's known as a flash sync speed. This is the fastest shutter speed you can use when the entire sensor is exposed to the flash's pulse – and for most modern DSLRs, a flash sync speed of 1/250sec is the norm. Any faster and the second curtain would be recorded as a black line across your shot, but you'll find that your camera will

automatically recognize this anomaly and refuse to fire.

If you're using flash as your primary light source, the shutter speed used (as long as it's slower than your flash sync speed) will not affect the main subject, only the ambient light in the background. This is because the flash pulse is delivered incredibly quickly – far quicker than even the camera's flash sync speed, with the power output controlled via the camera's flash meter to achieve a correct exposure. So it doesn't matter whether you shoot at 1/250sec or 1/60sec, it'll still retain the same exposure, only the surrounding ambient light will differ.

To control this, set your camera to shutter-priority. For a dark background, use the highest shutter speed possible. If you prefer to bring more of the ambient light in and a more natural look, experiment by slowing the shutter speed to achieve a longer exposure for the natural light. Remember to check your screen regularly to see if you've got it right.

GUIDE NUMBERS EXPLAINED

THE FIRST MISTAKE people make when using flash is to assume their camera's built-in pop-up flash unit will light up an entire football stadium. Sadly, a single flash unit just isn't powerful enough to do that, and will always result in a disappointing shot.

Even so, your pop-up flash unit is still very useful – you just need to work within its limitations. First off you need to know that its maximum output is determined by its guide

vary from camera to camera, but as an example, a Nikon D60's built-in flash unit has a GN of 13/43 (m/ft) at ISO 100.

How does knowing the flash's GN help you? Well, if you can roughly guess the distance to your subject in metres and you know the aperture (f/number) you're using, you can work out whether the flash is powerful enough to reach your subject using the equation:

DISTANCE FROM SUBJECT x F-NUMBER = GN

For instance, with a D60 set to ISO 100 and an aperture of f/4, a subject 3m (10ft) away would be fully illuminated, as this gives a GN of 12.

If you were 5m away, however, you would find that your flash's burst wouldn't reach, as you'd need a GN of 20 instead – surpassing the camera's built-in flash GN of 13.

Dedicated and accessory flashguns offer much higher guide numbers (often up into the 40s), so they offer better reach. See page 80

HOW TO USE SLOW SYNCH FLASH

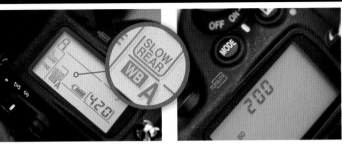

1 SET FLASH MODE AND METER Set your camera's flash mode to SLOW REAR and then select aperture-priority mode. Roughly frame-up, then stop down your aperture so you have a shutter speed between 1 second and 1/15sec depending on how much blur you want to achieve.

2 REDUCE ISO IF NEEDED It's best to try this technique when there's limited light – late afternoon or when you're indoors, for instance. If you find your shutter speeds are too fast, take the ISO down as low as you possibly can – ISO 100 or 200 – setting this via your camera's menu.

3 PAN AND FIRE Frame up the shot again and track your subject into the picture area, firing off your shutter, while continuing to track your subject until the flash has fired at the end of the exposure. It may take a couple of attempts to get the effect you want, but it's worth the perseverance.

If the fill-in flash effect is too harsh, you can knock back the power of the flash using your DSLR's flash exposure compensation.

EASY POP-UP FLASH TECHNIQUES

It may seem a bit daft using flash in broad daylight, but it can be really useful – especially with portraits. Trying to get a good shot in the full glare of the sun is often impossible – the harsh light can result in unflattering shadows and, as your subject will more than likely be squinting, they'll be uncomfortable, too.

The answer is to have the subject turn their back to the light, creating a pleasing halo effect round their hair. Now, to light their shaded face, add a bit of fill-in flash. Not only will it lift your subject, adding a bit of sparkle to your shot, it'll also add some appealing catchlights in their eyes. Simply pop your built-in flash up and, making sure your shutter speed isn't faster than your flash sync speed, fire away. Your camera's advanced flash meter will balance the exposure but if it's too bright, most DSLRs have a flash compensation button, allowing you to reduce the flash by one to two stops.

Another arty pop-up flash technique to master is slow sync flash (see above). Most DSLRs include this option in the flash menu, normally with a couple of options to choose from (see below): front curtain slow sync, with the flash firing at the start of the exposure, or rear curtain slow sync, with the flash firing at the end of the exposure. If your DSLR only offers one slow sync option, it'll be front curtain sync.

FRONT CURTAIN SLOW SYNC
This is great for low-light portraits using a tripod, where a blip of flash at the beginning of the exposure will highlight your subject, and the shutter will then remain open to expose for the darker background. It can also be used creatively too, as above, in mixed lighting at a wedding. With the exposure continuing after the flash has fired, the camera records any after-flash motion as a blur, conveying a real sense of movement.

REAR CURTAIN SLOW SYNC
Because the flash is fired at the end of the long exposure, it makes it more suitable for panning with your subject, especially if there are lights involved, as any movement leads up to the subject. If you used front curtain slow sync in this scenario, it would make the subject look as though it were moving backwards. This blend of movement and static main subject can create some really dynamic shots.

OFF-CAMERA FLASH

ON-CAMERA FLASH

OFF-CAMERA PORTRAITS

Let's see how to use off-camera flash on a simple portrait set-up. Shooting with the flash pointed directly at the subject produces an acceptable shot, but the lighting is quite flat and unappealing. By positioning your flashgun just to the left of the model, we can get some subtle directional light into the image to produce a much more pleasing result. Line up your flashgun with your subject by popping it on a tripod, then position it just to one side. Try not to place it directly on the floor as the lighting will be pointing up at the subject, producing quite a harsh light.

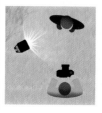 

Manufacturers' flashguns (right) offer complete dedication, but there are some great third-party options to choose from.

OFF-CAMERA FLASH

Don't restrict your creativity by confining yourself to your built-in pop-up flash. As you become more proficient and confident with flash, you may feel restricted by the pop-up unit's size, power output (GN) and creative options.

There are many types of off-camera flashgun available, offering more power and advanced, creative features. Choosing which one is best for you can seem daunting, but they're easily categorized to make the decision easier.

BUYING A FLASHGUN

Moving up from a built-in flash is the accessory flashgun, made by third-party manufacturers such as Metz, Sigma, Sunpak and Vivitar. Packing in more power than your built-in flash, they slot onto your camera's hotshoe, and lock in place.

These varieties can be split into two camps – those which are dedicated and those which aren't. A dedicated model is designed to work with a specific camera brand, such as Canon or Nikon. Although most manufacturers share a physically identical hotshoe (with the exception of Sony DSLRs which have their own unique design), the contacts vary from brand to brand. As such, a dedicated model has contacts on the bottom that allow it to communicate with a specific camera brand's TTL (Through The Lens) flash metering system to get balanced-looking exposures.

Non-dedicated models offer more basic controls as there's usually just a single contact, which restricts you from taking full advantage of your DSLR's own sophisticated flash system. The other thing to watch out for with non-dedicated flash (especially older, pre-digital models) is compatibility with your DSLR. Some flashes should never be directly attached to the hotshoe of your camera as they can fry the circuitry of a DSLR through their high-voltage output. If you still want to use an old, non-dedicated flash, invest in a Wein Safesync. This slots onto your hotshoe and will regulate the degree of voltage from the flash mounted on top of it, keeping your camera safe from high-powered older guns.

MANUFACTURER FLASHGUNS

Moving up another notch are fully dedicated manufacturer flashguns (known as Speedlites/Speedlights on Canon and Nikon systems), which are incredibly versatile pieces of kit. Designed to offer a complete flash solution, they work seamlessly with your DSLR's advanced flash metering system to offer a range of creative options, including remote flashgun control. There are usually two or three models in each manufacturer's range, varying in power and features.

SPECIALIST FLASHGUNS

Specialist flashguns, mainly macro and twin flash units, are engineered to work at extremely close range. Designs vary from a single ring flash or as a series of miniature flash tubes arranged around the front of the lens controlled via a separate commander unit. Each tube can be controlled independently for tailor-made lighting effects. While these kits provide bags of light for macro work, they can also produce some interesting results with portraits, too.

STUDIO FLASH

This is where your camera's own complex flash-monitoring system becomes redundant. Studio flash is completely separate from your camera, controlled manually and triggered either by a sync lead connected from your camera to the flash unit, or via a wireless trigger (see page 41).

Studio flash systems comprise one or more flash heads on stands, positioned round your subject, usually with a variety of flash modification units on the front to variously reflect the light, diffuse or channel it.

Each flash unit can produce plenty of power, so studio flash kits require a mains power supply or a (reasonably bulky but still portable) power pack if you need to shoot on location.

Studio flash offers the ultimate in lighting control, producing stunning results – but at a price. Amateur kits are available too, with generally smaller flash heads, lighter weight stands and generally less output.

HOW TO TRIGGER REMOTE OFF-CAMERA FLASH

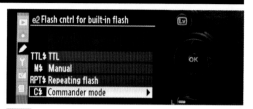

1 SET UP FLASHGUN In this step-by-step, we're using a Nikon DSLR and dedicated flashgun, but the principle remains the same for other camera systems. Refer to your camera/flash manual for specific menu options. First, set your flashgun to its Remote mode via its menu. This tells the flashgun that it's not attached to the camera and will be triggered remotely.

2 NAVIGATE THE FLASH MENU Pop-up your DSLR's built-in flash unit, which can be used as a trigger for the off-camera flashgun. Go into your camera's menu and find the Bracketing/Flash sub-menu. Select Flash ctrl for built-in flash, then Commander mode. This is the part of the camera's menu where you can control, not only the built-in flash, but also a series of off-camera flashguns, too.

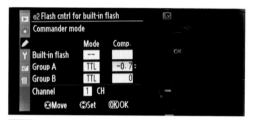

3 CONTROL FLASH Set the built-in flash mode to --. This will force the built-in flash unit to fire a pre-flash to trigger the off-camera flashgun, but won't affect the exposure of the shot. Now set Group A's Mode to TTL and Comp to 0. Make sure you select OK and then set the camera to aperture-priority mode, with an aperture of f/5.6. Increase aperture if the shutter speed is above the flash sync speed (normally 1/200sec–1/250sec).

4 TAKE THE SHOT Frame-up and fire the shutter. With the off-camera flash triggering, check the rear screen to review your results. If the light is too intense, either move the flash away from the subject or go back to the camera's Commander mode and dial in –0.3 or –0.7 flash exposure compensation for the Group A flash. Once you've got the hang of it, don't be scared to move the flash around to experiment with different lighting positions.

HOW TO BOUNCE AND DIFFUSE FLASH

THERE ARE MANY ADVANTAGES to using a dedicated accessory flashgun over a built-in model – not least the extra power, but also the ability to direct the light. Most dedicated flashguns allow you to rotate the head – upwards or to the side, known as "bounce" and "swivel" – both of which can have a dramatic impact on your lighting.

There is a risk of colour casts, so to avoid this, always bounce the flash off a plain white surface.

Some flashguns also come with attachable diffusers, fitting over the flash window and softening the flash, but still putting out plenty of power. The pictures shown right demonstrate the various effects of the different on-camera flash positions and what happens when you use a diffuser to soften the light.

DIRECT FLASH	BOUNCE FLASH	DIRECT DIFFUSER	BOUNCE DIFFUSER

Flash pointed direct at subject = harsh light with hard shadow

Flash bounced off ceiling = softer effect with soft shadow

Flash pointed direct with a diffuser = softer effect, slight shadow

Flash bounced with diffuser = softest, smoothest result

Useful contacts

**Adobe Systems Europe Ltd
(Imaging software)**
Market House, 34-38 Market
Street, Maidenhead, Berkshire SL6
8AD
Tel: 0208 606 1100
Web: www.adobe.com/uk/

Alba Photographic Society
Netherton Community Centre,
Old Manse Road, Netherton,
Wishaw, ML2 0EW
Tel: 01698 372983
Web: www.albaps.co.uk

**The Association of
Photographers**
81 Leonard Street, London, EC2A
4QS
Tel: 020 7739 6669
Web:www.the-aop.org

**Australian Photography
Association**
Web: www.australianphotograph-
yassociation.com

Australian Photographic Society
Suite 4, 8 Melville Street,
Parramatta, NSW 2150
Tel: +61 2 9890 6933
Web: www.a-p-s.org.au

**Bowens International
(studio lighting)**
355-361 Old Road, Clacton on
Sea, Essex
CO15 3RH
Tel: 01255 422807
Web: www.bowensdirect.com

**British Association of Picture
Libraries and Agencies**
BAPLA, 59 Tranquil Vale,
Blackheath,
London, SE3 0BS
Telephone: 020 7713 1780
Web: www.bapla.org.uk

**British Institute of Professional
Photographers**
1 Prebendal Court, Oxford Road,
Aylesbury,

Bucks, HP19 8EY
Tel: 01296 718530
Web: www.bipp.com

Calumet UK (major retailer)
Promandis House,Bradbourne
Drive, Tilbrook,
Milton Keynes, MK7 8AJ
Tel: 01908 366 344
Web: www.calumetphoto.co.uk

**Canon (UK) Ltd (cameras, lenses,
system accessories)**
Woodhatch, Reigate, Surrey
RH2 8BF
Tel: 01737 220000
Web: www.canon.co.uk
www.canon.co.uk

**Casio Electronics Co. Ltd
(compact cameras)**
Unit 6, 1000 North Circular Road,
London,
NW2 7JD
Tel: 020 8450 9131
Web: www.casio.co.uk

Corel (imaging software)
Sapphire Court, Bell Street,
Maidenhead
Berks SL6 1BU
Tel: 0800 376 9272
Web: www.corel.com

**Color Confidence/TypeMaker
Ltd (colour calibration devices)**
Spectrum Point,
164 Clapgate Lane, Birmingham
B32 3DE
Tel: 0121 684 1234
Web: www.colourconfidence.com

**Daymen International (Lowepro
bags, Giottos tripods, B+W
filters, Gorillapod tripods)**
Merryhills Enterprise Park,
Park Lane,
Wolverhampton, WV10 9TJ
Tel: 0845 2500790
Web: www.daymen.co.uk

Disabled Photographers Society
PO Box 85, Longfield, Kent, DR3

9BA
enquiries@
disabledphotographers.co.uk
Web: www.
disabledphotographers.co.uk

**Epson (UK) Ltd (printers, inks,
papers and peripherals)**
Westside, London Road,
Hemel Hempstead,
Herts, HP3 9TD
Tel: 0871 4237766
Web: www.epson.co.uk

The Flash Centre
68 The Brunswick Centre,
Marchmont St, London WC1N 1AE
Tel: 020 7837 5649
Website: www.theflashcentre.com

**Flight Logistics (sun position
compass)**
8 Lion Court, Swynford Gardens,
London NW4 4XL.
Tel: 020 8202 5667
Website: www.flight-logistics.com

**Fotospeed Distribution (wet
darkroom chemistry and digital
papers)**
Unit 6B, Park Lane Industrial
Estate, Corsham,
SN13 9LG
Tel: 01249 714 555
Web: www.fotospeed.com

Gary Fong (flash diffusers)
BBJ Imports, 31 Monkswood,
Welwyn Garden
City, Hertfordshire AL8 7EF
Tel: 01707 694 320
Web: www.garyfongestore.com

Guild of Photographers
30 St Edmunds Ave,
Newcastle-Under-Lyme,
Staffordshire, ST5 0AB
Tel: 01782 740526
Web: www.photoguild.co.uk

**Hahnemühle UK (art printing
papers)**
Suite 6, St Mary's Court, Carleton

Forehoe,
Norwich, NR9 4AL
Tel: 0845 3300129
Web: www.hahnemuehle.com

**Hama (UK) Ltd (bags, memory
cards, lenses and filters)**
Unit 4 Cherrywood,
Chineham Business Park,
Basingstoke, Hampshire,
RG24 8WF
Tel: 0845 230 4262
Web: www.hama.co.uk

**Hewlett Packard (printers, inks
papers and peripherals)**
3000 Hanover Street, Palo Alto,
CA 94304-1185,
USA
Tel: 0870 013 0790
Web: www8.hp.com/uk

**Ilford Photo
(wet darkroom, digital papers)**
Ilford Way, Mobberley, Knutsford,
Cheshire, WA16 7JL
Tel: 01565 684000
Web: www.ilfordphoto.com

**The Imaging Warehouse (Inkjet
paper, inks and darkroom gear)**
1A Black Hill Industrial Estate,
Warwick Road, Stratford-Upon-
Avon, Warwickshire CV37 0PT
Tel: +44 (0) 1789 739200
Website: www.
theimagingwarehouse.com

**Interfit Photographic (studio
lighting, flashgun accessories)**
Unit 4 Cleton Business Park,
Cleton Street,
Tipton, West Midlands, DY4 7TR
Tel: 0121 522 48001
Web: www.interfitphotographic.
com

**International Freelance
Photographers Organization**
P.O. Box 42, Hamptonville, NC
27020-0042
Tel: 336 468 1138
Web: www.aipress.com

Intro2020 (Samyang lenses, Seculine, Lensbaby, Crumpler bags, Hoya filters, Sunpak flashguns, Tamrac bags, Tamron lenses, Velbon and Silk tripods)
Intro 2020, Unit 1, Priors Way,
Maidenhead,
Berks SL6 2HP
Tel: 01628 674411
Web: www.intro2020.com

Just Ltd (sensor cleaning)
The Old Shop, Hook,
Swindon, Wiltshire,
SN4 8EA
Tel: 01793 855663
Web: www.cameraclean.co.uk

Kenro Ltd (Tokina lenses, Nissin flash, Marumi filters, Kenro studio lighting)
Greenbridge Road,
Swindon, SN3 3LH
Tel: 01793 615836
Web: www.kenro.co.uk

Kodak Ltd (cameras, printers and accessories)
Hemel One, Boundary Way,
Hemel Hempstead,
Herts, HP2 7YU
Tel: +44 (0) 1442-261122
Web: www.kodak.co.uk

Lastolite (Studio and lighting accessories)
Manfrotto Lighting Ltd, Bridge House, Heron Square, Richmond, Surrey TW9 1EN
Web: www.lastolite.com

Leica (compacts and rangefinder cameras)
Leica Camera Limited, 34 Bruton Place, Mayfair,
London W1J 6NR
Tel: +44 (0) 207 629 135
Web: www.leica-camera.co.uk

Lumiquest (flash diffusers)
Newpro UK Ltd, Old Sawmills Road, Faringdon,
Oxon, SN7 7DS

Tel: +44 (0) 1367 242411
Web: www.lumiquest.com

Master Photographers Association
Jubilee House, 1 Chancery Lane, Darlington, County Durham,
DL1 5QP
Tel: +44 (0) 1325 356555
Web: www.thempa.com

Micron Consumer Products Group Europe, 12 Redwood Crescent, Peel Park Campus, East Kilbride G74 5PA
United Kingdom
Tel: +44 (0) 1355 586033
Web: www.lexar.com

Nikon UK Ltd (cameras, lenses, system accessories)
380 Richmond Road,
Kingston upon Thames,
Surrey, KT2 5PR
Tel: 0330 123 0932
Web: www.nikon.co.uk

The North American Nature Photography Association
10200 West 44th Avenue,
Suite 304, Wheat Ridge,
CO 80033-2840
Web: www.nanpa.org
Tel: 303 422 8527

Olympus UK (cameras, lenses, system accessories)
KeyMed House, Stock Road,
Southend-on-Sea, Essex, SS2 5QH
Tel: 0800 111 4777
Web: www.olympus.co.uk

Panasonic (cameras, system accessories)
Panasonic House,
Willoughby Road, Bracknell,
Berkshire, RG12 8FP
Tel: 0844 844 3852
Web: www.panasonic.co.uk

Paterson Photographic (wet darkroom, lighting, Benbo tripods)

2 Malthouse Road, Tipton,
West Midlands,
DY4 9AE
Tel: 0121 520 4830
Web: www.patersonphotographic.com

Pentax (DSLRs, compact cameras)
Pentax House, Heron Drive,
Langley, Slough SL3 8PN
Tel: 0870 7368299
Web: www.pentax.co.uk

Redeye Photographic Network
Redeye, c/o Chinese Arts Centre,
Market Buildings, Thomas St,
Manchester M4 1EU, UK
Web: www.redeye.org.uk

Royal Photographic Society
Fenton House,122 Wells Road,
Bath, BA2 3AH
Tel: 01225 325733
Web: www.rps.org

Samsung (cameras, lenses, system accessories)
Samsung House, 1000 Hillswood Drive, Chertsey, Surrey, KT16 0PS
Tel: 01932 455000
Web: www.samsung.com

Sigma Imaging (cameras, lenses, system accessories)
13 Little Mundells, Welwyn Garden City,
Hertfordshire, AL7 1EW
Tel: 01707 329999
Web: www.sigma-imaging-uk.com

The Society of Wedding and Portrait Photographers
6 Bath Street, Rhyl, LL18 3EB
Tel: +44 (0) 1745 356935
Web: www.swpp.co.uk

Sony UK Limited (cameras, lenses, system accessories)
Jays Close, Viables,
Basingstoke, RG22 4SB
Tel: 0844 8466555
Web: www.sony.co.uk

Tenba (bags)
Profoto Ltd, 385 Centennial Avenue, Centennial Park, Elstree,
Herts, WD6 3TJ
Tel: +44 (0) 20 8905 1507
Web: www.tenba.com

Tiffen (Domke bags, Tiffen filters, Steadicam)
Pinewood Studios,
Iver Heath, SL0 0NH
Tel: 0870 100 1220
Web: www.tiffenco.uk

Vanguard
11 Basepoint Business Centre,
Enterprise Close, Aviation Business Park, Christchurch,
Bournemouth, Dorset BH23 6NX
Tel: 01202 651281
Web: www.vanguardworld.co.uk

Warehouse Express (major retailer)
The Showroom, Unit B Frenbury Estate,
Drayton High Road,
Norwich, NR6 5DP
Tel: 01603 486413
Web: www.warehouseexpress.com

Index